DATE DUE

THE LITTLE MAN'S
BIG FRIEND

James E. Folsom, December 18, 1945.
(Courtesy of Auburn University
Archives, Knox Collection)

THE LITTLE MAN'S
BIG FRIEND

James E. Folsom in Alabama Politics 1946–1958

George E. Sims

THE UNIVERSITY OF ALABAMA PRESS

Library of Congress Cataloging in Publication Data

Sims, George E., 1954–
    The little man's big friend.

    Bibliography: p.
    Includes index.
    1. Folsom, James Elisha. 2. Alabama—Governors—
Biography. 3. Alabama—Politics and government—1865–
1950. 4. Alabama—Politics and government—1951–
I. Title.
F326.F755S56 1985   976.1'063'0924   84-24057
ISBN 0-8173-0239-5

For
Florence Mooring,
Wayne Flynt,
and
Dan Carter

Contents

Illustrations

Acknowledgments

This study could not have been completed without the support and aid of a great number of professional associates and personal friends. I cannot adequately express my gratitude to all of them in this brief space, but I do wish to acknowledge the contributions of a few outstanding people.

Miriam C. Jones and Joseph Carver of the Alabama Department of Archives and History provided invaluable assistance in locating primary source materials housed in Montgomery, Alabama. Allen Jones guided me to relevant materials in the archives of Auburn University. William D. Barnard of the University of Alabama gave me the benefit of his own knowledge of Alabama politics during frequent conversations. I especially appreciate his generosity in sharing his own research notes with me. Patricia Sullivan graciously shared information relevant to my study that she discovered in the course of her own research.

The research for this study would have been greatly hindered except for a scholarship I received from the Colonial Dames of America in the State of Georgia. The scholarship was only one example of the admirable manner in which the Colonial Dames promote the study of American history.

While interviewing friends of James E. Folsom and the Alabama political leaders who served with him, I enjoyed the hospitality of many people throughout the state. I am grateful to Sue Crockett of Dothan; Marlene Rikard and Leah Atkins of Samford University; Ann and Ed Blount of Mountain Brook; and Charles Beard of Huntsville; my grandmother Ruth Epley of Gadsden; my wife's parents,

Molly and Louis Guice of Mobile; and my own parents, Sarah and Elwood Sims of Selma.

I owe profound debts of gratitude to Wayne Flynt of Auburn University, Leah Atkins of Samford University, and Dan T. Carter of Emory University. Wayne Flynt helped me gain access to materials in the Auburn University Library and broadened my perspective with many suggestions as he listened to my ideas. Leah Atkins guided me with her knowledge of Alabama history while reading and criticizing my manuscript. Dan Carter gave me the benefit of his expertise as a writer while suffering heroically through the first drafts of this work.

Finally, I treasure the love and support which my wife, Ellen, has given me over the last five years.

THE LITTLE MAN'S
BIG FRIEND

1

Raised on Politics

Alabama in 1946 bore a remarkable resemblance to the nine-teenth-century America that Robert Wiebe described in *The Search for Order*. Like Americans before 1877, Alabamians still oriented their lives toward the "island" communities in which they lived. They lived with the confidence that the lifestyle they controlled in their autonomous hometowns was superior to any other way of life. They believed that the true test of an economic concept, social practice, or ethical principle was its ability to produce visible, bene-ficial results in their community. Their religion, a commonsense version of Protestant Christianity, taught the lessons of honesty, sobriety, forgiveness, and charity necessary for harmonious com-munity relations. Their schools concentrated on training students to become productive, loyal community citizens. Their political ideas subordinated ideology to the practical tasks of defending community stability and distributing the benefits of government among themselves.[1]

The localism of Alabamians throughout the first half of the twen-tieth century established the boundaries within which the state made political decisions. In the state government, local leaders representing individual counties made up the Alabama Legislature. Responsible for making law for the entire state, legislators com-monly behaved as if they were ambassadors from the sixty-seven counties to the state government. A good legislator proved his worth by defending the interests of his home county from new legislation and by securing state revenue for public works in his hometown. The pervasive localism also narrowed the perspective of

1

the governor of Alabama, a state official with a statewide constituency. During a time when mass communication was limited, gubernatorial candidates depended on county committees to conduct local campaigns, get out the vote, and ensure that local officials counted the vote fairly. Once elected, the governor distributed the patronage at his disposal to win legislative votes for his proposals. Throughout his tenure, the governor had to consider carefully the effect his actions might have on locally oriented supporters.

Localism even pervaded the activities of Alabama's most influential interest groups: the Alabama Education Association, the Alabama Farm Bureau Federation, the Alabama League of Municipalities, and the Association of County Commissioners. Two groups, the League of Municipalities and the Association of County Commissioners, were made up of local government officials. The Alabama Farm Bureau Federation promoted the special interests of farmers, especially the large-scale farmers of central Alabama's Black Belt. The leading members of the Farm Bureau were also the leading citizens of their hometowns. Thus, the concerns of the Farm Bureau and the interests of Alabama's rural counties rarely conflicted. Similarly, the Alabama Education Association (AEA) exerted its influence on behalf of the goals of most local citizens. Alabama's most effective interest group, the association urged legislators to appropriate funds for better school buildings and higher teacher salaries. Community leaders who saw education as a means of training local citizens shared AEA's concerns.

The local orientation of most Alabamians made the political relationships within counties fundamental to political action across the state. And political relationships within the counties were dominated by the stable, controlling influence of "courthouse rings." No courthouse ring in any rural county ever existed as a formal political organization. Rather, it was usually a relatively small group of men who exercised decisive influence by virtue of their long residence, economic security, social prominence, and business interests. Although one of the ring members usually served as the county's probate judge or sheriff, the elite's influence did not inhere in any particular office. County leaders normally exerted influence through personal relationships with one another and with other citizens of the county. Their decisions emerged gradually from scores of casual conversations that took place while getting the mail at the post office, visiting the bank or the courthouse, or drinking coffee. By forming and shaping opinions so subtly, members of the county political elite seemed to act more as spokesmen for community consensus than as power brokers.

The evidence of courthouse ring influence lies in the long tenures of local leaders in major county offices. Five members of the Reeves family served as sheriff of Pike County between 1901 and 1954. The family's domination of that office ended only when Ben Reeves took a seat in the Alabama senate and later became probate judge. W. O. Brownfield served eleven elected terms as circuit clerk of Lee County between 1911 and 1955. In Pickens County, citizens demonstrated their confidence in B. G. Robinson by electing him probate judge six times between 1916 and 1952. Support for A. L. Hasty in Marengo County was even stronger: he occupied the probate judge's office continuously from 1901 through 1943.[2]

Members of Alabama's county elites dominated local government because their neighbors had confidence in their economic acumen, cultural values, and leadership ability. Their leadership received further support from the political structures that white Alabamians had erected in defense of white supremacy. The poll tax, the literacy test, and other voter qualifications barred the uneducated and the poor from the ballot box. Since only Democratic candidates won elections in Alabama, the party's primary was the only election of significance. And since the Alabama Democratic party identified itself as the bastion of white supremacy, no Negro voter could conscientiously support it. The voting restrictions and the "white" primary reduced the number of voters and ensured social and cultural homogeneity within the electorate. These structures also made it easy for a courthouse ring to represent the consensus among voters while exercising inordinate local power.[3]

The orientation of most Alabamians toward life in their island communities was only one facet of their resemblance to the nineteenth-century Americans that Wiebe described. In *The Search for Order,* he argued that Americans of 1877 lived on the verge of profound intellectual and cultural transformation, the result of rapid industrialization and urbanization. Alabamians of 1946 lived in an analogous situation. The economic, technological, and political forces that would catapult Alabamians into the mainstream of twentieth-century American life were already in motion.

Alabamians in the northern third of the state were just becoming accustomed to the miraculous achievements of the Tennessee Valley Authority (TVA). An innovation of the New Deal, the TVA had already built dams that controlled flooding and erosion, created large reservoirs that were ideal for water sports and recreation, helped thousands of farm families find new homes, produced fertilizers that improved agricultural productivity, and generated cheap hydroelectric power that was lighting rural homes for the first time. Within a few years of 1946, TVA's cheap electricity would attract modern industries to the region. During the 1950s, the inexpensive power would help make Huntsville an urban center of aerospace research. New industrial plants would make cities out of towns like Decatur and Florence. Soon, northern Alabama farmers and hillbillies would move to the cities, learn new skills, and begin new lives as industrial and clerical workers.

Other New Deal programs produced dramatic changes in the lives of rural Alabamians. Rural landlords received substantial payments under the provisions of the Agricultural Adjustment Act and other farm legislation. Using the payments for capital, they replaced their tenant farm families with modern agricultural machinery. For those who continued to live on the farm, the Rural Electrification Administration was electrifying isolated households that the Alabama Power Company had not reached. Many families did not immediately realize the impact that electricity would have on their lives. Not only did it make possible the use of electric lights and labor-saving appliances, but it also brought the radio, a constant supplier of news and information about the world that existed beyond the boundaries of their county.

Before Alabamians could acclimate themselves to the changes produced by the New Deal, the bombing of Pearl Harbor disrupted their lives even more. During World War II, over 200,000 young Alabamians served in the U.S. military. They traveled to places in Europe and in the Far East that no one from their hometowns had ever visited. They learned to value the camaraderie of fellows who hailed from diverse ethnic and cultural backgrounds. They saw sights and felt emotions that went far beyond anything they might have encountered in Alabama. Their experiences changed them. Then, with GI Bill benefits and poll tax exemptions, Alabama's military veterans came home in 1945 determined to lead their communities into the mainstream of modern American life.

The end of the war in 1945 did not slow the pace of change in Alabama. Rural homes which had recently welcomed electricity soon enjoyed the spread of rural telephone service. Communities no longer content with the available health care used U.S. funds provided by the Hill-Burton Act to construct modern county hospitals. As the number of automobiles and trucks multiplied, state and county governments paved rural roads. Because veterans could obtain vocational training or college educations, an eighth grade education was no longer sufficient for anyone. Modern communication technologies entered the state in the form of new radio stations and television broadcasting. As the communication media improved, they helped trigger the single most important social change in the state's history. By the 1950s, black Alabamians learned that they could use the media to transcend the power of white political elites and appeal to the conscience of the nation for their rights as citizens. Taken all together, after 1946, economic, technological, and political forces undercut the isolation of the island community in Alabama. For at least the next decade, Alabamians would struggle to accommodate themselves and their political institutions to this transformation.

James Elisha Folsom served as governor of Alabama for eight of the twelve years that followed 1946. During his two gubernatorial administrations, from 1947 to 1951 and from 1955 to 1959, his eccentric personality made him one of Alabama's most colorful governors. A generation after his first election victory, Alabamians still traded stories about the ridiculous and often ribald deeds of the Folsom administrations. Unfortunately, the drama and color of Folsom anecdotes overshadow the fact that Folsom's life and his public service confronted all the tensions that accompanied the thrusting of a locally oriented society into the confusion of America's mass culture.

By birth, James E. Folsom acquired an intimate introduction to the localism of Alabama politics. His father, Joshua Marion Folsom, belonged to Coffee County's ruling political faction when Jim was born on 9 October 1909. After completing one term of service as a county commissioner in 1910, J. M. Folsom won election to the office of tax collector and moved his family from their six-hundred-acre farm to Elba, the county seat. The sixth of seven children,[4] Jim Folsom occasionally followed his father to the courthouse. There he listened to fascinating conversations about politics. He probably did not understand whether his father's friends were discussing maneuvers to win support, the loyalty of fellow citizens, or plans for election campaigns. But he did know that politics was a man's business and the most exciting occupation for anyone.[5]

Between the ages of ten and thirteen, Jim Folsom witnessed the dramatic fall of one political faction and the emergence of another in Coffee County. The political transition affected the young Folsom personally because it began with the death of his father. Despite Eulala Folsom's aversion to liquor, J. M. Folsom enjoyed an occasional bout of drinking with his friends. On a Florida fishing trip in 1919, he contracted lead poisoning from moonshine whiskey and died within a few days. Governor Thomas Kilby appointed Jim's brother Fred to complete their father's fourth term as tax collector. Then, on the night of 18 February 1921, the 1921 tax collection records disappeared from the courthouse. The disappearance occurred in the middle of the period during which citizens paid property taxes and it forced Fred Folsom to rely on his memory while collecting unpaid taxes. Confusion reigned and Folsom inevitably alienated citizens who could not prove that they had already paid their taxes. In the 1922 local elections, the old faction disintegrated as a new faction, headed by J. A. Carnley, won election to four of the six major county offices.

While the Folsom family introduced Jim to political factionalism, the vital political culture of Coffee County shaped his understanding of political issues. Located in the Wiregrass section of southeastern Alabama, the county had never had the antebellum planter elite that dominated Black Belt counties and led the state government. Nor did Coffee County have the large Negro population that forced the Black Belt counties to view all issues within the context of racial relations. Agrarian protest during the 1890s left an indelible mark on county politics. When Jim Folsom was growing up, candidates who sought votes in Coffee County did not forget to criticize the corrupt power of "big business" or to praise democracy as it worked on the local level.

Coffee County's political rhetoric continued to distinguish it from the more conservative Black Belt counties during the years that Jim Folsom matured. During the 1920s, the *Elba Clipper* not only advised voters to approve bond issues for the construction of farm-to-market roads, but the county seat's weekly paper also endorsed the efforts of the Farmers Educational and Cooperative Union to organize local farmers. In the election campaign of 1922, legislative candidates promised the usual fare of lower taxes, new road construction, and honesty in government. Two who campaigned in Coffee County also promised to support tax reforms that would require large utility companies to pay a fair share of state taxes. They promised to oppose the centralization of law enforcement in the state and advocated the restoration of all power over law enforcement to the county sheriff. The candidates in Coffee County even endorsed the principle of collective bargaining and advocated a "progressive labor law." Later, the county became a stronghold of support for Dr. Francis Townsend's old-age pension plan. By 1936, more than five hundred county citizens had signed petitions and organized clubs to promote the pension program. For a young man already enamored of politics, Coffee County provided a fertile environment in which to learn.[6]

Of course, not all of Jim Folsom's childhood experiences involved politics. His mother, Eulala Folsom, exerted influence over the development of her son's character. A deeply religious Baptist, Mrs. Folsom taught all her children the moral lessons of the Bible. Even though Folsom was never a pious man, his respect for the dignity of all people and his sensitivity to the needs of the poor demonstrated the lasting impact of his mother's instruction. By example, Mrs. Folsom taught her family the virtue of extending generous hospitality to friends and strangers alike. That hospitality characterized Governor Folsom's management of the governor's mansion, where the expenses of food and entertainment always exceeded budgetary appropriations.[7]

Like other Elba boys, Jim Folsom went to school, played sports, held a series of part-time jobs, and learned about his community and about people while loitering around town. As a young scholar, Folsom was less than diligent. Only in subjects that related to politics, history, and government, did he earn consistently high marks. The other subjects bored him and elicited only enough effort to secure passing grades. Outside the classroom, Folsom's size gave him advantages that other boys did not have. On his way to a height of six feet eight inches, Jim Folsom was a stellar performer on Elba High School's football and basketball teams. After his first jobs delivering papers for the *Montgomery Advertiser* and the *Elba Clipper*, Folsom's size and strength qualified him for jobs stacking lumber in the yard of a local sawmill and handling cotton bales at the town's gin.[8]

Jim Folsom's quest for higher education was a relatively short one. With his friend Phillip Hamm, he left Elba and enrolled in the University of Alabama for the fall term of 1928. Folsom wanted to major in history and political science, and Hamm chose a teachers' training curriculum, but both freshmen quickly involved themselves in campus politics. Associating with other students who were independent of the Greek-letter fraternities, Folsom and Hamm contributed to the election of Albert Boutwell, a law student from Birmingham, as president of the student body. In the process, however, Folsom's grades suffered, and he decided to transfer to Howard College. At the Alabama Baptist college in Birmingham, Folsom's extracurricular interests continued to detract from his studies. When the Pea River flooded during the spring of 1929, Folsom was passing only two of his five courses. He told school officials that his mother needed his help to repair the flood damage. He did not return to formal academic pursuits after that spring.[9]

When the nation entered the Great Depression, Jim Folsom was a deck hand on a freight ship. He had left Elba in the middle of 1929 and taken the only full-time job of his life that did not have political implications. Folsom somehow avoided the despair that economic hard times brought to other people. During the worst of the depression, he adventurously explored American and foreign ports, satisfying his curiosity about the world. Even when he was unemployed between voyages, he did not suffer. The winter of 1931 found him out of work in New York City. Needing a job to earn living expenses, he noticed that the Paramount Theater wanted to hire a barker. When he answered the job advertisement, Folsom joined a line of applicants that extended for more than two blocks from the theater's entrance. From a half block away, the theater manager noticed Folsom's exceptional height and heard his booming voice. Folsom worked as a theater barker until he could sail on another freighter.

After three years of sailing, Jim Folsom was still seeking his life's vocation. When he returned to Elba in 1932, he could not find work.[10] Instead, he found old friends who were also out of work and spent the next few months hunting and fishing, playing poker, and courting girlfriends with them. At the age of twenty-two, Folsom was a giant with a congenial personality who had yet to prove himself adept at any special skill. He had an addiction to politics that was a product of his family's involvement in local factionalism and his community's political rhetoric. At this point in his life, his future a matter for speculation, Jim Folsom loitered around Elba's town square with his friends.

2

Getting Acquainted

Generalizations are inadequate to explain the political conduct of Alabamians. The state whose capital prides itself as the "Cradle of the Confederacy" was also the home of the unionist "Free State of Winston." While state legislators in Montgomery enacted restrictions on the rights of Negroes during the early 1900s, Booker T. Washington had already built a world famous center of black education in Tuskegee. Alabama's Hugo Black entered politics as a member of the Birmingham Ku Klux Klan and ended his political career as a consistently liberal U.S. Supreme Court Justice. The cosmopolitan heritage of French Catholics in Mobile existed in the same state with the bigotry that produced the Scottsboro trials. In 1955, while the Confederate Battle Flag flew over Alabama's capitol dome, the pastor of the Dexter Avenue Baptist Church, only two blocks away, became the leader of the nonviolent civil rights movement.

Still, there were at least two statewide political considerations of which all Alabama politicians, especially ambitious novices like Jim Folsom, needed to take cognizance. One of these principles was the pervasive localism of Alabama voters. The political scientist V. O. Key referred to it as the friends-and-neighbors effect. Alabama voters rarely identified with candidates on the basis of issues. Instead, they tended to give greatest support to the candidate whose home was nearest their own. The friends-and-neighbors effect was the most pronounced in the regularly scheduled Democratic primary where voters had to choose from among a half dozen or more candidates for major state offices. If no candidate received a majority of the votes, a common occurrence, the party held a run-off election between the two leading candidates. Obviously, a candidate had to have the support of his home county in order to have a chance of nomination in the "second" primary.[1]

Candidates for political office in Alabama also had to consider how they would operate within the context of intrastate sectionalism. Even though the dynamics of local political leadership remained essentially the same from county to county, geography and history divided Alabama into self-conscious sections. Differences of natural resources and wealth among the sections meant that each section made slightly different demands on the state government.[2]

The Black Belt, its crescent of prairie soil stretching across central Alabama from Georgia to Mississippi, had long been the dominant section of the state. The fertile soil gave the section its name and had enabled the earliest settlers to become slaveholding planters. Alabama's wealthiest section before 1865, the Black Belt continued to have the greatest concentration of Negro population after Reconstruction. Its white sons were born to lead and received the finest educations available. Their training and poise made them governors and outstanding legislators throughout the nineteenth century. The Alabama Constitution of 1901 preserved Black Belt leadership by overrepresenting Black Belt counties in the Alabama Legislature. As demographic and economic shifts gradually reduced the proportion of Negroes in the Black Belt and allowed other sections to surpass its population and wealth, the failure of the legislature to reapportion itself allowed the Black Belt to retain its political power. After World War II, Black Belt legislators and state officials took advantage of legislative malapportionment to protect planters from high property taxes and white citizens from the threat of Negro rule.

The fastest growing center of power in twentieth-century Alabama was Birmingham. Its conveniently located coal, limestone, and iron ore deposits enticed Yankee investors to build a booming steel town in Jefferson County during the late 1800s. The town grew so rapidly that boosters hailed it as the "Magic City." Leadership belonged to the officers of the corporations that controlled Birmingham's economic base: U.S. Steel, the L&N Railroad, the coal mining companies, and the public utilities. Since the home offices of these firms were located outside Alabama, their officers exercised power through the Alabama attorneys they retained. In a state where ambitious gubernatorial candidates labeled them "Big Mules," Birmingham's business leaders found that their interests complemented the goals of the conservative Black Belt politicians. Like the planters, the industrialists favored low property taxes and opposed state legislation that threatened to interfere with the management of their work force. Their interests were so similar that industrial leaders did not worry as population shifts left Jefferson County severely underrepresented in the Alabama Legislature. Instead, the "Big Mules" relied on the overrepresented planters to maintain a status quo that was favorable to them both.

The legislative influence of the northern third of Alabama and the southeastern Wiregrass counties was perennially inferior to the power of the Black Belt and Birmingham. The mountains and pine-covered hills of northern Alabama and the sandy soil of the Wiregrass discouraged the predominantly white population of both regions from engaging in large-scale farming. Although the original legislative apportionment in 1901 had been fair, the population of northern Alabama and the Wiregrass had grown more rapidly than the Black Belt during the following decades. However, Black Belt leaders repeatedly convinced the other sections that legislative reapportionment would threaten white supremacy and would allow the large populations of the urban counties (Jefferson, Mobile, and Montgomery) to lord it over the smaller, rural counties. By failing to win their rightful share of legislative representation, northern Alabama and the Wiregrass also forfeited their fair shares of the patronage and public works that each governor distributed in order to win legislative support.

Statewide election campaigns proved to be even more frustrating for northern Alabama and the Wiregrass than legislative politics. After World War II, the majority of Alabama voters lived in the two sections. Obviously, every candidate for statewide office set out to appeal to the interests of these voters. They regularly pledged to work for legislative reapportionment, more public works, and tax reforms that required corporations to pay higher taxes. Some of the boldest candidates even promised to reform Alabama's cumulative poll tax law, a burden on poor farm families because unpaid taxes accumulated from year to year. Once elected, however, former candidates faced the prospect of working with a legislature dominated by planters and "Big Mules." Soon the governor forgot his campaign promises, the Black Belt received the lion's share of state benefits, and the voters of northern Alabama and the Wiregrass felt betrayed again.

In addition to the four sections (the Black Belt, Wiregrass, northern Alabama, and Birmingham), there were several small enclaves of Alabamians with particular interests. In Mobile, merchants and officials of shipping companies generally sympathized with the conservative political outlook of the "Big Mules," but because the city depended on its port, they favored state taxes and bond issues to improve its port facilities. Also, Mobile's location and the French Catholic heritage of its leading families isolated Mobilians from many of the social concerns of the rest of the state. Laborers in the mines and industrial plants of Birmingham and Gadsden had come from the hills and pine woods of northern Alabama and usually shared the political views of their rural cousins. But despite their background, their work experiences led them to join CIO (Congress of Industrial Organizations) unions and to become constituents of the liberal wing of the Democratic party. Although they rarely formed unions, workers in Alabama's cotton mills and lumber camps were similarly cut off from the social and political institutions of their rural county homes across the state.

Localism and sectionalism were established political facts in Alabama when Franklin Roosevelt entered the White House and Jim Folsom began his political career. If Folsom dreamed of holding important public offices in 1933, and he did, these facts defined the most logical course for his political future. He would eventually be a candidate for state office. When the time for that race arrived, his Coffee County upbringing would help him articulate the concerns of voters throughout northern Alabama and the Wiregrass. His work experiences would even support his appeals to industrial laborers, coal and ore miners, and cotton mill workers. However, before embarking on such a campaign, Folsom worked patiently to spread his name across the state. For Jim Folsom, political success required getting acquainted with as many of Alabama's "friends and neighbors" as possible.

Jim Folsom made his political debut as a "wet" candidate for Coffee County's seat in the state constitutional convention called to ratify the Twenty-First Amendment. The young candidate, twenty-three years old in 1933, supported ratification because he wanted to enhance personal liberty and because he blamed the "noble experiment" for his father's death. Folsom's opponent was Charles Dozier, a "dry" candidate who had the support of J. A. Carnley, the probate judge. Dozier won the election, but Folsom succeeded in achieving his larger goal. His candidacy acquainted Coffee County with his name and his desire for public office. The race also drew favorable attention from the probate judge.[3]

In a relationship few people would have anticipated, J. A. Carnley took Folsom under his tutelage. Carnley, who had allegedly master-minded the 1922 plot to discredit the established political faction by stealing the county tax records, was somber, reflective, and scholarly. In contrast, Folsom tended toward impulsive, spon-taneous activity. However, the two men shared interests in history and politics, and their conversations ranged freely from stories of the Founding Fathers and Andrew Jackson to contemporary politi-cal analysis. Carnley always maintained a consistent ideological perspective. He claimed, and his disciple agreed, that political his-tory demonstrated how selfish business interests had corrupted American democracy and infringed on the liberties of the people.[4]

The probate judge was not the only Carnley who attracted Jim Folsom's attention. The judge's daughter Sarah had graduated from Elba High School just before Folsom and had gone on to earn a degree at Judson College in Marion. After teaching high school in Houston County for a short time, Sarah had been involved in an automobile accident. She returned to Elba and was recovering from her injuries when Folsom came home from the sea. They became friends during 1932 when they were both unemployed, and friend-ship later evolved into courtship. In 1933 the couple separated when Sarah became a social worker in Winston County, a poor Republican county in the hills of northwestern Alabama. There she worked under the supervision of Frank M. Johnson, Sr., the probate judge, and lived in the Johnson home. For three years Folsom main-tained a long-distance courtship, and then, in 1936, he proposed marriage.[5]

In the meantime, the New Deal provided Jim Folsom with a job and an introduction to "friends and neighbors" in northern Ala-bama. The U.S. government allocated funds in 1933 for work relief in the states. In Alabama, state officials hired administrators to supervise the work relief program in each of the counties. Since the most common project for work relief involved road construction, Folsom applied for a job as a county administrator, claiming that he had learned to supervise road construction from his father, a for-mer county commissioner. The claim was bogus, but Folsom ob-tained the position of work relief director for Marshall County, a mountainous county in north-central Alabama. Folsom moved to Albertville, the county seat, where he opened an office and quickly hired several hundred men. The job had obvious political advantages. The men hired under his supervision became his loyal partisans in future election campaigns, and O. H. Finney, Jr., whom he hired as his office manager, served as an indispensable aide in five campaigns and two gubernatorial administrations. Folsom took advantage of this opportunity for eighteen months, until bureaucratic adjustments placed the work relief program under the control of the Agricultural Extension Service. Because Folsom had no friends among Extension Service officials, someone else replaced him in Marshall County.[6]

Unemployed once again, Jim Folsom joined the flood of ambitious young men who swept into Washington and the New Deal's expanding bureaucracy. With Judge Carnley's support, Folsom found a place in the Project Control Division of the Public Works Administration (PWA). As one of four men working directly under the division director, he helped prepare plans and paperwork for PWA projects in the Southeast. The job placed Folsom in position to extend his acquaintances among Alabama political leaders. By expediting paperwork for Alabama projects, he made the most of this opportunity and received commendations from Congressman Frank Boykin of Mobile. Still, bureaucratic desk work was not Folsom's idea of an exciting career in public service, and he left Washington in early 1936 to initiate his second political campaign.[7]

Wishing to spread his name beyond Coffee County while learning how to conduct a larger campaign, Jim Folsom sought the Democratic nomination for Congress in Alabama's Third District. Entering the race, Folsom chose a formidable opponent: Henry B. Steagall, a veteran of eleven terms in Congress; chairman of the House Committee on Banking and Finance; co-author of the Emergency Banking Act of 1933 and the Banking Acts of 1933, 1934, and 1935; and a sponsor of Federal Reserve System reforms and the Federal Deposit Insurance Corporation. Folsom had no realistic chance of unseating Steagall. Nevertheless, he campaigned optimistically as an advocate of the Townsend Old-Age Pension Plan, federal appropriations for public education, federal farm relief, and rural electrification.[8]

The Folsom campaign operated simultaneously on three fronts. Up in Marshall County, O. H. Finney typed and mailed campaign correspondence. In Coffee County, Judge Carnley campaigned for Folsom in speeches and articles written for the *Elba Clipper*. While promoting the "tall sycamore" as a man of the people, Carnley

associated Steagall with the corruption of big business: "Mr. Steagall has expended all his efforts during these twenty-two years in
Congress in the interest of the big bankers and about the only thing
the farmers have gotten out of his efforts are some banking laws
that have resulted in their losing their homes by means of mort-
gages given to the Federal Land Bank." Under Carnley's leadership,
the *Clipper* and Elba's leading citizens made enthusiastic endorsements of "Long Jim." Meanwhile, the candidate conducted a personal campaign. He appealed to voters on their front porches and
attended their church services. He visited general stores on remote
rural roads, where he traded stories with the farmers. In the end,
Folsom could not defeat Steagall, but he made a vigorous effort and
won a majority in Coffee County and 38 percent of the votes in the
district.[9]

When the congressional campaign had ended, Jim Folsom turned
his energies toward a new career, one that would prepare him for his
eventual state election races. During 1936 six Elba investors formed
the Emergency Aid Insurance Company, and J. Ross Clark, one of the
six and the husband of Folsom's older sister, invited Folsom to be a
salesman. Emergency Aid offered a variety of insurance plans, but it
specialized in burial insurance, a cheap imitation of life insurance
sold to people who could not afford better protection. In return for a
small monthly or weekly premium, the insurance promised standard mortuary, funeral, and burial arrangements for the pol-
icyholder. Although the premiums were small, only a dollar or two
per month, the business was lucrative. Policyholders who faithfully
paid their monthly premiums eventually invested more in the policy
than the cost of funeral and burial services. Policyholders who allowed the policy to lapse lost all the money already invested in the
policy. Either way, small insurance companies like Emergency Aid
and insurance salesmen like Jim Folsom profited handsomely.

The job suited Folsom's talents and ambitions ideally. He was a
personable man cultivating the art of persuasion. His manner of
speaking—confident, sincere, and informal—convinced people
throughout the Wiregrass that they needed Emergency Aid's insurance policies. Folsom enjoyed his freedom from a confining office
job with complex paperwork and tight schedules. He loved explor-
ing the remote places and the crossroads communities of southeastern Alabama while meeting ordinary people who would talk
about politics with him. Like Huey Long of Louisiana, everywhere
the salesman went he learned about the issues that concerned

people most, and he learned how to appeal to the voters for support. The job also suited Folsom's personal interests. With the secure income it provided, Folsom was ready to marry Sarah Carnley on Christmas Day, 1936.[10]

Folsom quickly became his company's leading salesman and helped establish Emergency Aid as a secure, small insurance company in the Wiregrass. After he ran a second unsuccessful campaign for Congress in 1938, Folsom's employers chose him to manage the company's expansion into northern Alabama. In addition to their confidence in his salesmanship, they knew that Jim and Sarah maintained friendships with people in Marshall and Winston counties. Recognizing it as an opportunity to cultivate his political fortunes in northern Alabama, Folsom accepted the promotion and chose Cullman for his family's permanent home. After moving, Folsom spent most of every week traveling and selling insurance. His hard work produced a network of Emergency Aid agents in northern Alabama who sold policies and handled claims. Even after this network was formed, Folsom traveled constantly, training new agents, selling more insurance, and enlarging the number of his friends. His energy made Emergency Aid's expansion successful while it spread his name through the counties of northern Alabama.

While Jim traveled, Sarah Carnley Folsom remained at home and attempted to establish an orderly family life. It was not easy because Jim usually spent only three nights each week at home. Mutual respect and long friendship, however, tied them together in a relationship that survived his absences. Strong-willed and secure, Sarah did not let her husband's size or occasional brashness intimidate her. At times, she was even so bold as to drag him home from poker games when he had played long enough. Although Folsom often boasted that "I always keep my wife barefoot and pregnant," Sarah was his equal and lent stability to his otherwise rootless life.[11]

When Jim Folsom boasted that he kept his wife pregnant, he came close to describing an actual situation. During the eight years of their marriage, Sarah was pregnant four times. The first pregnancy, begun soon after the wedding, ended in a miscarriage. Sarah had barely recovered when she began carrying a second child, a daughter named Rachel. Less than three years later, she was pregnant again. This pregnancy was difficult and her second daughter, whom she named Melissa, was delivered by Caesarian section. A fourth pregnancy, begun during the winter of 1943–44, ended tragically. Complications related to her earlier pregnancies led to high blood pressure and infection. The doctors in Cullman could not treat the disorder successfully, and Sarah died suddenly in the local hospital. Her death created a void in Folsom's family. Even though his younger sister Ruby brought her family to Cullman to take care of Rachel and Melissa, Jim Folsom dealt with his grief silently and alone.[12]

Having lost the congressional campaigns of 1936 and 1938, Jim Folsom did not offer himself as a candidate again until 1942. In that year, two years before Sarah's death, he launched his most ambitious political venture yet when he entered the Democratic gubernatorial primary. No one, except perhaps Folsom himself, believed that the Cullman insurance salesman could be a contender in the race. Few voters outside the Wiregrass and northern Alabama even knew his name. An even greater obstacle to Folsom's success was the fact that he had no connection with either of the dominant factions of Alabama Democrats. Former governor Bibb Graves, running for his third term in 1942, led the faction of Alabama Democrats who supported increased public works appropriations and aligned themselves with President Roosevelt's New Deal. Economy-minded, anti–New Deal, and anti-Graves Democrats lined up behind Chauncey Sparks, a former legislator who had earned the nickname "the Bourbon of Barbour (County)." Knowledgeable Alabamians assumed that Graves would win easily because he had devoted his two previous terms in office, from 1927 through 1931 and from 1935 through 1939, to popular programs of highway and school construction. Graves had also used the patronage of the governor's office skillfully to build the most cohesive political organization in recent Alabama history. Jim Folsom could not expect to defeat such opposition.[13]

Since Folsom had never won an election, his entry into the 1942 gubernatorial primary appeared to defy common sense. Alabamians never understood why he did it. Some would later claim that Folsom had advance knowledge of Graves's poor health. Thus, he entered the race on the chance that Graves might withdraw and leave him as the logical leader of progressive Alabama Democrats. Folsom himself later explained that the campaign began when he was angry over state insurance regulations. During the administration of Governor Frank Dixon, Folsom claimed, the superintendent of insurance tightened state insurance regulations in a way that favored large life insurance companies which had made campaign contributions. The tighter regulation reduced Emergency Aid's margin of profit and forced it to cut agent commissions. Since Folsom's income depended on agent commissions, the situation and its political origins angered him. The circuit court judge A. A. Griffith of Cullman, who owned an interest in another small insurance company, shared Folsom's anger. Griffith invited Folsom to his office one afternoon and suggested that Folsom run for governor. After Griffith offered to help Folsom borrow the qualifying fee, Folsom decided to enter the race. Both explanations of Folsom's entry, however, overlook one undeniable consideration: there was no better way to acquaint voters with his name than through a statewide campaign.[14]

Whatever Folsom's motivation in 1942, he was one of six candidates to qualify for the gubernatorial primary. During the first weeks of March, he and four other candidates began their public campaigns while front-runner Bibb Graves lay in a hospital bed at Johns Hopkins in Baltimore. While the doctors attempted to treat a kidney ailment, Graves instructed his organization to begin the campaign without him. Graves's managers issued optimistic reports of their candidate's recuperation and even implied that Graves was waiting to discuss national defense with President Roosevelt. Alabamians of all political factions mourned the former governor's death in mid-March.

Graves's death reduced the field of candidates to five and confounded the clear-cut alignment of Democratic factions. Chauncey Sparks was the most widely known candidate remaining in the race. For that reason, the majority of the Graves organization decided to ignore Sparks's conservative legislative record and give him support. Chris Sperlock, a former highway director in the Dixon administration, had entered the race in hopes of winning the votes of conservatives who felt that Sparks was too much of a moderate. When Graves's partisans threw their support to Sparks, Sperlock remained the only unequivocal conservative in the race. Folsom's campaign program—which included farm-to-market roads, improvements in public education, old-age pensions, and opposition to selfish interests—identified him as the candidate most sympathetic to Graves's ideas. By virtue of Judge Carnley's influence (Carnley had been a Graves supporter himself), a small number of Graves men joined the Folsom campaign. However, Folsom did not have enough name recognition throughout the state to attract the former governor's entire organization to his banner.

The realignment of Democratic factions produced a bizarre campaign. Chauncey Sparks, supported by the Graves organization, seemed invincible. Chris Sperlock and Jim Folsom appeared to be running a distant second and third, respectively. For Sperlock to overtake Sparks, he and Folsom needed to win enough votes between them to deprive Sparks of a majority in the Democratic primary. Then, by winning Folsom's endorsement during the run-off campaign, Sperlock might snatch the nomination away from Sparks in the second primary. Assuming that he would run second behind Sparks, Sperlock's hopes depended on Folsom's campaign as much as on his own. Folsom's campaign leaders understood Sperlock's position. Therefore, when Folsom ran out of money before the end of March, they appealed to Sperlock for help. Believing that he was helping himself, Sperlock subsidized the Folsom campaign until the Democratic primary in May.

Sperlock's machinations proved futile. Alabama Democrats awarded the party's nomination to Sparks on 5 May 1942 without the necessity of a run-off primary. Altogether, Sparks garnered more than 51 percent of the vote and left his four opponents to divide the remaining 48 percent. Sparks had drawn strong support in every section of the state and won pluralities in fifty-one of the sixty-seven counties. He seemed to be most popular in the Black Belt and least popular in the Wiregrass, but the sectional differences were not large enough to constitute a significant pattern.

Sparks's victory did not surprise political prognosticators, but Folsom's strength did. No one had expected the relatively unknown candidate to displace Chris Sperlock as the runner-up. Within the context of Alabama's sectionalism and localism, however, Folsom's success was not startling. In general, his campaign received strongest support in the Wiregrass and in northern Alabama, the two sections that dissented from Black Belt political leadership most often. Within each section, Folsom's ability to win votes varied significantly. In the five northern Alabama counties where he won pluralities, his share of the vote exceeded 45 percent. At the same time, Winston County gave him less than 30 percent of its ballots. Folsom led the races in three Wiregrass counties, but less than one-third of the voters in the section's other counties supported him. In both regions, Folsom's pluralities came from contiguous counties in which he had sold insurance. Apparently, Folsom's sectional appeal was most effective in local areas where he had established personal contact with voters.[15]

Running second in the 1942 gubernatorial primary did not discourage Folsom. At age thirty-three, he had acquainted Alabamians with his name and established a solid foundation of support for future races. Looking forward to the 1946 primary, Folsom decided that he could best prepare for the election by joining the army. Soon after he enlisted and joined both the American Legion and the Veterans of Foreign Wars, however, he realized that he had no ambition to be a combat soldier. While he sweated at basic training, Judge Carnley and an Alabama congressman secured his discharge. For the record, the army discharged him because it could not outfit a soldier who was six feet eight inches tall and wore a size fifteen-and-a-half boot. Folsom then went on to prove his patriotism by joining the U.S. Merchant Marine, in which he served until 1944, when he returned to Cullman just before Sarah's death.[16]

Neither Sarah's death nor World War II hindered Jim Folsom's efforts to keep his name before the voters. In a final rehearsal for 1946, Folsom entered the 1944 Democratic primary as a candidate for delegate-at-large to the Democratic National Convention. The campaign allowed Folsom to measure his popularity without expending either the money or the energy demanded in an election campaign. The results were encouraging. Folsom won a delegate-at-large seat by placing third in the field of ten candidates. Only Governor Sparks and Congressman Frank Boykin received more votes than Folsom, and Folsom's total exceeded the number of votes he received in 1942 by almost 27,000. The voting returns seemed to indicate that Folsom had completed his political apprenticeship and was ready to be a leading contender in the next gubernatorial campaign.[17]

3

"Suds for Scrubbing"

During one of his campaigns for Congress, Jim Folsom solicited votes on a rural road in the southwest corner of Geneva County. Since he had no car that day, Folsom walked the unpaved lane greeting passersby and speaking to farmers in the fields. At each house, he knocked on the door and received a warm welcome from the residents. They interrupted their activities to serve him cool glasses of buttermilk and sit on the front porch while he explained his political platform. Periodically, a passing vehicle raised a thick cloud of choking dust that settled just before the next vehicle passed. By the end of the day, Folsom was making a new promise, a promise to pave that road when he won an elective office. Years later, Governor Folsom returned to rural Geneva County for the ceremonial opening of the "buttermilk road." The grateful residents who attended brought buttermilk in earthen jugs for "the little man's big friend" to take back to the governor's mansion.[1]

The story of "buttermilk road" is typical of the political campaign Jim Folsom ran in 1946. He went directly to average people, many of whom believed that political leaders had forgotten them, and asked for their support. His act of seeking them out told them that he considered them to be important. Blessed with a sharp memory for faces, he recognized them when he met them again. His words and his manners showed that he understood their needs because he was one of them. He seemed to care nothing for the votes of courthouse rings, interest groups, or even the elite of rural county seat towns. Of course, as a gubernatorial candidate, Folsom did not have time to sit on every front porch in Alabama, but he wanted to, and he communicated that neighborly spirit in his campaign talks and political advertisements.

To some, Folsom's campaigns might have seemed simple exercises in democratic nostalgia, campaigns designed by a man raised on myths of pure Jacksonian democracy. However, behind Folsom's authentic neighborliness lay the irony of his public life. In 1946, rural Alabamians were reeling from the impact of events beyond their control. The New Deal, World War II, economic development, and federal court decisions were ending the self-determination and autonomy of Alabama communities. With all of his country-boy folksiness, Jim Folsom reassured them. He offered hope that a friend would have the authority to protect the interests of ordinary citizens. Ironically, Folsom's campaigns belonged to the politics of the coming mass culture. He bypassed traditional community leaders in order to appeal directly to the mass of voters and undermined the influence of local political leaders in state and national election campaigns. In so doing, Folsom unwittingly prepared voters for the time when state and national candidates could use mass communication techniques and appeal directly to the voters' sentiments and prejudices.

On 12 January 1946, four candidates filed documents with the Alabama Democratic Executive Committee and became official candidates for the party's gubernatorial nomination. Lieutenant Governor Handy Ellis; the president of the Public Service Commission, Gordon Persons; the commissioner of Agriculture and Industries, Joe Poole; and the probate judge Elbert Boozer of Calhoun County entered the race on the first day of qualifying. The four candidates represented the two major factions of the Alabama Democratic party, but they produced campaign programs that were remarkably similar. Each promised to support road construction, improvements in public education, welfare benefits for the elderly, and aid for World War II veterans. They agreed to promote the return of gasoline taxes paid on tractor fuel to farmers, and each took a slightly different stand on the issue of conducting a state liquor referendum. Their plans for disposing of the treasury surplus that had accumulated during World War II varied only in detail.[2]

The subtle differences that existed between the four candidates sufficed to associate each with one of the Democratic factions. Handy Ellis and Gordon Persons identified themselves with the more progressive faction, the faction of Bibb Graves. Ellis had earned the support of most Graves partisans by working for Graves in the Alabama senate and on the campaign trail during the 1920s and 1930s. Persons was running to "get acquainted" and to attract the progressive faction's support in later campaigns. He showed his agreement with the ideas of pro—New Deal Democrats by pledging to work for rural electrification and against Alabama's Bradford Act, a 1943 law that restricted organized labor.[3]

Judge Boozer and Commissioner Poole represented economy-minded, anti—New Deal, and anti—Bibb Graves Democrats. Boozer, a resident of Anniston, succeeded in business before entering politics, and his program bore the marks of his businessman's outlook. He made all of his promises for road construction, educational improvements, and veterans benefits conditional upon the efficient use of existing state revenue. He emphasized that new public services would not require increased taxes. Joe Poole had proved his conservatism during four terms in the Alabama Legislature. Because he always supported the interests of Black Belt farmers like himself, Poole enjoyed the endorsement of the Alabama Farm Bureau and Agricultural Extension Service leaders. He promised to use the state's treasury surplus to reduce property taxes. This promise won him the backing of Alabama's largest landowners, the industrial corporations. Just as the old Graves organization made Ellis the leading progressive candidate, support from Black Belt planters and industrial "Big Mules" made Poole the foremost conservative in the 1946 race.[4]

Grover C. Hall, Jr., a *Montgomery Advertiser* columnist, called Joe Poole's platform "the composite political comprehension he has gained in twenty-odd years of politics."[5] Hall's commentary was equally appropriate for the platforms of Ellis, Persons, and Boozer. The issues that each addressed—increases of state services, proper use of state funds, and the distribution of the tax burden—had been the staples of the past "twenty-odd years of politics." In the early 1920s, Governor Kilby showed Alabamians that expenditures for public works and state services were investments in the economic future of the state. Bibb Graves capitalized on the concept, sometimes identified as "business progressivism,"[6] to carry out extensive and expensive programs of highway and public school construction. Political opponents criticized Graves's building program. They called it an extravagant, politically partisan program that jeopardized Alabama's fiscal integrity. Two governors, B. M. Miller of Camden and Frank Dixon of Birmingham, won election by reacting to the Graves administrations with promises of economy and efficiency. In 1946, the first four candidates to enter the race sought the magic balance between progressive programs and fiscal responsibility that would lead to election.

The candidates' platforms were not the only monuments to "twenty-odd years of politics." The campaign techniques of Ellis, Poole, and Boozer further demonstrated their reliance on conventional political wisdom.[7] During the first stage of the race, each candidate attempted to draw sheriffs, probate judges, leading businessmen, and other local influentials into county campaign committees. The county committees not only carried the campaign directly to the voters, but they also received and disbursed local campaign funds. The candidate hoped to consolidate the local units into a cohesive statewide organization by the time he delivered his first campaign speech. Handy Ellis had the advantage in 1946 because he inherited most of the Graves committees from Chauncey Sparks. Joe Poole almost matched Ellis's organization. The Agricultural Extension Service had county agents in every county. Because Poole received the endorsement of the Extension Service leaders at Alabama Polytechnic Institute, the county agents efficiently cooperated with members of the Farm Bureau to set up Poole's local committees.

After months of organizing, each candidate began the public campaign with a large, festive kick-off rally in early March. Organizational leaders and friends attended the rally to hear the candidate present his platform and to eat barbecue. Veteran journalists could predict the success of the campaign by noting how many prominent people were present. After the opening rally, the candidate began a county-by-county tour of the state. At each stop, he conferred with local leaders and contacted influential residents who might swing blocs of votes to him. He also delivered at least one campaign address, usually in the county seat. Because the campaign lasted less than sixty days and candidates spent time meeting local committees, no one could speak more than once or twice in any one county. This was the type of campaign that Ellis, Poole, and Boozer chose to run in 1946.[8]

"Big Jim" Folsom, the candidate who would defy all conventional political wisdom, officially entered the 1946 gubernatorial primary several weeks after the first four candidates. Although the giant-sized insurance salesman was a nonconformist by nature, his success in 1946 depended, in part, on his ability to distinguish himself from the other candidates. A young man of thirty-seven years, Big Jim entered the race with very few of the conventional prerequisites for a successful campaign. He had never held an elective office and did not have a record of service that he could present to the voters. He did not have the political friendships and associations that other candidates had amassed during "twenty-odd years of politics." Most Alabamians knew his name by 1946, but few considered him strong enough to attract the support of major interest groups or generous campaign contributors. Despite the 1942 campaign, the state's news media did not believe that Folsom could win and did not give consistent attention to his campaign. Lacking all these conventional advantages, Jim Folsom could not conduct a conventional campaign and expect to defeat Handy Ellis.

In place of the advantages he lacked, Jim Folsom relied on personal attributes that no other candidate could match. He was the only candidate who could claim to be a veteran of World War II. He was the only candidate who was a widower and the father of two young girls. He was the only candidate who had never held public office and could boast of his independence from "professional politicians" and special interests. He was unquestionably the most handsome candidate to hit the campaign trail. His dark hair, twinkling eyes, natural smile, and great height attracted favorable attention whether he was dressed in surplus khakis and army boots or in a conventional suit and polished loafers.

His manner of speaking held the attention of his audiences and further distinguished him from the other candidates. Jim Folsom did not deliver campaign orations. Rather, he talked calmly, using familiar idioms and images to present himself as a genuine friend. Because of this talent, one reporter observed, Big Jim was never a politician in the eyes of most people. Instead, he was just the friend next door or the neighbor down the road. Folsom enriched his speaking ability with a store of anecdotes that perfectly communicated his thoughts to his audiences. His unique abilities made him a matchless campaigner in 1946.[9]

When he presented his campaign promises, Folsom was equally intent on distinguishing himself from the other candidates. He began by insisting that he did not offer a campaign platform. A campaign platform, he said, was similar to the loading platform at a railroad station. A candidate used the platform only to board the political train and left it behind as the train pulled out of the depot.[10] Instead of publishing a "platform," Folsom talked of what he would do for the people and referred to his plans as the "People's Program."

The differences between the People's Program and the platforms of other candidates were more than semantic. Borrowing ideas from the age of Jackson and J. A. Carnley, Folsom advocated the repeal of the cumulative poll tax, the reapportionment of the Alabama Legislature, and a revision of the Alabama Constitution of 1901. These reforms were essential, Folsom argued, to the restoration of true American democracy in Alabama government. The cumulative poll tax was undemocratic, Folsom said, because it restricted the people's ability to participate in their government. The 1901 constitution deprived people of their "liberties" with its limits on the power of county and city governments to decide local questions. The malapportionment of the Alabama Legislature, which had not been reapportioned since 1901, allowed less than one-third of the state's population to elect a majority in both legislative houses. The People's Program promised long-overdue reforms that would restore true American democracy to Alabamians.[11]

Even when the People's Program addressed issues that were standard in other platforms, Folsom made his plans unique. Other candidates promised to support rural road construction, but Folsom said he would pave every farm-to-market road in the state. Like other candidates, Folsom wanted to provide financial relief for retired citizens who were not eligible for Social Security benefits. However, while the others promised welfare benefits for the elderly, Big Jim assumed that a retired farmer deserved a monthly income just as much as a retired factory worker deserved his Social Security checks. Thus, Folsom recognized the pride of elderly people and promised to provide the "old-age pensions" they had earned while they worked. Each of the candidates pledged to increase state appropriations for public education. Folsom made the issue his own by promising teachers a minimum salary of $1,800 per year. Folsom could not explain how he would provide the $600 pay raise, but his specific promise implied a definite commitment to improve public education.[12]

The rest of the People's Program included positions on minor issues that no one else would take. Folsom was the only candidate to endorse the right of workingmen to organize and bargain collectively. He also appealed to industrial workers with calls for revisions of the workman's compensation and unemployment compensation laws. Jim Folsom promised to fill his administration with young men like himself, men who were war veterans and independent of the "professional politicians." Finally, Folsom's People's Program ignored an issue that every other candidate addressed. While everyone else talked about a state liquor referendum, Folsom told a reporter, "Liquor has been a problem for two thousand years and wiser men than I have failed to find a solution." As far as Folsom was concerned, there were more important issues to debate in 1946 than the stale issue of liquor.[13]

The operation of the Ellis, Poole, and Boozer campaign organizations in 1946 resembled the operation of an army. Members of the county committees, like soldiers, did the actual campaigning. The candidates toured the state during March and April like generals. They reviewed their troops before battle, exhorted them to greater efforts, and coordinated the efforts of all. No such division existed within the Folsom campaign. Rather, Big Jim Folsom was the campaign. The candidate himself took his program to the voters and sought their support. Obviously, he needed the backing of an office staff, financial contributors, and a traveling entourage of entertainers and stage hands. However, all of those people worked in order to put the Cullman insurance salesman in front of an audience where he could sell his program and himself. Unlike the other four gubernatorial candidates, the candidate's appearance at a campaign rally was the heart of the Folsom campaign.

Behind Folsom's personal appearances was a campaign "organization" that was never really organized. It was an incongruous collection of friends and associates who supported Big Jim for diverse personal and ideological reasons. Bill Drinkard, who served as the campaign manager but never held the title; Robert and O. H. Finney, the managers of the campaign office in Cullman; and Bill Lyerly, Folsom's driver throughout the campaign, were all men who worked in the campaign out of genuine personal loyalty to Big Jim. In western Alabama, from Tuscaloosa to Mobile, Folsom's number one campaign worker was Ward McFarland, an acquaintance Folsom had made at the University of Alabama and a nonideological Tuscaloosa attorney. McFarland worked for Folsom for the same reason he had supported Bibb Graves: political activity promised to enhance business contacts around the state. Birmingham attorney Horace Wilkinson had ambitions of becoming the power behind an Alabama governor when he joined Folsom's ranks. Neither Wilkinson's reputation for race-baiting or shady political deals prevented Folsom from welcoming the lawyer's advice and political influence. Gould Beech, the editor of the *Southern Farmer,* began 1946 as a supporter of Handy Ellis. However, the progressive promises of the People's Program appealed to the young journalist, and after a personal interview Beech became Folsom's press adviser and occasional speech writer. Without job descriptions, hierarchy, or ideological consistency, these men, and the many others Folsom attracted, constituted the only campaign organization Big Jim had in 1946.[14]

Bill Drinkard, a Cullman mortician and close friend of Folsom, handled most of the preliminary preparations for Big Jim's campaign tour. In addition to making arrangements for meals and nightly accommodations, Drinkard scheduled between five and ten appearances for Folsom on every day, Sundays excepted. The first appearance usually began at 9:00 A.M. and was followed by other rallies at intervals of at least one hour. On many days, Folsom delivered his last talk at an evening meeting held in a county seat town. It was a rigorous schedule that lasted from January through April and exhausted everyone except the candidate himself. Folsom's years as a traveling salesman and his ability to take catnaps in the car between appearances gave him the stamina to endure the ordeal.

Folsom gave Drinkard two general guidelines for scheduling campaign appearances. First, most of the rallies were to be held in crossroads communities barely large enough to have their own post offices. Since no other candidate went to "the brush arbors and the forks of the creeks," Folsom would have no difficulty drawing a crowd or convincing the voters that he was the candidate most sensitive to their needs. Also, Folsom figured that voters in rural areas made regular trips to the county seat. He believed that as they went, they would carry news of Folsom to the people who lived in town. According to the second guideline, the campaign itinerary moved Folsom rapidly from one section of the state to another. In a typical week of campaigning, he might begin with rallies in north-central Alabama, move into counties on the Georgia-Alabama line by midweek, and finish in the heart of the Black Belt. Sweeping through the state rapidly, Folsom believed, would build the momentum of the campaign in every section at once. His schedule also made it possible for enthusiastic supporters to bring friends to hear him speak at any of his several visits to their general vicinity.[15]

With the campaign itinerary set, Folsom depended on his office staff to help attract voters to each rally. Approximately one week before Folsom campaigned in a particular locality, his office manager Robert Finney put together a campaign circular. The circular consisted of a form letter to the voter printed on paper bearing

Folsom's letterhead. In the circular, Big Jim invited the voter to attend one of the campaign rallies near his home and listed the places and times of nearby rallies. The letter closed with a re-production of Folsom's signature and a postscript that urged voters to write Big Jim about their problems. Either Bill Drinkard or Bryce Davis, a Cullman lumber mill owner, arranged to have the circular printed. Campaign volunteers—including the Finney brothers, Folsom's sister Ruby, and all the neighbors they could enlist—folded the circulars and mailed them to every rural boxholder on a schedule that allowed the circulars to arrive in local mail boxes about two days before Folsom's appearance. Since rural Alaba-mians were not accustomed to receiving form letters, the circular proved an effective advertisement of Folsom's candidacy and his program.[16]

While the campaign staff in Cullman struggled to mail each batch of circulars on schedule, Big Jim toured the state with an entourage of less than a dozen men. In addition to Folsom, the company included five musicians known as the Strawberry Pickers, a hillbilly band that Folsom had recruited to entertain voters before, during, and after his talks. Bill Lyerly, a combat veteran who joined forces with Folsom in March, lent the candidate his new Lincoln convert-ible and served as Folsom's chauffeur. Phillip Hamm—Folsom's childhood friend, college roommate, and wedding attendant—mingled with the crowd at each rally, taking the names of local voters who volunteered to work for Folsom for the remainder of the campaign. Several other men, like Johnny Steifelmeyer of Cullman, went along to perform vital manual duties. They preceded Folsom to every campaign stop, collected campaign contributions, and dis-tributed literature. The entire group learned to work together so smoothly that they could easily conduct up to ten rallies a day.

The typical Folsom rally took place in the middle of a small Ala-bama town. A few minutes before the rally began, the Strawberry Pickers and a small group of campaign workers arrived to prepare the area from which Folsom would speak, usually the steps of a public building or the back of a flatbed truck. As soon as possible, the Strawberry Pickers began to play and sing while the other cam-paign workers spread out through the town inviting everyone to attend the rally. Meanwhile, Bill Lyerly pulled his car off the road just outside the town, woke Folsom from his nap, and allowed him a few minutes to prepare for another appearance. When he arrived at some rally sites, Big Jim would announce that he was tired and wanted to rest. He would then look for a shady spot, remove his army boots, and recline on the bare ground. After a few minutes, Folsom would sit up, brush the dirt from his sockless feet, and amble to the front of the crowd for his campaign talk. At other campaign rallies, Folsom omitted the nap and mingled with the crowd as he made his entrance. Unlike most politicians, Big Jim shook hands with voters as if he already knew them. Asking "What's your name?" of some and making up nicknames for others, he worked his way through the crowd and left each person with the sense of having met a friend.[17]

When Folsom was ready, the Strawberry Pickers concluded their concert, and Big Jim began to talk. He talked about his promises to pave farm-to-market roads, increase schoolteachers' salaries, and provide adequate old-age pensions. When speaking in northern Alabama, he told audiences about legislative reapportionment and poll tax repeal. In industrialized areas, Folsom declared his support for organized labor and advocated revisions of labor laws. As he discussed his program, Big Jim assured his audiences that he understood Alabama's needs in the same way that an ordinary citizen understood them. "I don't need to tell you what's wrong with Alabama," Folsom would begin. Any housewife who saw the dust from an unpaved road soil her clean laundry knew what the problem was. Every farmer who had to pull his truck out of the mud knew what needed to be done. Parents understood the issues when their children had to attend overcrowded schools where salaries were too low to retain the best teachers. Retired citizens, frustrated because they did not have enough money to live with dignity, knew what needed to be done. These problems had obvious, commonsense solutions, the solutions that Jim Folsom promised to provide.

Jim Folsom's campaign talks included many evidences of his identity with the average citizen. Throughout the campaign, he wore an old pair of army boots, "the only war veteran in the governor's race" as one advertisement announced. In a famous part of his campaign talks, Folsom discussed his favorite food, turnip greens. With both words and motions, Big Jim proved that he was a genuine farmboy as he described the proper way to pick, wash, and cook turnip greens. He claimed that his mother, who died during the middle of the 1946 campaign, had always cooked the best turnip greens in the world. At one point in the campaign, Handy Ellis tried to project the same "country boy" image by distributing a photograph of himself behind a plow mule. However, in Ellis's picture, the mule was incorrectly hitched to the plow. It was such an obvious mistake, Folsom used the picture as evidence that Ellis was just another "professional politician" trying to fool rural folks.[18]

After establishing his identity as the people's candidate, Big Jim explained why the state government had not acted in the interest of the average Alabamian. His analysis omitted tenant farming, the Great Depression, and World War II. It focused instead on the "professional politicians" and selfish interest groups that dominated both the governor's office and the Alabama Legislature. Folsom claimed that the industrial corporations and planters—the "Big Mules" and the "Gotrocks"—bought special favors by financing the election campaigns of their candidates. At the same time, the legislature's malapportionment gave Black Belt planters excessive power in the Alabama house and senate. With so much power, Folsom argued, the "Big Mules" and the "Gotrocks" diminished the "liberties" of the people. Furthermore, the power of the selfish interest groups was so deeply entrenched that they could, and did, ignore with impunity the needs of the people.

Big Jim followed his critique of Alabama's old political leaders with symbols of his independence from established political cliques. He did not have a political organization, Folsom boasted. He did not need "professional politicians" to support and manage his campaign. Instead, the only campaign managers he would ever have were "you and you and you." With the people as his managers, the "professional politicians" would never control "the little man's big friend." Folsom illustrated his political independence with a favorite joke. He solemnly announced that the politicians and their newspapers were spreading a vicious lie about him. After a pause, he continued. They had misled thousands of voters into believing that Big Jim wore a size sixteen shoe. In mock seriousness, Folsom protested that he had never worn a shoe larger than a size fifteen and a half. To prove his point, Folsom lifted one giant foot to display a large "15½" painted on the sole of his army boot.

Folsom concluded his campaign talks with the most memorable of his gimmicks. Because the big mules and the gotrocks had corrupted the state government, Folsom announced that it was time for Alabamians to clean the selfish interests out of the capitol. Producing a corn-shuck mop and a wooden bucket bearing the words "Suds for Scrubbing," he compared his political goal with his mother's annual spring cleaning. When she finished scrubbing the house, Folsom recalled, it was sparkling clean and filled with the "cool, green breeze" that flowed through the open windows. Brandishing the mop in front of his audience, Folsom explained that Alabama needed a leader who would let the "cool, green breeze of democracy" into halls that had been soiled by years of corrupt politics.[19]

At this point Big Jim converted his metaphor into an appeal for campaign contributions. He explained that a good scrubbing job required a bucketful of suds and that the election of the people's candidate required campaign funds. Therefore, if the voters wanted Big Jim to scrub out the capitol, they would have to provide him with the suds to do the job. With the promise, "You give me the suds and I'll do the scrubbing!" Folsom handed the bucket to a campaign aide. People dropped their pennies, nickels, and dimes into the suds bucket while the Strawberry Pickers played and Folsom mingled with the crowd.

Folsom spent the final minutes of his campaign rally greeting people in the audience. Of course, he had his own way of doing this. As he met women in the crowd, he leaned over and gave each a kiss, usually a kiss on the forehead or cheek. This was his customary greeting and earned him the nickname "Kissin' Jim." After several greetings, Folsom would turn aside and observe loudly that the girls in this town were prettier than the girls in the last one he visited. Opponents criticized the practice, especially after Folsom and an attractive young lady posed for a *Life* photographer. But for Big Jim Folsom, kissing was just another small token of his friendliness and regard for the voters of Alabama.[20]

The Folsom compaign treated Alabamians to a display of effective campaigning assembled in an imaginative, entertaining package. Folsom presented himself as an alternative to four conventional candidates. He reminded voters of the influence that a few leaders and interest groups exercised over state government. With anecdotes and unforgettable symbols, Big Jim told voters that he could return control over state government to them. Along with the political messages, Folsom's campaign rallies advertised Big Jim at his best. He was sensitive to the people's needs, constantly energetic, personable and friendly, and completely independent.

During March and April, the two months of active campaigning before the 1946 primary election, the contrast between Big Jim Folsom and his four opponents was profound. While Folsom promised poll tax repeal and legislative reapportionment, Ellis, Poole, Boozer, and Persons debated the proper use of Alabama's treasury surplus, a state liquor referendum, and the social services that Alabama's existing revenue sources could provide. While Folsom went to the "brush arbors and the forks of the creeks," the conventional candidates reviewed their county committees and delivered addresses in county seats. Big Jim sought support from "you and you and you," but his opponents courted the leaders of local factions and interest groups. Folsom entertained his audiences as he spoke his political message. None of his competitors intended to bore his audience, but each attempted to make the serious, dignified, responsible appearance that befitted a governor. As Folsom attempted to speak to the needs of the voters, the other four candidates seemed determined to rehash the well-known differences between conservative and progressive factions of the Alabama Democratic party.[21]

The conventional campaign of 1946, which ignored Folsom, began with the kick-off rallies of Ellis, Poole, Boozer, and Persons. Afterward, Persons initiated a series of radio broadcasts and the other three embarked on speaking tours. Throughout March, the candidates devoted their speeches to affirmative representations of themselves and their programs. Each attempted to convince the voters that he offered the most reasonable approach to the campaign's major issues. When comparing his platform with those of his opponents, each candidate stressed the wisdom of his promises and implied the stupidity of his rivals' pledges. Observing proper etiquette, the candidates did not mention each other by name. Aiming criticisms at "some people" or at "one of my opponents," they kept "personalities" out of an "issue-oriented" campaign. In this fashion, the gubernatorial campaign remained superficially polite, dignified, and serious throughout March 1946.[22]

Since courteous candidates created little political news, Alabama newspapers spent the campaign's first month making endorsements and recording the endorsements of others. Most newspapers conducted "nonpartisan" studies of the candidates before publishing their official endorsements. Handy Ellis received the overwhelming support of the press and could count the state's most influential dailies, the *Montgomery Advertiser* and the *Birmingham News,* among his supporters. By contrast, Folsom received endorsements from only four small-circulation weeklies. Meanwhile, the Railroad Brotherhoods recommended the election of Handy Ellis, and the Alabama Farm Bureau formally announced its support for Joe Poole. Jim Folsom received a citation from the CIO's political action committee, which referred to him as the only candidate "in step with the times."[23]

The tempo of the gubernatorial race increased as the first days of April approached. The front-running candidates, Ellis and Poole, discarded their courteous regard for one another, and the newspapers displayed increased partisanship. Joe Poole struck the first blow when he accused Ellis of accepting excessive legal fees for services rendered to the state during the second administration of Bibb Graves. Poole said that Handy Ellis had received substantial support from Alabama liquor licensees. These contributions, Poole charged, were the result of a "shake down" of state liquor dealers by the chairman of the Alabama Alcoholic Beverage Control Board (the ABC Board). Poole's supporters introduced racial prejudice into the campaign when they complained that Ellis's organization had regimented Negro voters in a recent local option election that legalized the sale of liquor in Colbert County. Finally, Poole alleged that Lieutenant Governor Ellis had expedited individual pardon and parole cases in return for extralegal fees.[24]

Lieutenant Governor Ellis met Poole's accusations with effective refutations and powerful counterattacks. Since the issue of excessive legal fees had come up in previous campaigns, Ellis simply produced the evidence that had previously cleared him of the charge. Ellis took the offensive by scrutinizing Poole's legislative record. He found that during four legislative terms, Poole had abstained on more than half of the roll-call votes. Legislative records indicated that Poole abstained most often when controversial or progressive legislation came before the legislature. In another line of attack, Ellis claimed that fifty-two Alabama corporations which actively supported Poole would save more than nine million dollars annually in property taxes if Poole's program were enacted. In a final charge, Ellis accused the former governor Frank Dixon of directing the "reactionary forces" behind Poole's campaign.[25]

While Ellis and Poole slugged at each other, the press forfeited its nonpartisanship in order to aid favorite candidates. The *Montgomery Advertiser* consistently gave front-page coverage to the Ellis campaign and buried news of the other candidates in the back pages. The *Advertiser*'s editorials made explicit what the front page implied. According to the editor, Charles Dobbins, Poole's personality would prevent cooperation with the Alabama Legislature, Poole's plan for property tax reduction would hurt public education, and Poole could not be elected because he had identified himself with big business, the Farm Bureau, and former governor

Dixon. Fifty-five University of Alabama journalism students wrote the *Birmingham News* to protest similar partisanship. In a frank letter of reply, the newspaper explained that regular newspaper ethics did not apply to news of political campaigns. Therefore, the Birmingham newspaper felt no responsibility to confine its political opinions to the editorial page.[26]

In the midst of the fighting between the front-runners, Ellis, Poole, and the Alabama press agreed that Jim Folsom would not win the election. Poole predicted that Folsom could not beat either him or Ellis. Ellis laughed at the candidate who was "trying to fiddle himself into the Governor's office." The *Montgomery Advertiser* said that Folsom "emphasizes music instead of a program for the state," and Hugh Sparrow of the *Birmingham News* claimed that most people attended Folsom's rallies to hear the Strawberry Pickers. The *Baldwin* (County) *Times* warned that Big Jim would be a "disgrace" to Alabama. The *Huntsville Times* took comfort in the belief that Folsom, "a demagogue pure and simple," could not win.[27]

To have been so certain of Folsom's defeat, veterans of Alabama political campaigns were remarkably unsure about predicting the race's winner. Several commentators noted that the candidates had not shaken the public from its apparent indifference. No candidate, it seemed, generated enthusiasm among the voters. Political journalists complained that the campaign had been the quietest gubernatorial race in recent years. The *Huntsville Times* reported that not even the professional politicians on the local level could forecast the outcome of the gubernatorial primary. Only Atticus Mullins, a *Montgomery Advertiser* reporter for more than fifty years, attempted to guess who would lead the field on 7 May. After visiting almost one-third of the counties, Mullins confidently predicted that Ellis would win a plurality and would compete against Joe Poole in the run-off. Few people had Mullins's confidence, but they accepted his prediction for lack of contradictory evidence.[28]

On 7 May 1946—a pleasant, overcast spring day—Alabama Democrats lined up "just like women waiting to buy nylons" and cast their ballots. The voting returns shocked Alabama's political establishment: Jim Folsom led the field with 104,152 votes, 28.5 percent of the ballots cast. Handy Ellis trailed the leader with 88,459 votes and earned the right of facing Folsom alone in the run-off election. Joe Poole, Elbert Boozer, and Gordon Persons finished behind the leaders in that order.[29]

Alabama newspapers registered the shock of the political experts as they learned of Folsom's success. The *Gadsden Times* confessed that it had not given serious consideration to Folsom's candidacy before 7 May. The *Birmingham News* reporter Hugh Sparrow credited Folsom with conducting the "most surprising and upsetting" gubernatorial campaign in Alabama history. Columnist Grover Hall reported, "A few days before the election there were many politicians just back from state tours to say that Folsom was definitely in the run-off. But never once did any suggest that Folsom would place first." *Alabama,* a newsmagazine published in Birmingham and financed by industrial advertisers, reacted outspokenly. *Alabama's* editor warned that the CIO would go to great lengths during the run-off campaign to put Big Jim in the governor's office. The *Huntsville Times* was vituperative. A *Times* editorial warned that Folsom did not have the ability to direct the state government. He was, in effect, "a direct threat to orderly, well-directed government" in Alabama.[30]

When the votes in the Democratic primary had been counted, the gubernatorial race resumed. The first events in the run-off campaign were the announcements of support by the candidates who had been eliminated. Gordon Persons, already looking forward to the 1950 campaign, quickly declared his support for Ellis with the explanation, "Jim Folsom is a nice boy, but he does not have the experience to operate a $100,000,000 business." More than a week of behind-the-scenes politicking gave rise to rumors that Folsom was making significant concessions, involving both policies and patronage, in an effort to win support from Poole and Boozer. Finally, the two defeated candidates announced that they were giving their support to Folsom in return for his promise to consult an advisory board of experienced leaders before making policy decisions as governor.[31]

News of the endorsements further confounded an already confused political race. In any conventional campaign, the leader of the progressive faction of the Alabama Democratic party should have run as the more progressive candidate. However, Folsom's promises of greatly expanded state services and constitutional reforms forced Handy Ellis into the unaccustomed role of the campaign's more conservative candidate. Yet Poole and Boozer had represented the leaders of Alabama's most conservative Democrats and they had endorsed Folsom. Their endorsements seemed to undermine the integrity of the Folsom program. As in 1942, Folsom's presence in the gubernatorial campaign had contributed to the blurring of any ideological distinctions that may have existed among the candidates.[32]

Since Ellis ran second in the Democratic primary, he launched an aggressive run-off campaign, a three-pronged offensive against Folsom's lead. Focusing first on the CIO's endorsement of Folsom, Ellis claimed that the radical, northern-based union was using Folsom in an effort to seize control of the Alabama state government and dictate state labor legislation. The pro-Ellis editor of the *Dothan Eagle* associated the CIO's political action committee with "the communist fringe" working with the NAACP to abolish racial segregation in Alabama. The *Birmingham Post*'s John Temple Graves devoted his daily column to making rural Alabamians understand that Folsom was the choice of the CIO, "forces which needed expression here in the 1930's but have dangerously overreached themselves in the 1940's and must be stopped."[33]

In a second line of attack, Ellis concentrated on Folsom's apparent agreement to appoint a group of experienced advisers. He regarded the "advisory board" as Folsom's straightforward confession of inability to govern Alabama. If Folsom needed advisers, then he did not have the knowledge and experience to be an effective governor. Going further, Ellis's supporters challenged Folsom to identify the men who would be his advisers. When he ignored the challenges, they speculated that the "advisory board" would include a representative of the CIO leader Sidney Hillman, the race-baiting politician Horace Wilkinson, and members of the industrial and agricultural interests that had supported Joe Poole. As the Ellis campaign described the situation, Folsom's victory would give power to leaders whom the voters would have never placed in state offices.[34]

For those who could not be stampeded by fears of CIO domination or rule by committee, Ellis and his supporters offered estimates of how much the People's Program would cost. Ellis claimed that a monthly old-age pension of fifty dollars paid to every elderly Alabamian would completely drain the state treasury. The *Birmingham News* and the *Montgomery Advertiser* both estimated that Alabama would have to double its revenue to pay Folsom's old-age pensions. The *Huntsville Times* reported that the cost of paving the farm-to-market roads in Madison County alone would exceed the assessed value of all property in the county. The *Birmingham Post* columnist John Temple Graves claimed that "gasoline will have to sell for ninety-five cents a gallon" to pay for Folsom's promise of farm-to-market roads. Although many of the estimates seemed arbitrary, Ellis argued that Folsom's promises would require hearty tax increases. Thus, if Folsom continued to promise that he could provide additional state services without raising taxes, then he was either a liar or lacked the intelligence to be governor.[35]

Where Ellis's criticisms of Folsom left off, his supporters continued with ridicule. Without question, the master of political ridicule was John Temple Graves. He claimed that Folsom won votes because he had "put a hex on some Alabamians." Graves explained,

> The hypnotic word is simple, and easy to say. It is "fokes." Folsom just stands up before our fine farm people and says "fokes." And then he says it again—"fokes." And then he says it a few more times— "fokes," "fokes"—and you begin to feel all warm and happy and careless. You stop noticing what he is saying, you overlook the promises that can't be kept and that only a professional would make, the political tricks like the suds bucket and string band that professionals before him developed, the record of the man as a light-footed wanderer utterly unfit for the great job he wants, the fact that while he may be Big Jim in stature he is very little Jim in ability and experience. You just go to sleep and sign up in a happy-go-lucky dream, dear fokes and fellow Alabamians.[36]

Jim Folsom handled the criticisms and the ridicule superbly. In campaign talks, he observed that no one had worried about the CIO until the people's votes upset the "professional politicians." Furthermore, Folsom said, he had not solicited the union's endorsement as other candidates had done. Folsom also minimized the dire warnings that his election would bring financial ruin to the state of Alabama. Big Jim claimed that the state could raise sufficient revenue for his program if it taxed large corporations and planters at the same rate it taxed ordinary citizens. According to Folsom, his opponent's estimates of costs only proved that the conventional politicians would not expand state services for the people. For the most part, however, Folsom answered his opponent's criticisms by ignoring them and conducting the same kind of campaign that he conducted before 7 May. He remained the independent candidate who took his program to "the brush arbors and the forks of the creeks." He accepted no public help in the campaign from either Boozer or Poole. In so doing, Big Jim convinced more people that he was "the little man's big friend."[37]

On 4 June, the people of Alabama upset the "professional politicians" again when they awarded the Democratic gubernatorial nomination to Big Jim Folsom. With 58.7 percent of almost 350,000 ballots, Folsom received more votes than any other candidate for state office had ever received in Alabama. His margin of victory reflected the sectionalism of Alabama politics. While Handy Ellis won majorities in the Black Belt and southwestern Alabama, Big Jim was unbeatable in the northern half of the state and throughout the Wiregrass.[38]

As they had after 7 May, newspaper editorials revealed the bewilderment of Alabama's conventional political leadership in response to Folsom's success. Both the *Birmingham News* and the *Montgomery Advertiser* considered Folsom's victory part of a popular move for change, but neither paper could predict the direction or significance of that movement. The *Huntsville Times* seemed most upset. It described the election as a popular revolt against proven leadership, "a blind unreasoning revolt, hitting good men as well as bad." As if the state which had just nominated Folsom needed reassurance, the *Anniston Star* and the *Mobile Register* urged their readers to have confidence in the Alabama Constitution and the Alabama Legislature as bulwarks against Folsom's radicalism.[39]

Obviously, Alabama newspapers and the political interests for which they spoke did not comprehend the meaning of Folsom's nomination. And there is reason to doubt whether Folsom or his supporters grasped the significance of the campaign any better. On the surface, Big Jim was conservative, a candidate who called for a return to the democratic methods and manners of the past. He used the traditional idioms, music, and symbols of the rural South in a campaign in which he advocated the restoration of political power to the people of Alabama. Yet, even as he called for a return to true democracy, Folsom was permanently altering political campaigns in the state. Folsom's campaign bypassed county and community leaders in every section of Alabama as he appealed directly to Alabamians for their votes. Claiming to be independent of the "professional politicians," Big Jim led Alabamians to disregard the advice of traditional local leaders and to vote as individuals. After 1946, every other candidate for state office would have to seek the votes of individual citizens too.

4

No Plans at All

According to columnist Atticus Mullins, Jim Folsom's triumph over Handy Ellis placed him on "the summit" of Alabama politics in 1946.[1] With assurance of his election as governor and a popular mandate for the People's Program, Folsom indeed held a commanding position. However, while surveying the political landscape from the summit, Folsom could not afford to overlook the continuing power of his opposition. He could not afford to forget that a majority of the Alabama senate[2] and practically all of the state's newspapers had publicly endorsed Ellis. Nor should he fail to notice that both the League of Municipalities and the Association of County Commissioners had supported his opponent. Despite Folsom's victory, state legislators, local officials, and newspaper editors retained the power to enact Folsom's programs and to interpret his proposals to the general public. Folsom should have realized that the election campaign was over and that his success as governor would depend on his success in converting opponents into supporters.

Winning the support of influential Alabamians was not impossible for Folsom in the summer of 1946. Obviously, he would never find support for tax equalization among the "Big Mules," backing for legislative reapportionment among Black Belt legislators, or sympathy for racial equality among white Alabamians. However, the rhetoric of Handy Ellis's run-off campaign had exaggerated the ideological distance between Folsom and the more progressive faction of Alabama Democrats. Big Jim was not a bona fide radical or a minion of the CIO. Although most realized that the reforms could

40

not win legislative approval, progressive candidates had regularly promised constitutional revision and poll tax repeal in previous campaigns. The expansions of state services that Folsom promised—road construction, improvement of public education, and welfare benefits for the elderly—were essentially the same services that progressive Alabama Democrats had supported since the first Graves administration.

In spite of this common ground, Jim Folsom had not sought the support of the progressive Democratic faction during the gubernatorial campaign. Instead, he had included them among the "professional politicians" whose control of state government he blasted. With the nomination won, Folsom now had seven months during which to prepare for assuming office. From June until January, Alabamians looked for signs of leadership from the man who would next occupy the most powerful position in the state government. Progressive Democrats especially wanted to know which of Folsom's campaign promises would receive his most active support and how his pledges would be written into legislative proposals. They looked to see how Folsom would exercise his prerogative of organizing the new house of representatives. And because of his impressive victory, they waited for evidence that Folsom wanted their support and would provide gubernatorial leadership worthy of it.[3]

If the nominee for the governorship understood the crucial importance of the interim between nomination and inauguration, his public behavior did not reflect that comprehension. Instead of spending the months winning supporters and planning a legislative program, Folsom accomplished little beyond the selection of his office staff and some of his department heads. He underestimated the importance of discussing legislative plans with sympathetic legislators and almost lost the opportunity to direct the organization of the house of representatives. Instead of cultivating cordial relations with the Alabama press, he rarely informed newsmen of his activities, and he continued to antagonize editors with hostile public statements. Folsom frequently repeated a slogan to newsmen, "Make no small plans, they have no magic to stir men's blood." But as far as potential supporters in the legislature or the general public could see, Folsom was making no plans at all.

Immediately after he won the gubernatorial nomination, a delicate personal problem distracted Folsom. Instead of planning for his administration, he spent the summer of 1946 extracting himself from a two-year-old love affair with Christine Putman Johnston.[4] The affair began shortly after Sarah Carnley Folsom's death in 1944. Christine was a clerk at the Tutwiler Hotel, the hotel Folsom frequented when business trips took him to Birmingham. By March of 1945, they were deeply in love, but marriage was out of the question. Christine was young, beautiful, and divorced, and Folsom could not risk marrying her less than one year after his wife's death. Instead, the couple dated and engaged in occasional sexual relations while waiting for their eventual wedding.

In September 1945, Christine discovered she was pregnant. Folsom seemed happy to hear the news, but he instructed her to leave Alabama so that the pregnancy would not jeopardize his political career. Christine agreed to hide until after the 1946 Democratic primary and left for New Orleans. Following his instructions, Christine later moved to Louisville and Fulton, Kentucky, before Folsom took her to Nashville for the last weeks of the pregnancy. After the baby was born on 17 April, Christine continued to hide with an aunt who lived in Michigan until she and the baby joined Folsom in a Jacksonville hotel room during June 1946. Then she spent the summer traveling from Memphis to Mobile, to Fairhope, back to Nashville, and finally to Tuscumbia.

Sometime during that summer, Folsom realized that he could not marry Christine. It was a decision he agonized over even as he continued to express deep affection for her. However, at the end of a three-day visit in September 1946, Folsom revealed his decision when he returned their infant son to Christine and said, "Take care of my boy always and don't let anything happen to him!" Once she was certain there would be no wedding, Mrs. Johnston sought to establish the child's paternity. She contacted the Birmingham attorney Roderick Beddow in October and asked him to help protect her own and her child's legal rights. Beddow advised her that she had neither the financial resources nor the emotional stamina to win a court battle against Folsom. He contacted Folsom's attorneys and negotiated a cash settlement instead. In return for her signed pledge that she would do nothing to embarrass, humiliate, or hurt the political career of Folsom, Christine received $5,000. After honoring her pledge for one year, she received another $5,000. Bill Drinkard and Bryce Davis gladly raised the money with confidence that Christine Putman Johnston would never trouble Big Jim Folsom again.

Jim Folsom's love affair with Mrs. Johnston revealed aspects of his character that had not exhibited themselves during his campaigns. When he first became romantically involved, Folsom allowed his emotions to overwhelm his political sense. Because he yielded to his feelings, Folsom eventually had to choose to marry Christine or protect his political future. In giving priority to his own career, Folsom demonstrated that no commitment, not even his love for his first-born son, was more important to him than political success. Ironically, Folsom's commitment to politics did not make him ruthless. He supported Christine throughout the pregnancy, even phoning her regularly after long days of campaigning. He never denied that the child was his own and he could not face Christine with the decision that their wedding would not take place. Even after the settlement was negotiated in October 1946, Folsom made certain that his son had everything he needed.

The most striking of Folsom's qualities was his incredible carelessness. Obviously, if the couple had abstained from sexual relations or practiced contraception, there would have been no pregnancy to force their separation. During the months that Christine was in hiding, Folsom visited her several times and paid their hotel bills with his own personal checks. When Christine was four months pregnant, Folsom escorted her to an Alabama-Kentucky football game. During his 1946 campaign, he placed long-distance phone calls to Christine through hotel switchboard operators. When Christine and Jim met in Jacksonville, Folsom registered under the name of Bill Lyerly, even though anyone looking for Folsom would have recognized Lyerly's name. For more than a year, Folsom carelessly left a broad trail of obvious clues that any investigative reporter could have followed with ease.

Most important, the affair with Christine Putman Johnston preoccupied Folsom at a politically critical time. From June through September, it demanded his attention, drained him emotionally, and forced him to avoid newsmen and publicity. During that summer when Alabamians were forming their estimates of the next governor, the only information they received came from occasional glimpses of Folsom's public behavior. Because of the affair and his general inexperience with press relations, those glimpses showed a Folsom who was uncooperative, unprepared, or simply foolish.

Jim Folsom mishandled his relations with the Alabama press from the date of his nomination. On the evening of 4 June, he issued a public statement thanking Alabama Democrats for their votes and expressing special appreciation to his supporters. Then

Folsom slipped out of the state unannounced for his vacation in Florida and his visit with Christine. Alabama journalists did not even know where to find him until he popped up in Daytona Beach to meet the mayor and answer the questions of local reporters. He appeared next in Montgomery on 16 July. Meeting with reporters there, Folsom merely repeated his campaign promises and promised to open an office in the capital around the first of September.[5]

Folsom's public reticence continued when he made a triumphant tour of Washington, D.C., during August. The guest of the Democratic party chairman, Robert Hannegan, Folsom visited with President Truman, members of Alabama's congressional delegation, and officials in the Commerce Department and the Social Security Administration. The Democratic chairman hosted a banquet in Folsom's honor which was attended by Truman and other Democratic leaders. At the banquet, it seemed that the nation's liberal political leaders celebrated the discovery of an oasis of southern liberalism between the conservative deserts of Herman Talmadge's Georgia and Theodore Bilbo's Mississippi.

Everywhere Folsom went in Washington, he happily posed for photographs with other officials. But when newsmen asked him about his conversations with them, Folsom either replied, "No comment," or he offered friendly, meaningless responses. Journalists had to guess what Folsom was doing. Some said that the Social Security Administration might help Folsom provide the old-age pensions he had promised. Others speculated that the Commerce Department had surplus military machinery that could help pave the farm-to-market roads. There was even the possibility that Folsom discussed the 1948 presidential campaign with President Truman. No one knew for sure, and Folsom would not release any information. Finally, Grover Hall, Jr., concluded that the Washington junket held no deep significance. All it showed, Hall wrote, was that no one knew who Jim Folsom was and that everyone, including the president, wanted to get Big Jim on his side.[6]

After returning from Washington, Folsom continued to avoid public discussions of the plans for his gubernatorial administration. He visited Governor Ellis Arnall of Georgia to study the accomplishments of Arnall's administration. At their joint press conference, Folsom said he favored programs that would encourage Alabama investors to develop Alabama's own natural resources. However, even when questioned, Folsom could not describe how his administration would pursue that objective. Later, in a speech at Luverne,

Alabama, Folsom completely omitted references to Alabama and his administration in order to speak on U.S. foreign policy. He criticized the Marshall Plan, calling it a program for "dumping American money overseas" and warning that it would not buy international friendship or respect for the United States. The speech provoked political commentators to complain that Folsom ought to concentrate on the concerns of Alabamians at home rather than addressing issues beyond his control.[7]

The dearth of information Folsom provided Alabama's news media in 1946 demonstrated both his preoccupation with Christine Putman Johnston and his general inexperience with press relations. Paradoxically, his behavior also betrayed both cynicism and naïveté concerning the role of the press in shaping public opinion. Big Jim did not trust the Alabama press. He identified the *Montgomery Advertiser* as the consistent voice of corporations like the Alabama Power Company and assumed that the Birmingham dailies always articulated the interests of the "Big Mules." Convinced that the state's press would not report the truth, Folsom used "no comment" so frequently that Grover Hall, Jr., claimed Folsom would answer no question "more controversial than whether or not it was snowing." When he had no answers for reporters' questions, Folsom often joked, "Boys, you can write anything about me you like—just spell the name right."[8]

During the 1946 campaign, Folsom had benefited from the newspapers' lack of credibility among rural folks. In May, John Temple Graves had visited Scottsboro and asked Jackson County farmers what they thought about the CIO endorsement of Folsom. Graves reported, "I had the amazing reply that this was just a lie spread by a Birmingham newspaper." After the election campaign ended, Folsom continued to take advantage of the popular distrust of the press. In November, Folsom told a Cullman audience that he would have to make periodic reports to the people concerning the progress of the People's Program. These reports would be necessary, Folsom explained, because the people could not rely on the "lying newspapers" to report his administration's work objectively. Cynically, Folsom used the daily newspapers as popular whipping boys and thereby forfeited the goodwill of both reporters and editors.[9]

Because he distrusted the press too much to cooperate with it, Folsom made himself vulnerable to the news media's ridicule and criticism. During early June, *Life* published a series of photographs for which Folsom had posed during a campaign stop in Cullman. Most of the pictures were typical campaign fare: the candidate giving a speech, the candidate's audience, the candidate and his campaign aides. However, three of the pictures caught the more undignified side of Big Jim. One showed Folsom embracing a young lady tightly and kissing her on the lips while two equally attractive women awaited their turns. A second photograph captured the Folsom family eating supper at home. Folsom posed for this picture dressed in wrinkled khaki pants and an undershirt and eating with his hands. He sat with his chair pushed back from the table so that the photograph could include his own and his daughters' bare feet in the picture. Finally, *Life* showed how Big Jim ended each day of campaigning. For this shot, Folsom lathered up and sat in a bathtub so small that he had to raise his bent knees as high as his shoulders.[10]

Life's title for the pictures, "Alabama Election," embarrassed many Alabamians with its implication that the antics of Big Jim Folsom were typical for the state. An Associated Press photograph distributed several weeks later embarrassed the state again. In the picture, the mayor of Daytona Beach, Florida, dressed in a businessman's suit, extended his city's official greetings to Alabama's nominee for governor. Folsom appeared for the momentous occasion in his flowered tropical shirt, swimming trunks, and bare feet. The picture sparked editorial complaints in Alabama. It seemed that Folsom cared nothing for the dignity of the state, that he was more impressed by his celebrity status than by the responsibilities of his position, that he openly flouted conventional moral standards, and that he spent too much time traveling around the country making a spectacle of himself. Several newly elected legislators expressed essentially the same feeling: "Big Jim can't help it if he's a fool, but he could stay home."[11]

If the objectives of a governor-elect were the same as the goals of a candidate, Folsom's affair with Mrs. Johnston and his mishandling of press relations would never have hurt him. None of the pictures or even the rumors lessened his popularity among voters on "buttermilk road." However, once his election was assured, Folsom confronted the task of winning legislative support for his campaign program. That challenge would have been difficult for anyone who had made the promises Folsom made. The Black Belt planters, and their "Big Mule" allies, dominated the Alabama Legislature and were always ready to fight like Spartans against efforts to repeal the poll tax, reapportion the legislature, rewrite the state constitution, and reform the tax structure. They even frowned on new state services that threatened to increase taxes. Furthermore, Folsom scared the legislative leaders. He had supported Henry Wallace for vice-president in 1944; he had received the endorsement of the CIO; a protégé of the liberal agricultural reformer Aubrey Williams was among his closest campaign aides; and he had circumvented traditional community leaders to win the 1946 gubernatorial nomination. Then, as if all of that was not enough, Folsom spent the summer and fall of 1946 gallivanting across the country, posing for silly pictures, and making no overt effort to prepare for taking office. Folsom's behavior discredited him in the eyes of most legislators and made a difficult challenge almost impossible.

The political consequences of Folsom's behavior were immediately evident as he almost lost his opportunity to direct the legislature's organization. By custom, the nominee for governor announced his choices for Speaker of the house and president pro tem of the senate as soon as he won the Democratic nomination. When the legislature convened the following January, the legislators followed his recommendations as they elected their leaders. In 1946, Folsom waited until November, after he had won election to the governor's office, to announce his choice of legislative leaders.[12]

Folsom's neglect of his leadership responsibilities gave his legislative opponents an opportunity to organize the lawmakers for themselves. During July, W. L. "Doc" Martin of Greene County and Charles Norman of Bullock County became candidates for Speaker of the house. Among the newly elected senators, Bruce Henderson of Wilcox County, Joe Poole's 1946 campaign manager, declared himself a candidate for president pro tem. All three represented the traditional political leaders against whom Folsom had campaigned. They were experienced politicians, with a total of twenty-eight years of legislative experience. All three made their homes in the Black Belt and supported the section's conservative political interests. Bruce Henderson's family owned a plantation with a work force of several hundred Negro tenants. Martin also owned a Black Belt farm, while Norman owned and edited a weekly newspaper in a Black Belt county seat.[13]

Doc Martin, Charlie Norman, and Bruce Henderson spent the summer of 1946 securing pledges of support from legislative colleagues, but Jim Folsom was occupied with other matters. By September, when he finally began holding conferences with legislators, he knew what kind of man he wanted to nominate for Speaker of the house: a military veteran, an experienced legislator, a supporter of Folsom's campaign program, and a representative from northern Alabama. Folsom announced his choice of William M. Beck, DeKalb County's representative, on 15 November. Beck had served in the U.S. Army after World War I, the National Guard during the 1920s, and the U.S. Marine Corps during World War II. A county seat lawyer in Fort Payne, Beck had led county Democrats since they overthrew a Republican courthouse ring in 1934. He served one term in the legislature before returning to military service during World War II. Beck promised to support Folsom's program loyally, even though neither he nor DeKalb County had supported Folsom in the Democratic primary on 4 May. Although some people said Beck made financial contributions to both the Ellis and Folsom campaigns during the run-off, Folsom nominated Beck for Speaker of the house without questioning his promise of loyalty.[14]

By the time Folsom announced his support for Beck, Martin, Norman, and Henderson appeared to have already secured the votes of a majority of the legislators. When Representative Walter Givhan, the Farm Bureau legislator from Dallas County, announced his support for Doc Martin, observers declared that Martin had enough support to become the next Speaker. Certainly the pledged supporters of both Martin and Norman constituted a majority of the Alabama house. Among Alabama senators, Bruce Henderson had enough votes to ensure his election as president pro tem. Instead of fighting Henderson, Folsom announced on November 19 that the Black Belt senator had agreed to support the People's Program and would be his candidate for president pro tem.[15]

On the surface, Folsom's support of Henderson was inexplicable. He had campaigned on a program of expanded state services and fundamental political reforms. Henderson was a Black Belt planter, a leading Alabama prohibitionist, and Poole's 1946 campaign manager. Most journalists explained Folsom's announcement as political double-talk intended to disguise the fact that Folsom could not defeat Henderson. This explanation did not take into account, however, that Folsom, Poole, Boozer, and Horace Wilkinson had met secretly a few days after the primary on 4 May. At that meeting, Poole and Boozer exchanged promises of support for Folsom in the run-off for his pledge to allow each of them to make one-third of the governor's patronage decisions. If the politicians discussed legislative organization, Folsom may have obligated himself to support Poole's candidate for president pro tem. Since Beck was a Democratic leader in a county that gave a plurality of its votes to Boozer in the Democratic primary, Folsom may have chosen him for Speaker of the house for the same reason.[16]

The candidacies of Doc Martin and Charlie Norman forced Jim Folsom into an expensive and intense legislative battle before he assumed office. Beginning in mid-November, Folsom and his aides set up individual conferences with legislators. At each, Folsom argued that the house should elect Beck because the people expected the legislature to enact Folsom's program. When Folsom's words failed to convince, his aides employed other means of persuasion. Most commonly, the Folsomites offered highway construction projects and influence over patronage. In a few cases, Folsom's men arranged for legislators to purchase new personal automobiles through the state government, taking advantage of the state's post–World War II priority. A representative of one western Alabama county decided to support Beck after a Folsom supporter threatened to publicize evidence of peonage on the legislator's farm. A Folsom supporter in Montgomery helped a local legislator reduce his gambling debts in return for a vote for Beck. With persuasion, promises, and pressure that bordered on blackmail, Folsom battled to win the Speaker's gavel for William Beck.[17]

As Alabama legislators arrived in Montgomery for their organizational session in January 1947, the race for Speaker of the house was too close to predict a winner. Even though 61 of the 106 had given written pledges of support to Doc Martin, the Folsomites continued to solicit votes for Beck. On the eve of the legislature's first meeting, Martin realized that more than one-third of his backers had succumbed to the administration's pressure. Rather than seeking to win the votes back, Martin released all his supporters from their pledges. On the following morning, Folsom grinned from ear to ear in the gallery as the house of representatives chose Beck by a vote of fifty-eight to forty-four.[18]

Folsom celebrated Beck's election as the first major legislative victory of his administration. However, the defeat of W. L. Martin and Charles Norman was a Pyrrhic victory for the governor-elect. Before he had taken office or proposed the first piece of legislation, the contest for Speaker of the house had forced him to concede public works projects and patronage appointments. In spite of these efforts, more than 40 percent of the representatives still voted against the governor-elect's candidate. Beck's victory was even more costly in light of the fact that the struggle had been unnecessary. By exerting his leadership immediately after he won the run-off primary, Folsom could have prevented Martin and Norman from becoming serious candidates.

Folsom made a similar blunder with regard to the leadership of the Alabama Democratic Executive Committee. The committee derived its importance from the fact that it supervised the Democratic primary elections, the only elections offering Alabama voters a choice between viable candidates. The chairman was the most important officer on the committee because he had authority to call committee meetings, prescribe the agenda for each meeting, and conduct the business of the Alabama Democratic party whenever the executive committee was not in session. Since the 1920s, each new governor had nominated the new committee chairman in the same way he nominated the Speaker of the house and the president pro tem of the senate. When Folsom ran for governor in 1946, the chairman of the Alabama Democratic Executive Committee was Gessner T. McCorvey of Mobile, a conservative on economic issues and a staunch believer in white supremacy. Before Folsom took office in 1947, he assumed that he needed McCorvey's support in order to lead a successful administration. Therefore, without seeking a pledge of loyalty from McCorvey, Folsom telegraphed him and asked him to serve a second term as chairman of the Alabama Democratic Executive Committee. When McCorvey accepted, both the party chairman and the president pro tem of the senate were men with whom Folsom could not agree on major political issues.[19]

As the day of Jim Folsom's inauguration approached, he no longer stood on the summit of Alabama politics. His personal problems had distracted him from planning, and his inept handling of the news media made him seem unprepared and foolish. Men who would not follow his leadership had acquired leadership positions in the Alabama senate and the Alabama Democratic Executive Committee. Before officially assuming office, he had spent irreplaceable stores of patronage in an unnecessary struggle to elect the Speaker of the house. Throughout the interim between nomination and inauguration, Folsom failed to prove that he was capable of leading Alabama's progressive politicians in achieving the goals that he and they shared.

5

"Weaning Time . . . Squealing Time"

"Have you heard of the terrible tragedy?" one former legislator joked on 20 January 1947, the day Jim Folsom took office. "Twelve adults and six children have been stranded in Cullman." The joke captured the Jacksonian spirit of Folsom's inauguration. More than 100,000 Alabamians braved winter temperatures to hear James E. Folsom swear his oath of office and deliver his inaugural address. "Now I am *your* Governor!" he began. "My hands are untied . . . I am free to serve you, you and you and you!" Like the mobs that celebrated "Old Hickory's" inauguration in 1829, the people overwhelmed Montgomery all day. After the inaugural parade and swearing-in ceremony, they jammed receptions in the capitol and in the governor's mansion. Later, as guests at Folsom's inaugural ball, the voters packed a Maxwell Air Force Base hangar so tightly that dancing was almost impossible.[1]

On 21 January 1947, the celebration ended and Big Jim's rural constituents returned to their homes at the "branchheads."[2] As they left Montgomery, their new governor confronted the greatest challenge of his public career, the challenge of leading the Alabama Legislature to enact the People's Program. This was not a challenge that Folsom could master with a suds bucket, a hillbilly band, and a bunch of campaign circulars. The legislature comprised 149 local politicians, like the community leaders Big Jim circumvented in his election campaign. Chief among them were the representatives and senators of the Black Belt counties, whose influence depended on the poll tax, legislative malapportionment, and the unrevised state constitution. In the same situation, other governors had forgotten their promises of substantive reform in order to win votes for appropriations and budgets. Instead of forgetting his pledges, Governor Folsom began his tenure fighting to exert legislative leadership on behalf of the People's Program.

Before Governor Folsom could give his undivided attention to the Alabama Legislature, he had to spend time installing his family in the governor's mansion and his administration in the capitol. Actually, Folsom depended on his sisters, Ruby and Thelma, to supervise the establishment of the Folsom household in Montgomery. Ruby and her family, the Charles Ellis family, had been living with Big Jim ever since 1944, and she had already agreed to serve as his official hostess. Thelma and her husband, Ross Clark, joined the governor's household temporarily. The older sister, Thelma, helped Ruby make the transition to Montgomery and learn the etiquette of official entertaining.[3]

While the governor's sisters moved the family into the mansion, Folsom worked to organize his official family. As his administration took shape during January, it followed the same lines of personal loyalty that had prevented ideological consistency during the campaign. The most prominent positions went to Folsom's best friends. Bill Drinkard served as finance director, Bryce Davis as chairman of the Alabama Alcoholic Beverage Control Board, and Phillip Hamm as revenue commissioner. In the governor's office, Bill Lyerly was chief of staff, O. H. Finney was executive secretary, and Kenneth Griffith—the son of the circuit court judge A. A. Griffith—became the governor's legal adviser.

Governor Folsom gave the remaining positions in his cabinet to men who had made his election campaign successful. From the ranks of the old Bibb Graves organization, Folsom selected Frank Boswell to direct the Department of Corrections, Bert Thomas to head the Conservation Department, and L. L. Gwaltney, Jr., to be superintendent of insurance. For his work in the counties of west-central Alabama, Folsom made Ward McFarland the director of the Highway Department. Recognizing the contributions of organized labor, the governor asked R. R. Wade, a former president of the Alabama State Federation of Labor, to direct the Department of Labor. In gratitude to his friends in Cullman, Folsom appointed the Cullman County sheriff, J. D. Mitchell, as the director of public safety. Folsom did not reward Birmingham attorney Horace Wilkinson with a state job, but he did follow Wilkinson's recommendation in appointing Henry W. Sweet as director of the Alabama State Docks.[4]

As he made his cabinet appointments, Governor Folsom adhered to a Jacksonian philosophy concerning patronage. He assumed that each man was competent for any job within the administration. Thus, he made a mortician his finance director and selected a schoolteacher as his commissioner of revenue. The only qualification he expected from his appointees was absolute loyalty to the administration. For this purpose, he collected a resignation dated 20 January 1948 from each of his cabinet members before his inauguration. Finally, since he assumed the loyalty of his appointees, Governor Folsom took public responsibility for the actions of any of them. During later years, whenever a member of his administration received public criticism, the governor defended him publicly and explained that the voters would have an opportunity to commend or censure at the next election. As far as Folsom was concerned, this was the only way that state employees could be made responsible to the democratic process.[5]

Folsom's distribution of minor patronage plums inspired the first criticism of his administration as opponents charged that he was using the state payroll to reward his political supporters. For example, three members of the Strawberry Pickers went to work as engineering assistants for the Highway Department. The Conservation Department hired another Strawberry Picker as a game farm supervisor, while the fifth musician found work as a deputy fire marshal in the Commerce Department. Under a law that allowed him to hire additional office help on a temporary basis, Folsom increased his clerical staff from twelve to twenty-nine. While a few of the "temporary clerks" actually did office work, more than a dozen of them became Folsom's "special investigators." Hired in recognition of their political support, the investigators performed a wide variety of ad hoc duties. Cecil Folsom checked the political backgrounds of citizens Folsom considered for local appointments. "Special investigators" helped the ABC Board to combat the flow of untaxed whiskey from Mississippi into Alabama. Folsom's men worked with the Revenue Department to catch gasoline distributors who shipped fuel into Alabama without paying the state gasoline tax. Governor Folsom even used his most trusted investigators to lobby the Alabama Legislature on behalf of administration bills.[6]

While making patronage appointments during January, Governor

Folsom precipitated his first direct conflict with the legislature. Alabama Polytechnic Institute (API), located in Auburn, was Alabama's land grant college and the home of the Alabama Agricultural Extension Service. Its Board of Trustees included one trustee from each of Alabama's ten congressional districts, the governor, and the superintendent of education. The ten appointed trustees served staggered, twelve-year terms. As a result of unusual circumstances, Folsom began his administration with an opportunity to appoint five new trustees: three to begin full twelve-year terms and two to complete the unexpired terms of late trustees. Although the appointments required senate confirmation, Folsom's five appointments appeared to give him immediate control of the API trustees. On 30 January, Folsom exercised his prerogative by nominating Gould Beech, Reuben Wright of Tuscaloosa, and Guy Lynn of Huntsville to the Board of Trustees.[7]

Alabama's agricultural leaders and Black Belt politicians suddenly realized that Folsom's trustees threatened their interests. Dr. Luther Duncan, the president of API, had already announced his desire to retire. During Duncan's tenure, API had given first priority to agricultural education and had given preference to the "Ag" school in the allocation of resources for salaries, physical plant, and student scholarships. The president's retirement presented an opportunity for the trustees to evaluate and possibly to redirect the educational emphasis. Furthermore, the API Board of Trustees governed the work of the Agricultural Extension Service. Since the 1930s, the Extension Service had been an instrument of Black Belt political influence in Alabama. Working closely with members of the Farm Bureau, Extension Service leaders had campaigned for Joe Poole in 1946 and for gubernatorial, legislative, and congressional candidates in earlier elections. In 1947, agricultural leaders feared that Governor Folsom and his trustees would punish the Extension Service director, P. O. Davis, or his assistant Jimmie Lawson for this illegal political activity. Some of Folsom's opponents even speculated that the governor would attempt to use the Extension Service to build his own political machine.[8]

Governor Folsom's nomination of Gould Beech particularly alarmed Alabama agricultural leaders. As editor of the *Southern Farmer,* Beech had persistently criticized both the Extension Service and the Alabama Farm Bureau. Beech's mentor was Aubrey Williams, an ardent New Dealer during the 1930s and a backer of agricultural reformers in the Resettlement Administration and the

Farm Security Administration. Like Williams, Beech supported the Rural Electrification Administration and the Farmers Union, an agricultural organization created to serve the needs of farmers outside the Farm Bureau Federation. *Alabama* identified Beech as an "eager young leftist" who was "thoroughly steeped in all the various socialistic schemes, share-the-wealth plans, and racial equality goals of the party-line followers." Since Folsom had nominated Beech, *Alabama* assumed that the governor was planning "the Extension Service purge program engineered by Aubrey Williams, Gould Beech, and other leftists." Judge F. W. Hare of Monroeville, an API trustee, shared the same anxiety. Before attending the first meeting of 1947, he wrote to Dr. Duncan, "I hope very much to be present at this meeting to see what our new 'boss' has in store for us. I hope we are not in the hands of the Philistines."[9]

The API trustees' meeting on 21 February confirmed the fears of agricultural leaders and politicians. With the support of the superintendent of education, Austin Meadows, and one incumbent trustee, Folsom and his appointees adopted a strongly worded resolution criticizing the Extension Service. The resolution cited the Extension Service leaders for political activities, interference in the affairs of the Alabama Farm Bureau, and failure to serve the needs of all Alabama farmers. The Board of Trustees also invited P. O. Davis and Jimmie Lawson to answer the criticisms at the board's next meeting. Governor Folsom elaborated on the criticisms in a speech to the API student body on the same day. Folsom declared that the Extension Service needed appropriations and personnel sufficient to serve all Alabama farmers. However, Folsom continued, "the Extension Service has got to get out of politics. And I mean all kinds of politics. Local politics. State politics. National politics. My kind of politics. Your kind of politics. Government politics and farm organization politics. The farmers in every Alabama county have got enough sense to run their own farm organization."[10]

Reaction throughout the state to the trustees' resolution followed the traditional division between progressive and conservative Alabama Democrats. Speaking for the more progressive faction, the *Montgomery Advertiser* and the *Birmingham News* welcomed the criticisms. The *News* editorialized, "Long since there has been a need for a complete airing of this situation and the charges and counter-charges it has evoked. The Auburn Trustees have taken an important step." *Alabama* voiced the objections of conservative Alabama Democrats as it warned readers of "the Folsom-Beech purge campaign against the Extension Service" and of the obvious class hatred in Folsom's speech to the students. The president of the Alabama Farm Bureau, Walter Randolph, was even more vociferous. He called the resolution an attempt by the Farmers Union and the CIO to seize control of the Extension Service and to destroy the Farm Bureau. It was Folsom's way, Randolph declared, of repaying the CIO for its 1946 campaign endorsement.[11]

The actions of the Farm Bureau president proved the seriousness of his sentiments. On behalf of the Farm Bureau, Randolph entered suit in Alabama's Fifteenth Judicial Circuit challenging the legality of the API trustees' meeting on 21 February. The suit argued that the meeting was not official because Folsom's nominees had participated in it without having first been confirmed by the Alabama senate. Although the nominees' participation followed an accepted precedent, Randolph's argument was constitutionally sound.[12]

When Governor Folsom recognized the validity of Randolph's contention, he devised a legislative scheme to circumvent the inevitable court decision. On Saturday, 1 March, Folsom summoned the Alabama Legislature to meet in special session on Monday, 3 March. In the proclamation, the governor asked the legislators to confirm his trustee nominations and call a constitutional convention. Irritated by the sudden summons and influenced by senators from Black Belt and industrial counties, the senate treated the governor with contempt. First, the senators resurrected two of Governor Sparks's nominations, Representative Earl McGowin and Frank Park Samford, an insurance magnate, and filled the two unexpired terms. Then, while Extension Service agents and Farm Bureau officials sat together in the gallery, the senate ignored the nominations of Beech, Wright, and Lynn in order to debate a constitutional amendment to make the API Board of Trustees a self-perpetuating body.[13]

On Tuesday, the second day of the special session, the senators were no more courteous than they had been on Monday. Ignoring a petition from the API student body, they did not consider confirming Beech, Wright, or Lynn. Venting the anger of the senate, Senator W. A. Gulledge declared that the students' petition was not worth the paper it was written on. Believing that the senate's opposition was implacable, Beech formally withdrew his name from consideration, and the governor withdrew the nominations of Reuben Wright and Guy Lynn. Having conceded defeat, Folsom negotiated with Bruce Henderson before replacing his initial nominations with the names of Senator V. S. Summerlin of Crenshaw County, Judge W. L. Parrish of Chilton County, and Redus Collier of Morgan County. The senate confirmed all three nominations without opposition. Governor Folsom then submitted the names of Representative Roberts Brown of Auburn and Joe Davis, a veterinarian of Marshall County, for two new vacancies on the Board of Trustees. In a final show of disrespect, the senate adjourned sine die, thereby ending the special session before considering either Brown or Davis.

Meanwhile, students at API reacted to Senator Gulledge's remark without knowing that the legislature had ended its session. Six hundred angry students left a mass meeting on the campus in an improvised march on the Alabama capitol. Their banners expressed their sentiments: "We Want Our Trustees," "Auburn Backs Big Jim," "Any Change Would Be an Improvement," and "To Hell with the Legislature!" The students' arrival in Montgomery was anticlimatic. Finding no legislature in session, they drove around the capitol a few times before heading back to Auburn.[14]

When the API Board of Trustees met again on 17 March 1947, Governor Folsom presided without making reference to the resolution adopted on 21 February. Instead, he made a brief presentation of charts and statistics to show that the productivity of Alabama farms lagged behind the productivity of other southern states. Concluding his remarks, he attributed Alabama's lag to the inefficiency and politicization of the Extension Service. When Folsom had finished, the trustees voted to recess for lunch while the Extension Service director, P. O. Davis, and his assistant, Jimmie Lawson, prepared to meet with them. The decision to recess indicated that a majority of the trustees did not support Folsom's position.

After the recess, Governor Folsom was resigned to humiliation and P. O. Davis was haughty. Davis began his report to the trustees with the comment, "Now I would like to give you this *real* information about Alabama agriculture." Presenting a list of county fairs, stocks shows, and similar activities, Davis asserted that the Extension Service had been very busy working for the Alabama farmer. He denied that the Extension Service involved itself in politics and produced a letter from his files that warned county agents to avoid political activity. Jimmie Lawson echoed his superior's argument, claiming that the charges of political activity were nothing but vague, undocumented rumors. Although three of the trustees questioned Davis and Lawson closely, no one could present specific evidence that contradicted their report. Finally, Frank Park Samford offered a resolution commending the Extension Service's agricultural leadership. Folsom watched passively as the Board of Trustees adopted Samford's resolution.[15]

When the conflict had passed, the defenders of the Extension Service had scored the first major political victory over Governor Folsom. Obviously, the overrepresentation of Black Belt counties in the Alabama senate made the victory possible. However, Governor Folsom himself contributed mightily to his own defeat. He blundered first by nominating men who were not API alumni. With forethought, he could have predicted that Gould Beech's nomination would stir controversy. Folsom made the further mistake of allowing the trustees to criticize the Extension Service before the Alabama senate confirmed his nominees. In his haste to avoid a defeat in court, the governor angered senators with his sudden special session. In fact, Folsom's hurry did not even allow his administration to discover how many of the thirty-five senators would endorse his choices. Once embroiled in conflict, Folsom's will to lead wilted. Instead of demanding that the senate give his nominees fair consideration, Folsom withdrew their names and compromised with Bruce Henderson. At the second meeting of the Board of Trustees, Folsom again failed to lead. His passivity allowed Davis and Lawson to evade the charges of inefficiency and political involvement. In spite of the fact that the Extension Service was guilty of political activity, Folsom's mistakes allowed his opponents to embarrass him.

After the legislature stormed out of town on 4 March, the Folsom administration concentrated on preparations for the biennial legislative session. Beginning on 6 May 1947, the house and senate would meet for thirty-six nonconsecutive days to provide for all of Alabama's legislative needs. Despite his poor preinaugural planning and the legislators' antipathy for him, Governor Folsom formulated a shrewd strategy for presenting the People's Program to the legislature. The Folsom administration decided that it would work hardest for public education, old-age pensions, and tax reforms during the early weeks of the session. Later in the session, Folsom would seek legislation for farm-to-market roads, legislative reapportionment, and poll tax repeal. Since the legislature ignored his call for a constitutional convention during its March special session, Governor Folsom would wait until a later session to press that issue again.

Governor Folsom had already taken steps to smooth the way for his proposals. During the legislature's organizational session in

January, the session during which the legislators elected their officers, Folsom recommended that the legislature create interim committees to study the long-term needs of Alabama and prepare specific legislation for the biennial session. Responding favorably to the idea, the legislature established seven committees to study public education, highways, agriculture, conservation, the judicial system, health and public welfare, and financial and tax matters. The Speaker of the house and the president of the senate, Lieutenant Governor Clarence Inzer, appointed members of their respective houses to the interim committees, choosing legislators for each committee primarily on the basis of the members' expressed preferences. Only for the committee on finance and taxation did the presiding officers attempt to balance the number of pro-Folsom, anti-Folsom, and nonpartisan legislators.[16]

As the interim committees studied the state between February and May, the Folsom administration presented its undiluted program to the relevant committees. Governor Folsom appeared before the interim committee on education to ask that the legislators raise the average teacher's annual salary from $1,276 to $1,800, provide for a standard nine-month school term, and supply public school students with free textbooks. Before the interim committee on health and public welfare, Folsom asked for monthly old-age pensions of forty-five dollars. He proposed a 30 percent budgetary increase to the interim committee on finance and taxation. Folsom argued that the increase was needed to improve public education, pave roads, and pay old-age pensions. The governor recommended that the committee propose a constitutional amendment that would divide the state's income tax surplus equally between public education and old-age pensions. Finally, he proposed that the committee write legislation to equalize all property tax assessments, repeal all exemptions to the state sales tax, and close miscellaneous loopholes in the tax laws.[17]

Folsom's tactic worked well. Because he took the People's Program before the interim committees, he could accurately claim to have represented the people's interest in the legislature. Because six of the committees studied specific areas of legislation, Folsom could rely on organized interest groups, like the Alabama Education Association, to promote his proposals. Because six of the committees were composed of legislators who had expressed interest in the committees' areas of concern, the governor was certain that his program would receive a sympathetic hearing. And because legislators themselves made the studies and drafted legislation, Governor Folsom would later be able to urge the Alabama Legislature to enact the bills which its own committees had prepared.[18]

This did not mean, however, that Folsom's ideas sailed through the committees on their way to easy legislative approval. Though the committees on education and on health and public welfare eagerly endorsed Folsom's recommendations, the legislators still confronted two thorny problems. The first was the problem of financing higher schoolteacher salaries and old-age pensions, a problem that fell within the jurisdiction of the interim committee on finance and taxation. From the committee's first day of deliberations, its chairman, Senator Bruce Henderson, had stressed the importance of "economy." "Economy" in 1947 meant that the interim committee on finance and taxation opposed any new taxes or any tax increases for the funding of expanded state services. For Henderson and other financially conservative legislators, "economy" offered a politically attractive way of opposing the expanded state services that Governor Folsom proposed.[19]

Since Henderson's committee would not consider raising taxes, the most attractive source of funds was the surplus revenue generated by the state income tax, and both the advocates of public education and the advocates of old-age pensions coveted those funds. When Alabama voters ratified the income tax in 1935, they designated its proceeds exclusively for the retirement of Alabama's floating debt and the reduction of property taxes.[20] Since the beginning of World War II, however, the income tax revenue had increased steadily and exceeded the need for debt retirement and tax reduction.[21] Thus, in 1947, the interim committee on education and the Alabama Education Association insisted that the income tax surplus be redirected to help finance improvements in the public schools. At the same time, Governor Folsom and the interim committee on health and public welfare wanted to divide the surplus revenue equally between education and old-age pensions. Even though the interim committee on finance and taxation sided with the public welfare advocates, there was no legislative consensus on the issue before the biennial legislative session began.[22]

The second major problem facing the legislators, especially the supporters of public education, was one of time. Since the state income tax had originally been established by constitutional amendment, another amendment was required to reallocate the income tax revenue. The constitution mandated that each amendment be ratified by a popular referendum held at least ninety days after the end of the legislative session in which it was proposed. Since the 1947 biennial session could last until October, only a special session of the legislature could propose an amendment in time to hold a referendum before the start of the 1947–48 school year. However, Governor Folsom refused to convene a special session of the legislature. Still smarting over his defeat in the first special session of 1947, Folsom claimed that there was no point in holding a special session until the legislators agreed among themselves how they would divide the income tax surplus. By delaying a call for a special session, the governor increased pressure on legislative supporters of education to aid in the effort to raise old-age pensions.[23]

The interim committees disbanded and the 1947 biennial session began before the legislators could resolve either problem. Addressing the legislature on opening day, 6 May 1947, Governor Folsom announced that he would call a special session for the purpose of reallocating the income tax surplus. The special session would convene, he explained, on 13 May 1947 during a recess of the biennial session. Continuing his address, Folsom reviewed every facet of the state government, recommending measures that closely followed the reports of the interim committees. Even the budget he proposed differed only in detail from that of the interim committee on finance and taxation. Going beyond the committee report, Folsom asked the legislature to repeal all sales tax exemptions, reform the collection of sales tax, and overhaul the corporate tax structure. In this detour away from the report of Henderson's committee, Folsom still followed the report of the Revenue Study Committee, a legislative interim committee created in 1945. The governor's strategy was astute. Because he relied on the work of the legislative committees, no opponent could fight his proposals with the argument that they were impractical or poorly planned.[24]

In response to the governor's announcement, the legislature recessed the biennial session and opened the special session on 13 May. Everyone knew that only quick action would allow for a state referendum before the school year started, but the legislators were deadlocked. Because reallocation of the income tax surplus required a constitutional amendment, any proposal needed at least two-thirds of the votes in both legislative houses. The supporters of education and the advocates of old-age pensions each had enough votes to defeat the other. Finally, on 16 May, the legislators reached a compromise. Legislators who favored diverting the entire surplus to public education promised to vote for an appropriation of $5.5 million for pensions when the biennial session considered the 1947–49 budget. Under the terms of this compromise, old-age pension advocates endorsed the constitutional amendment that allocated the entire income tax surplus for public education. Having acted, the legislature adjourned sine die on 22 May so that the referendum could be held on 26 August 1947.[25]

The work of the 1947 biennial session had scarcely begun when the session resumed on 3 June. At the top of the agenda were the biennial appropriation bills and a variety of new revenue measures. As prescribed in the state constitution, the house Ways and Means Committee was the first to study Folsom's budget proposals and the report of the interim committee on finance and taxation. The work proceeded quickly because the interim committee had completed all the preliminary investigative tasks. By the end of June, the committee reported an amended version of the governor's budget to the house for debate and action. After the representatives made a few minor amendments, the house of representatives voted to appropriate $39,250,128 for general fund expenses and $98,599,928 for public education.[26]

Meanwhile, the senate Finance and Taxation Committee chose to write its own budget proposals. As in the house, the work of the interim committee helped to expedite the deliberations. By late July, the senators had written bills that allotted $41,010,565 for general fund expenditures and $99,302,728 for Alabama schools. The full senate approved the committee's recommendations with only one notable amendment. That amendment made the appropriations for the University of Alabama and API contingent on the resumption of varsity football competition between the two schools.[27]

The conference committee appointed by Speaker Beck and Lieutenant Governor Inzer quickly reconciled the differences between the house and senate appropriation bills. After comparing each house's proposals line by line, the conference committee wrote a new budget that consisted of the larger appropriation for each item in the house and senate bills. When the conferees finished, they reported a general fund appropriation of $41,829,766 and an educational appropriation of $99,402,728 and had eliminated the varsity football amendment. When adopted by both houses, the 1947–49 biennial budget included the promised $5.5 million appropriation for old-age pensions and represented an increase of approximately $50 million over the appropriations for the preceding biennium.[28]

In addition to the biennial budget, the legislature acted on two administration revenue bills during the early weeks of the session. The first, introduced by Representative John Snodgrass, honored Folsom's campaign promise to equalize taxes by repealing all exemptions to the Alabama sales tax. However, by the time the bill emerged from the house Ways and Means Committee, lobbyists had persuaded the representatives to gut the proposal. As finally enacted, Snodgrass's bill repealed sales tax exemptions only on alcoholic beverages, cigarettes, and stock withdrawn for private use by retail store owners. The second bill, authored by Representative George Wallace, placed an additional 2 percent tax on liquor sales and earmarked the proceeds for the construction of four regional trade schools. While both the superintendent of education, Austin Meadows, and the Alabama Education Association lobbied for the bill, Governor Folsom privately urged his friends to support it also. With such strong backing, Wallace's bill easily won legislative approval.[29]

The income tax amendment, a large increase in funds for old-age pensions, the biennial budgets, a diluted sales tax exemption repeal, and revenue for four new trade schools made up an impressive record of legislative action for the first half of 1947. Although the legislature had not approved every proposal he made, Governor Folsom deserved a large measure of credit for the lawmakers' accomplishments. Since March, he had made a remarkable recovery from the humiliation of the first special session. He had stressed those portions of the People's Program that were most popular across the state and had used the interim committees to lead legislators to identify actively with improvements for public education and elderly citizens. While avoiding another disastrous confrontation with "Big Mule" and Black Belt power, Folsom had worked with lobbyists for education and public welfare to win support for his ideas.

In spite of the accomplishments of the legislature, Folsom's critics were unrelenting in their attacks on his administration and his personal conduct. Throughout 1947, the newspapers printed new criticisms of the governor almost as frequently as the sun rose over the capitol's white dome. At first, the critics protested that Governor Folsom intended to destroy the integrity of the state's civil service system. Within two weeks of the inauguration, four prison system administrators signed resignations under pressure from the prison director, Frank Boswell. All five of the Strawberry Pickers secured state jobs without taking a merit system qualifying examination. Folsom's appointees on the Alcoholic Beverage Control Board abruptly transferred nineteen employees to assignments outside of their hometowns, a proven tactic for coaxing resignations. Hubert Baughan of *Alabama* summarized the criticisms when he sarcastically defended Folsom's actions: "He was strong for the merit system, but only his friends had merit."[30]

Later, critics focused on evidence of extravagance and political favoritism in the Folsom administration. After coming into office, Folsom created fifty new jobs in executive departments, including seventeen new positions on his office staff. The governor assigned new state automobiles to his executive secretary, legal adviser, revenue commissioner, and the secretary of state, even though none of these officials had ever driven state vehicles before. Bill Drinkard arranged for the purchase of twenty-six new Fords from his brother's dealership, and the state did a booming business in selling used cars. Because of the post–World War II shortages, used cars sold for 20 percent more than the original purchase price even after they had traveled up to 70,000 miles. The Folsom administration showed political favoritism by channeling the sale of used cars through W. Cleve Stokes of Montgomery.[31]

Folsom's personality and conduct provided another favorite target for his critics. The Alabama State Docks maintained a sporting boat for the entertainment of its clients. Whenever the governor announced that he was going to inspect the operation of the docks or survey the shoreline of Baldwin County, he was actually planning a deep-sea fishing trip on board the state yacht. Likewise, whenever the governor left the capital in order to review the work of the Conservation Department, he and some buddies were taking a hunting trip. Even more embarrassing was the public notice that "Kissin' Jim" attracted. During the 1947 celebration of Mardi Gras, Folsom attended a ball in Mobile where girls lined up for a kiss. According to the *Dothan Eagle,* Folsom "didn't miss any of the volunteers, either." Visiting Cullman for the annual Strawberry Festival, Folsom stopped to meet a high school majorette. In his booming voice, the governor asked, "Want to get married?" Perhaps Folsom's behavior was not scandalous, but most Alabamians agreed that his conduct was not appropriate for the office he held.[32]

Governor Folsom handled the criticisms as if he had expected them. On the campaign trail in 1946, Folsom had predicted that the corrupt politicians and selfish interest groups would squeal like piglets being weaned when his administration threatened their privileges. So, when the newspapers began criticizing his conduct as governor, Folsom told a statewide radio audience, "Weaning time has gone by and squealing time is *here!*" He also used a political cliché to deny that any of the charges were true. "If I have made a mistake," Folsom said, "it was due to one thing. I have taken on too many enemies of the people's interests at one time."[33]

As legislative factions coalesced during 1947, Folsom enjoyed strongest support in the house of representatives where Speaker Beck had given the most strategic committee assignments to pro-Folsom legislators. Folsom's chief leader in the house was John Snodgrass of Jackson County, chairman of the house Ways and Means Committee. Although his Spartan personality did not approve of Folsom's personal conduct, "Captain John" believed that the governor's program served the interests of his northern Alabama constituents. His eight years of legislative experience and his reputation for principled honesty lent credibility to the administration's legislative efforts. Similarly, the legislative talents of George Wallace were assets for the Folsom administration. Despite his home in the Black Belt's Barbour County, Wallace recognized Big Jim's genius on the campaign trail and had ambitions of following Folsom's example in state politics. In the legislature, Wallace labored to master both the rules of procedure and the details of each piece of major legislation. He thereby made himself indispensable to the Folsom administration as a perceptive analyst of legislation and legislative maneuver.[34]

Behind the leadership of Snodgrass and Wallace, the Folsom administration could count on the support of representatives who shared in the administration's patronage. Among these, E. L. Roberts of Etowah County shared Wallace's ambitions of running for state office. Thus, the Gadsden attorney aligned himself with Governor Folsom because he believed political loyalty would increase his influence over local patronage decisions and allow him to consolidate his political base. Representatives G. B. Cox of Chilton County, Paul Coburn of Colbert County, and Emmett Wood of Washington County were all shrewd local politicians who wanted a portion of what Folsom called the "emoluments of office." Accordingly, all three loyally supported the administration in the legislature while accepting employment as "temporary clerks" or "special investigators."[35]

Among the thirty-five senators, Folsom's friends were few. Ordinarily, the president pro tem served as the administration's floor leader, but in 1947 Bruce Henderson was Folsom's chief opponent. Instead, Folsom received support from Joe Langan of Mobile, an independent and progressive legislator, and from Broughton Lamberth of Tallapoosa County, an undistinguished local politician with an appetite for patronage. Senators Rankin Fite of Marion County and Fuller Kimbrell of Fayette County provided able leadership for the senate's pro-Folsom minority. The two represented adjacent districts in the western part of northern Alabama and rode together to and from legislative sessions in Montgomery. Because both aspired to political power as legislators, they studied the rules of the senate during their weekly drives and helped each other become masterful legislative tacticians. According to an Alabama political legend, neither Fite nor Kimbrell was a Folsom supporter before 1947. However, after the first special session, the administration desperately solicited support with offers of road construction projects and other political favors. Surprisingly, most senators refused the offers. While driving between Fayette County and Montgomery one day, Kimbrell observed, "You know, Rankin, the state treasury divided by five is a lot more than the state treasury divided by thirty-five." Fite pondered the idea in silence for several miles before responding, "That's exactly right." So saying, Fite and Kimbrell became Folsom's stalwart defenders in the Alabama senate.[36]

In the house of representatives, the opposition faction represented the interests of the Black Belt and the industrial district. Walter Givhan of Dallas County spoke for the Alabama Farm Bureau throughout his more than thirty years of legislative service. Wallace D. Malone of Houston County, the president of a Dothan bank, was Folsom's most outspoken opponent. In one house debate, Malone violated legislative courtesy by accusing Folsom of "gross incompetence." Although never so outspoken, Doc Martin, Charlie Norman, Pugh Haynes of Lowndes County, Ira Pruitt of Sumter County, Hugh Kaul and J. Paul Meeks of Jefferson County, Thomas A. Johnston III of Mobile County, and L. W. Brannan of Baldwin County shared Malone's opinion. Only their exclusion from influential committee posts prevented these men from challenging Folsom's leadership of the house.[37]

The center of legislative opposition to Folsom was the senate, where Bruce Henderson held the office of president pro tem. With the cooperation of the president of the senate, Lieutenant Governor Inzer, Henderson awarded the most important committee assignments to anti-Folsom senators. Henderson received consistent support from fellow Black Belt senators Robin Swift, a lumber mill owner and veteran legislator from Escambia County, and James S. Coleman, a graduate of the U.S. Naval Academy and a bright, young attorney from Greene County. By giving his support to Henderson, Albert Boutwell of Jefferson County, an established corporation lawyer, demonstrated that Alabama's "Big Mules" endorsed the anti-Folsom faction. Senator James B. Allen of Etowah County, another corporate attorney, used his mastery of the senate rules and his detailed knowledge of every major bill for Henderson's faction in the same way that George Wallace aided the Folsom administration in the house.[38]

As factionalism intensified during the 1947 biennial session, Folsom's hope of securing political reform suffered first. In the house, E. L. Roberts introduced a resolution calling for a constitutional convention, and J. J. Benford authored bills that sought to reapportion the house according to county population and the senate by granting each county one seat. The Folsom administration also endorsed a bill to reduce the poll tax's cumulative feature to a maximum of two years. Constitutional revision and reapportionment died on the house floor in votes of sixty to twenty, forty-seven to thirty-four, and forty-nine to thirty-four, respectively. The house Constitution and Elections Committee killed poll tax reform when it failed to report the proposal for house action.[39]

Obvious political partisanship also blocked Governor Folsom's program for paving farm-to-market roads. The administration proposed legislation to authorize the issue of $40 million worth of Highway Department revenue bonds. The proceeds of the bond issue would be divided between the sixty-seven counties and the Alabama Highway Department. With the aid of Speaker Beck, Folsom's partisans eased the bond issue through the house on a vote of seventy-three to twenty-two. In the senate, however, the bill encountered fierce opposition. Some senators complained that highway construction costs were inflated in 1947 and that the state would save money by delaying new projects until prices declined. Other senators argued that the state could save money by issuing general obligation bonds instead of revenue bonds. The difference between the two was that whereas revenue bonds were secured by the promise of future Highway Department revenue, the general obligation bonds were backed by the full faith and credit of the state. Furthermore, general obligation bonds, unlike revenue bonds, required ratification in a state constitutional referendum. Behind these arguments, the senators hid the underlying political consideration: road construction was the currency in the commerce of political patronage. The senators opposed Folsom's road bond issue to keep the governor from supplementing his supply of patronage.[40]

In addition to opposing the political reforms and road construction bond issue, anti-Folsom legislators sought to reduce the governor's powers. A bill regulating the number and use of state vehicles sailed through the legislature in July. The house sustained Folsom's veto only after he imposed similar limitations on state automobiles by executive order. Fearing that Folsom might bankrupt the state, anti-Folsom legislators considered a recess of the biennial session at the end of the twenty-fourth legislative day so that the legislature could reconvene at any time during 1948 to protect the state treasury. When the plan proved to be impractical, the anti-Folsom faction turned its attention to the Office of the Examiner of Public Accounts. Since 1939 the state's primary auditing agency had worked under the supervision of the finance director, a gubernatorial appointee. Anti-Folsom senators wrote legislation to reconstitute the Examiner of Public Accounts office as an independent department under the legislature's supervision. Believing that the bill would silence criticisms of administration extravagance, Governor Folsom chose to endorse the plan. The legislature enacted it without a fight.[41]

Even the creation of the Department of Examiners of Public Accounts did not satisfy the anti-Folsom senators. With less than a month left in the biennial session, Senator Jim Allen introduced the "self-starter" amendment. The proposed constitutional amendment required the governor to call the legislature into session "whenever petitioned to do so by three-fifths of the members elected to each house." Allen presented the self-starter amendment as a progressive reform that would make the state government more responsive to the people. Governor Folsom correctly interpreted the amendment as a political attack on his administration and an assault on the constitutional separation of powers. Nevertheless, Folsom did not ask his followers to fight the amendment. Rather, he decided that the amendment would allow him to campaign personally against his senate opposition just before the state referendum on 6 January 1948. With Folsom restraining his supporters, the self-starter amendment won the approval of both the house and the senate.[42]

As the biennial session neared its conclusion, partisanship became so intense that no major legislation survived senate filibusters. Three bills appeared on top of the senate's calendar during those final days. The first was a bill to rebate to farmers five-sixths of the gasoline tax they paid on tractor fuel, a measure sponsored by the Farm Bureau. The second and third were administration bills, the road construction bond issue and a reapportionment bill known as the sixty-seven senator bill. To avoid opposing road construction or reapportionment directly, Folsom's opponents did not want either bill to come up for a vote. Meanwhile, Folsom was determined to defeat the tractor gas tax rebate if the Black Belt senators killed the administration measures. The anti-Folsom filibuster began on 12 September, when only ten days remained in the 1947 biennial session.[43]

The anti-Folsom strategy almost worked. On the next to the last day of the session, the reapportionment bill died because there was not enough time remaining for it to win house approval. The senate passed the tractor gas tax rebate bill with a vote of thirty-three to zero and sent it to the governor for signing. A filibuster against the road construction bond issue began. Angry at the senate, Governor Folsom retaliated. On the last day of the biennial session, he resubmitted his nomination of Roberts Brown to the API Board of Trustees. To avoid dealing with the trustee issue again, the anti-Folsom senators voted against considering any messages from the governor. Then Folsom sent the tractor gas tax rebate bill back to the senate with his veto. As the 1947 session expired, Folsom's supporters began their own filibuster and blocked the opposition from acting on Folsom's veto. They sacrificed the road construction bond issue in order to kill the Farm Bureau's bill and left the nomination of Roberts Brown in the senate *Journal* as a testimony to the anti-Folsom faction's obstructionism.[44]

When the Alabama Legislature adjourned sine die, the first nine months of Folsom's gubernatorial tenure came to a conclusion. During those nine months, Governor Folsom had led the legislature to provide additional funds to both public education and old-age pensions. However, the Folsom administration achieved those victories with the blessing of Alabama's conservative political and economic leaders. In direct confrontations between the governor and representatives of those conservative interests, Folsom's plans had been frustrated. The partisanship of the last weeks clearly demonstrated that no matter how much "squealing" transpired, the Folsom administration would not easily "wean" the established political interests from the Alabama government.

Folsom campaigning in Cullman in 1946. To his right are his daughter Rachel, his sister Ruby, and his daughter Melissa. (Courtesy of *Birmingham News*)

Listening to the Little Man's Big Friend, 1946. (Courtesy of *Birmingham News*)

Folsom and the Strawberry Pickers, 1946. (Courtesy of the Alabama Department of Archives and History)

Inauguration in 1947. (Courtesy of Auburn University Archives, General Photo Collection)

Henry Wallace's visit to Montgomery in September 1947. *Left to right:* Gould Beech, James Folsom, and Wallace. (Courtesy of Auburn University Archives, General Photo Collection)

The governor at the Barbizon School of Modeling, New York City, March 1948. (Courtesy of Associated Press)

Folsom campaigning in Montevallo in March 1954. (Courtesy of *Birmingham News*)

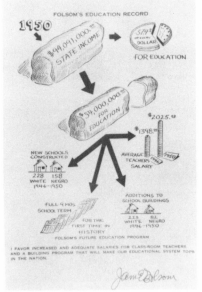

Above, left: Folsom on steps of U.S. Supreme Court Building, March 3, 1948, the day after Christine Putman Johnston filed paternity suit. *Above, right:* Jamelle and Jim Folsom reading congratulatory telegrams on May 6, 1948, the day after their wedding. (Courtesy of Associated Press)

Below, left and right: 1955 campaign circulars. (Courtesy of the Alabama Department of Archives and History)

Folsom campaigning in Warrior, March 1954. (Courtesy of *Birmingham News*)

Inaugural parade, 1955. Folsom and Lieutenant Governor Guy Hardwick. (Courtesy of *Birmingham News*)

Folsom on trial for driving while intoxicated, Jefferson County Courthouse, February 26, 1952. (Courtesy of *Birmingham News*)

At Congressman Frank Boykin's hunting lodge in late 1955, an intoxicated Folsom listens to Averell Harriman's speech. (Courtesy of *Alabama News Magazine*)

Left to right: James E. Folsom, Jr., Folsom, President Jimmy Carter, Jack Folsom and Jamelle, May 14, 1979, in the White House. (Courtesy of Associated Press)

One of Folsom's personal business enterprises. (Courtesy of Alabama Department of Archives and History)

Folsom campaigning in 1962. (Courtesy of *Birmingham News*)

Folsom at home in Cullman. *Left:* January 16, 1979. *Right:* September 2, 1982. (Courtesy of *Birmingham News*)

6

Stalemate

Political partisanship in the Alabama senate completely frustrated Governor Folsom's program during the second half of the 1947 biennial session. The defeat of his road construction bond issue and political reforms was evidence that Black Belt politicians and their allies still had enough legislative influence to ignore the mandate of a popularly elected governor. The defeats also fostered speculation that Governor Folsom was helpless. The *Montgomery Advertiser* called him a political "has-been," a governor whose ability to lead the state had vanished. Likewise, John Temple Graves of the *Birmingham Post* sarcastically consoled readers disillusioned with Folsom's ineffective leadership. The voters did not elect Folsom to lead the legislature, Graves wrote, but elected him for his "capacity as an entertaining campaigner. In a time of plenty and the peace that goes with it, he came to our electorate all youthful vitality and string band folksiness. We surrendered to the pleasing show."[1]

Not surprisingly, partisan reports of Folsom's political demise were somewhat exaggerated. The legislature had not destroyed Folsom's political influence. Rather, the governor and his legislative opposition had arrived at a stalemate. In the standoff, both sides retained strength to inflict occasional defeat on the other, but neither could dominate completely. Governor Folsom's power continued to rest on his genius as a campaigner and on the prerogatives of his office. However, the governor's embarrassing personal conduct augmented the conservative power of Black Belt leaders and the economic clout of the industrial corporations. Thus, as soon as the legislature adjourned, Folsom employed the

powers of his office, the patronage at his disposal, and the resources of the executive departments to achieve his goals. By January of 1948, he had reasserted his political leadership and won a
resounding popular endorsement in the self-starter amendment
referendum. Four months later, however, conservative political
forces used Folsom's behavior, his political mistakes, and rumors of
corruption to hand him a humiliating defeat in the 1948 Democratic primary.

Immediately after legislative adjournment in October 1947, Governor Folsom used his veto to kill three legislative interim committees. The first committee would have investigated the use of corporal punishment in state prisons. The prison director, Frank Boswell,
a former prison guard, had revived the practice of punishing vio-
lators of prison discipline with leather straps, six to eight feet long
and four inches wide. Boswell defended flogging by saying that only
brute force could control hardened criminals. Even more alarming
were reports that Boswell himself enjoyed wielding one of the
straps from time to time. The legislators intended the second committee to investigate allegations of graft in the Alcoholic Beverage
Control system, the state's monopoly of retail liquor sales. Since its
creation in 1937, the ABC had been a breeding ground for graft;
now the lawmakers suspected graft because the membership of the
ABC Board changed rapidly during 1947 and Folsom's appointees
to the Board had stocked the stores with unpopular liquor brands.
Governor Folsom interpreted both investigative committees as attempts to limit the powers of his office. Promising to conduct his
own investigations of departments under his supervision, Folsom
pocket vetoed both.[2]

The legislators proposed a third interim committee to study Alabama election laws. During 1946, the Boswell amendment to the
state constitution had altered voter registration procedures by giving local registrars complete discretion in assessing the qualifications of voter applicants. Alabama voters believed the amendment
would prevent the registration of Negro voters. Less than a year
later, chapters of the National Association for the Advancement of
Colored People (NAACP) had filed federal suits challenging the law.
The NAACP action frightened legislators. They feared that the suits
would open voter registration to all citizens and that Governor
Folsom would not act to defend white supremacy. Therefore, the
interim committee would prepare strategies for disfranchising
Negroes that would withstand the scrutiny of federal court judges.

Governor Folsom's pocket veto showed his ambivalence about the issue. In killing the bill, he supported the voting rights of Negroes. However, by killing it without public comment, Folsom hinted that his respect for Alabama's cultural conventions tempered his commitment to the civil rights of all citizens.[3]

While disposing of disagreeable legislation, Folsom also used patronage decisions to complete other legislative business. First, he dismissed Senator George Quarles of Dallas County from the position of executive officer of the State Military Department. Quarles had supported the filibuster of Folsom's road construction bond issue and publicly questioned the governor's competence. In his place, Folsom appointed Broughton Lamberth, the Tallapoosa County senator who supported Folsom while serving as the chairman of the interim committee on health and public welfare. Under the provisions of "temporary clerk hire," the governor put four other legislators on the state payroll. The Highway Department hired Representatives C. B. Cox and Paul Coburn as liaisons between the Highway Department and local government officials in planning for farm-to-market road construction. Before he became an assistant in the governor's office, Representative Emmett Wood worked as a "special investigator." A criminologist by training and a "good ol' boy" by nature, Wood was uniquely qualified to track moonshiners through the pine forests and swamps of southwestern Alabama. Ira Thompson, an attorney and pro-Folsom representative, performed legal services for the governor before officially replacing Kenneth Griffith in 1948 as Folsom's legal adviser. Ignoring critics who claimed the appointments violated the constitutional separation of powers, Folsom employed his patronage powers to reward supporters and advertise the advantages of cooperation with the administration.[4]

When all the legislative business was finished, Folsom's administration had made remarkable progress toward realizing his 1946 campaign promises. Although the legislature rejected political reform, Folsom used his position on the Board of Appointment of Registrars of Elections to ensure that at least one voter registrar in each county shared his commitment to the expansion of the suffrage. Although the legislature refused to enact any new tax measures, Folsom and his revenue commissioner, Phillip Hamm, increased state revenues. Although his road construction bond issue had been filibustered, Folsom's administration began an extensive farm-to-market road construction program. Without any legislative action, the Alabama State Docks initiated an ambitious expansion of its facilities. From October 1947 through 1948, the legislature's refusal to cooperate with the governor did not hamper the work of the Folsom administration.

The Board of Appointment of Registrars of Elections—composed of the governor, state auditor, and commissioner of agriculture and industries—appointed the three officials in each county who served as voter registrars. By tradition, each of the board members selected all three registrars in his home county and one of the three in every other county. When he made his appointments in October 1947, Folsom chose only persons who had supported him in 1946 and who agreed to follow his voter registration policy. Folsom instructed each of his appointees to interpret the legal qualifications for registration consistently. The governor especially urged them to approve the registration of all military veterans, regardless of race.

In spite of the racist opposition it encountered, Folsom's voter registration policy gradually contributed to the expansion of civil rights. In Tuskegee, the seat of Macon County, Folsom's appointee led the Board of Registrars to register new voters without racial discrimination for four months. Voter registration stopped, however, when one registrar resigned, a second refused to attend meetings, and Folsom's man could not accept or process new applications by himself. When the Board of Registrars in Jefferson County discriminated against Negro citizens, Folsom warned that its action would bring prosecution by Alabama's attorney general or the U.S. Justice Department. In 1950, the governor's special investigators went to Henry County to investigate reports of discrimination. Folsom's appointee to the Mobile County Board of Registrars, E. J. Gonzales, became a primary witness for the NAACP in its successful suit against the Boswell amendment. Admittedly, Folsom's contribution to voting rights was small and only gradually significant. Nevertheless, his appointees worked quietly to expand suffrage at a time when the Alabama Legislature sought new ways to disfranchise Negroes.[5]

Since the legislature had not enacted new taxes or tax increases, the Folsom administration devoted itself to increasing state revenues by reducing tax evasion. Although the voters had ratified the income tax during the 1930s, only a minority of Alabamians had ever filed tax returns and paid the tax. Whether they were ignorant of the law or simply chose to ignore it, lax enforcement measures had allowed them to evade the tax impunity. At Folsom's direction, Commissioner Hamm sent state employees to Washington to microfilm federal income tax records. Back in Montgomery, the Revenue Department compared the federal tax returns with the state returns that had been filed. Alabamians who had evaded the state tax soon received unexpected tax bills in the mail. Meanwhile, the special investigators improved the enforcement of the state sales tax law. The investigators first secured the records of whole-sale merchants. Comparing these with the tax records of retail stores, they looked for marked discrepancies that signaled tax eva-sion. If the retail merchant protested the tax bill he received, the Revenue Department collected the overdue tax through litigation.[6]

The Folsom administration also worked to increase the revenue generated by the state property tax. According to the law, all real property could be assessed at up to 60 percent of its market value for the purpose of taxation. In Alabama, however, property was rarely assessed at more than 15 or 20 percent of market value. Governor Folsom could do nothing to raise the assessments on most property because that was the responsibility of county tax assessors and county Boards of Equalization. However, his revenue commissioner did have the authority to assess the property of pub-lic utilities and foreign corporations.[7] With the expert legal advice of E. C. Boswell, the author of the Boswell amendment, Commis-sioner Hamm reassessed the property of public utilities and foreign corporations. In late October 1947, Folsom announced that the assessments of four rubber manufacturers had been raised from $4,389,356 to $8,650,000. In the following weeks, Hamm an-nounced similar increases for the Alabama Power Company, U.S. Steel's Birmingham mills, the Southern Railroad, and other major corporations. The "Big Mules" protested that the new assessments were discriminatory, but Folsom and Hamm had proven their power to increase tax revenues without legislative action.[8]

Between postwar inflation and the stricter tax enforcement, fiscal 1947–48 was the most prosperous year the state government had ever had. The number of retailers paying sales tax increased by 33 percent, while 40,000 more Alabamians filed state tax returns. The ABC system earned its greatest profits ever and the Alabama State Docks had doubled its income since the end of World War II. Fiscal 1947–48 was also the biggest year on record for the Department of Public Welfare. Increased state appropriations and federal match-ing funds provided $6 million more than the department had spent in fiscal 1946–47. Although it could not pay the pensions Big Jim had promised, the Department of Public Welfare was able to increase the average monthly check from $15.08 to $21.14 between June 1947 and June 1948, while enlarging its eligibility rolls from 27,000 to over 65,000 retired Alabamians.[9]

Record tax collections helped fund the Folsom farm-to-market road program. By the beginning of 1948, the Highway Department director, Ward McFarland, was supervising construction projects on 1,196 miles of highways and secondary roads. Revenue generated by the gasoline tax, both current receipts and the accumulated surplus from the years of World War II, financed all of the construction. In spite of the surplus, the Folsom administration stretched the road construction money by building modest thoroughfares at minimum expense. As a rule, Folsom's farm-to-market roads consisted of a strip of pavement eighteen feet wide with shoulders of at least three feet on either side. The pavement usually followed the route of an existing dirt or gravel road that was graded smoothly. Without straightening the curves or reducing the steepness of the grade, the Highway Department hired a contractor to cover the roadbed with at least one layer of tar and one layer of asphalt plant mix. The Highway Department rarely replaced narrow, rickety bridges with safer ones when paving an existing road. If the farm-to-market road followed an entirely new roadbed, the state economized by requiring the county government to secure the right-of-way. The counties' cost, however, was small because most rural landowners gladly donated land in order to have a paved road on or near their property. The farm-to-market roads were cheaply built, narrow, winding, and dangerous. As traffic increased, the pavement deteriorated more quickly than road crews could maintain it. Regardless, those paved rural roads were vastly superior to the dirt and gravel lanes over which people traveled before Folsom became governor.[10]

The Folsom administration began expansions of the Alabama State Docks in Mobile with enthusiasm equal to Folsom's interest in farm-to-market roads. The management of the docks rarely interested anyone except Mobilians, but Governor Folsom envisioned Mobile as a major international port. Under the direction of Henry Sweet, the State Docks Advisory Board decided to issue $4 million worth of revenue bonds for new construction. With that money, the State Docks built three new ship berths and invested in a new ore tipple. The expansion appeared to pay immediate dividends. In the fall of 1948, the Frisco Railroad announced plans to construct a new line to Mobile that would connect the docks with Frisco's national trunk lines.[11]

While his administration collected taxes, increased old-age pensions, built roads, and expanded the state docks, Governor Folsom did not forget about politics. The reassessment of corporate property might have been a dispassionate administrative process, but it was more likely an expression of Folsom's regard for the "Big Mule" corporations who had supported his legislative opposition. The fall and winter of 1947–48 presented other opportunities for Folsom to express himself politically. First there was a small-scale dispute concerning a rural electric cooperative. Then the campaign preceding the self-starter amendment allowed Big Jim to return to the "branchheads" and ask the voters to reaffirm their support for his leadership.

During the summer of 1947, the Alabama Electric Cooperative (AEC) asked the Rural Electrification Administration (REA) for a loan of $5,516,000. AEC sought the loan in order to construct an electric generating plant on the Conecuh River in Covington County near Gantt. Without the plant, AEC had to purchase power for the Wiregrass counties it served from the Alabama Power Company at wholesale rates established by the private corporation. With the plant, AEC would become independent of Alabama Power and would be able to compete with the private utility locally. The authority to approve the loan request belonged to John Shaffer, a civil service employee who directed the local Finance Division of the Alabama Department of Finance.[12]

Although the AEC loan application enjoyed the support of Governor Folsom, U.S. Senators Hill and Sparkman, and eight of Alabama's nine U.S. congressmen, Shaffer ruled against it. In October 1947, Shaffer decided that adequate sources of electricity were already available in AEC's service area and that private industry could generate sufficient power for AEC's customers more efficiently and less expensively than the cooperative. Bill Drinkard, the director of the Finance Department, quickly overruled Shaffer and approved the REA loan. The *Montgomery Advertiser* protested, and attorneys for Alabama Power filed suit in the Fifteenth Judicial Circuit of Alabama. Before Judge Walter B. Jones, the corporation lawyers argued that Drinkard had overstepped his authority because only the director of the Local Finance Division could rule on REA loan applications. The Folsom administration argued that

Shaffer's decision was only a preliminary opinion he had written pending consultation with Drinkard.[13]

On 5 December, Judge Jones ruled that Drinkard had in fact overstepped his authority in approving the AEC loan. Later, Judge Jones also ruled that Shaffer's decision had been correct, a decision that greatly pleased the Alabama Power Company. Despite the adverse decision, Folsom and Drinkard continued to look for ways to grant the loan. In January 1948, the Finance Department gave John Shaffer a leave of absence, and Drinkard selected Brooks Holleman as the new director of the Local Finance Division. When AEC resubmitted its loan application, Holleman held new hearings before approving an REA loan package in April. This time there was no legal ground on which Alabama Power could challenge the decision. Clearly, Governor Folsom had outmaneuvered the "Big Mule" corporation and won a decision in favor of the consumer owners of AEC.[14]

The conflict over the REA loan was a small skirmish when compared with the campaign for the self-starter amendment. As Governor Folsom and his legislative opponents clashed, it was more than a campaign over a constitutional amendment. It was a state referendum on Folsom's performance in office. "If the amendment is adopted," Grover Hall, Jr., wrote, "it will be a repudiation of Folsom and a stern warning to be heeded by him in the three remaining years of his term." John Temple Graves shared the same view: "God only knows what will happen to our great state if Jim Folsom gets what seems to be a vote of confidence." For once, the governor agreed with both journalists. He had not fought the self-starter amendment in the legislature because it presented an opportunity for him to revive the popular mandate for his 1946 campaign program.[15]

The legislators who opposed Folsom during the 1947 biennial session assumed leadership in support of the amendment. At the invitation of Senator Jim Allen, anti-Folsom legislators met to coordinate their efforts during October and November of 1947. Sixteen state senators and twenty-nine representatives eventually endorsed ratification. In addition, they spoke to businessmen and civic clubs and financed advertising in Alabama newspapers. Senator Bruce Henderson was the most prominent of the nine Black Belt and southern Alabama senators who promoted the self-starter amendment. Representative Walter Givhan, the Farm Bureau's advocate, delivered the most bitter anti-Folsom addresses of the campaign. Senators Allen, Albert Boutwell, and six of the seven representatives from industrial Jefferson County assumed leadership roles. All of these men represented the same Black Belt and "Big Mule" interests that had opposed Big Jim and the People's Program since 1946.[16]

The unprecedented defection of the Speaker of the house from the governor's supporters enlivened the campaign for the self-starter amendment. With the enthusiasm of a religious convert, William Beck accused Folsom of cynically misleading the people with his promises and deliberately stirring class hatreds with attacks on "Big Mules" and "Gotrocks." Beck claimed that Folsom's personal eccentricities were the primary source of the nation's poor image of Alabama and that Folsom supported roads, schools, and old-age pensions only in order to serve his own political interests. Folsom opposed the amendment, Beck claimed, only because he feared that a truly independent legislature would expose his administration's corruption.[17]

Beck's criticisms echoed the blistering campaign rhetoric of Senator Allen and other self-starter proponents. They predicted that Folsom would revive his $57 million tax program if the voters did not ratify the amendment. Senator Henderson portrayed the governor as a political fraud, because his campaign promises could never be fulfilled. Another senator bluntly labeled Folsom "a shame and a disgrace" to the state. *Alabama* reported that Folsom's brother Cecil and five other special investigators had remained on the state payroll while they solicited campaign contributions from firms that did business with the state government. Representative Givhan's speeches were the most virulent of all. According to Givhan, Folsom's entire legislative program was subversive and had earned the endorsements of Gould Beech, Aubrey Williams, and the *New York Daily Worker.* It was clear, at least to Givhan, that Folsom opposed the self-starter amendment because he held basic democratic rights in contempt.[18]

Ridicule was the favorite campaign tactic of the *Montgomery Advertiser* editor Grover Hall, Jr., and the *Birmingham Post* columnist John Temple Graves. Hall coined a multitude of derisive monickers for the governor. Folsom was "the number one peckerwood of the peckerwood administration," "His Excellency Slappity-Hap," or sarcastically, "His Excellency." In Hall's editorials, there was no Folsom administration, just "Big J and the Jaybirds." John Temple Graves's ridicule was equally imaginative. When the governor began to campaign against the self-starter amendment, Graves wrote:

> Big Jim is going back to the stump, where seldom is heard a dis-
> couraging word and the skies are not cloudy. Far from executive and
> administration routine and perplexing questions of statecraft, he and
> his Strawberry Pickers will live as the Lord expected them to live and
> their natures most suggest, with music and sweet cajolery around,
> applause sure, crowd psychology blessedly replacing the cold exam-
> inations of the Legislature, with every promise set to music and per-
> formance nothing strict.[19]

Although Graves wrote in derision, he exaggerated Folsom's enthusiasm for the campaign only slightly. Folsom did prefer the excitement of campaigning to the rigors of his office. He eagerly
opened his campaign against the self-starter amendment—Folsom
called it his "Report to the People"—in late October with speeches
in Luverne, Troy, and Elba. His campaign followed the authentic
Folsom format. Four to six times a day, Big Jim and the Strawberry
Pickers appeared in small communities and county seats. As they
went, Folsom rehearsed his familiar program of farm-to-market
roads, old-age pensions, and fundamental political reform. Where
he had complained of "Big Mules" and "Gotrocks" in 1946, however, the governor now focused his criticisms on legislative obstructionism. From the day he nominated the trustees for API until the
senate killed his road construction bond issue as the legislature
adjourned, selfish legislative interests had blocked his program.
According to Folsom, the self-starter amendment was one more
attempt by the professional politicians to "hog-tie Big Jim" and
"hamstring" his program.[20]

Of course, since Folsom was already in office, he did not carry his
mop and suds bucket with him. Still, the suds bucket had been
more than a means of collecting campaign contributions; it had
also been a method for involving voters in the campaign. So, in
place of the suds bucket, Big Jim asked his audiences to write
down their advice for him and drop it into the "Branchhead Hope
Chest." At every campaign stop, thirty or forty people wrote their
suggestions on the backs of used envelopes, campaign flyers, old
receipts from retail stores, business cards, and even the wrappers
off chewing gum and tobacco. Most of the letters were encouraging:
"I am for old-age pensions" or "Pave farm-to-market roads" or simply "I am for your program." A few supporters urged Folsom to
continue his fight against legislative opponents: "Give Bruce Henderson hell!" To each of the Hope Chest letters, more than three
thousand of them altogether, Folsom's office staff wrote a reply on

the governor's stationery. Since the office workers used different form letters for the most common suggestions, each author of a Hope Chest letter received what appeared to be a personal response from Big Jim.[21]

The only major innovation of Folsom's campaign against the self-starter amendment was the publication of a four-page campaign newspaper, *Folsom's Forum.* Although published anonymously, *Folsom's Forum* was primarily the work of Ralph Hammond, a military veteran from DeKalb County and a recent graduate of the University of Alabama. Folsom's campaign aides distributed *Folsom's Forum* at every campaign rally while the governor urged his audiences to read the only source of information that was independent of the "Big Mules" and "Gotrocks." *Folsom's Forum* appeared every other week throughout the self-starter campaign and reappeared under various titles in many of Folsom's later election campaigns.[22]

As 6 January 1948 approached, Folsom's forty-five legislative opponents repeated one of the mistakes of Handy Ellis's 1946 run-off campaign. Just as Ellis had overdramatized the significance of the CIO's endorsement, the legislators conducted their campaign with dire warnings of improbable disasters that would occur if the amendment did not win ratification. Representative Givhan was especially guilty of this. In a speech to the Alabama Farm Bureau, Givhan warned that Folsom endorsed communistic ideals, opposed basic American rights, and intended to undermine white supremacy. Instead of winning support for the self-starter amendment, such extremism helped convince voters that the legislators were as reactionary and obstructionist as Governor Folsom claimed them to be.[23]

Voter turnout on 6 January 1948 was relatively light, but the referendum was decisive. More than 61 percent of the voters opposed the self-starter amendment, including majorities in fifty-one Alabama counties. Ignoring the possibility that the voters had rejected the amendment on its merits, political analysts declared the referendum a victory for Jim Folsom. The will of the people seemed obvious. Even newspaper editors who had endorsed the self-starter amendment agreed that the referendum demonstrated the electorate's desire to see the legislature enact Governor Folsom's program.[24]

Once again it appeared that Jim Folsom was on the summit of Alabama politics. Both he and his opponents had treated the self-starter referendum as a referendum on his performance in office, and Folsom had won. This victory complemented his successes in increasing state revenues and old-age pensions, paving farm-to-market roads, expanding the Alabama State Docks, and securing an REA loan for the Alabama Electric Cooperative. However, once again Folsom's mistakes helped his opponents to recover from their defeat. During 1948, the governor's personal conduct again offended citizens who expected sober dignity from their political leaders. His frequent statements on controversial issues allowed opponents to portray him as a radical or a fool. Patronage decisions and unethical practices within executive departments led to public charges that he abused the powers of his office. Ironically, at the time when Governor Folsom was most successful, he again made himself vulnerable to political defeat.

For some reason, Governor Folsom could not resist an opportunity to perform for *Life* photographers. For the first of two late-1947 articles, Folsom allowed reporter Paul Deutschman to interview and photograph him. For Deutschman's benefit, Folsom rambled on about the "cool green breeze" and the virtues of democracy and democratic rule. While deep-sea fishing on the state yacht, Folsom underlined his democratic faith by repeatedly asking for a cane pole and a can of worms. One picture captured Folsom relaxing in an undershirt, unbuttoned trousers, and socks without shoes. Another showed Folsom sipping a cocktail in a Mobile hotel room. In the accompanying article, the reporter admitted that much of Folsom's behavior had been deliberate theatrics, but the pictures powerfully communicated the message that Alabama's governor was an eccentric, ignorant clown.[25]

A few weeks later, *Life* again spotlighted Folsom. In two pages of pictures, *Life* showed Kissin' Jim Folsom in action at an "Air Day in Texas" celebration in Harlingen, Texas. Photographers caught Folsom kissing seven different Texas beauties. The short article appearing with the pictures described Folsom's manners as he refused to attend a cocktail party for dignitaries or sit at the head table during a formal dinner because he felt either action would have been undemocratic. Although he agreed to judge a beauty pageant, the article reported, he almost slept through it. On the final morning of his visit, Folsom ordered beer with his breakfast in the hotel restaurant. After gulping down one bottle, Big Jim smacked his lips loudly and announced, "Only thing better than beer is whiskey."[26]

Governor Folsom soon proved that he could make a spectacle of himself even when *Life* was not looking. In October 1947, Brady Bynum of the *Columbus Ledger-Enquirer* snapped a candid picture of Folsom drinking an unidentified beverage from a paper cup during an API football game. When Bynum refused to destroy the photo, the governor ordered his special investigators to take the film. While two men held Bynum, a third ruined forty-five dollars worth of his film and equipment. In March 1948, Folsom's buffoonery claimed national attention again. The female students of the Barbizon School of Modeling in New York City elected Big Jim Folsom as "America's No. 1 Leap Year Bachelor" and invited him to visit their school. When Folsom arrived for his visit, three hundred models flooded Fifth Avenue to greet him. With traffic tied up in all directions and photographers snapping pictures, Kissin' Jim greeted each of the young ladies in his own way. Once again, respectable Alabamians groaned with embarrassment. Representative Earl Tucker repeated a phrase that was becoming more popular: "We reckon Jim can't help being a damn fool, but he could stay at home."[27]

While Folsom's impolitic conduct inspired Tucker to call him a "damn fool," his patronage practices made him equally vulnerable to criticism. In 1948, critics most frequently blasted Folsom's use of "temporary clerk hire" and his apparent attempts to undermine the Alabama civil service system. Governor Folsom used "temporary clerk hire" to pay his special investigators. These included men who had worked for his 1946 campaign and legislators who supported the administration during 1947. They had no clearly defined duties, but the state was paying them a total of $10,677 per month in salaries and all of their daily expenses while on "official business." For Folsom's opponents, the special investigators and the "temporary clerk hire" appeared to be an unabashed boondoggle. Sharing this view, the chief examiner of public accounts, Ralph Eagerton, challenged "temporary clerk hire" in a suit against Folsom in Alabama's Fifteenth Judicial Circuit. When Judge Walter B. Jones ruled that the governor had not violated state law, he recommended that Eagerton ask the Alabama Legislature to correct the abuse during its 1949 biennial session.[28]

In addition to hiring friends as "temporary clerks," Folsom appeared intent on undermining the operation of the Alabama civil service system. In November 1947, Bill Drinkard delayed the appointment of a new state purchasing agent because none of the qualified candidates was a Folsom partisan. Only the threat of litigation compelled the finance director to select J. B. King for the post. In April 1948, the governor stirred controversy when he instructed his department heads to send applications for all merit system jobs to his office for approval. Although Folsom's order did not actually violate the civil service law, it violated the law's intent and drew criticism from the director of the Alabama Personnel Department. Journalists found proof of Folsom's antipathy for the merit system when he pressed Mrs. Albert Thomas to resign from the Alabama Personnel Board. He had appointed Mrs. Thomas to a six-year term on the board that governed the merit system with the expectation that she would side with the administration on controversial decisions. When Mrs. Thomas did not become Folsom's advocate on the Personnel Board, he sent O. H. Finney to Auburn to demand her resignation. When she complained to the Alabama press, the story reinforced the claim that Folsom had no respect for the merit system.[29]

The purchasing and contracting procedures of Folsom's administration sparked even more criticism than its hiring practices. Because three politically sensitive areas—state purchasing, the ABC Board, and the Highway Department—did not conduct business by competitive bids, Folsom's opponents always suspected corruption and graft. *Alabama* reported that the Folsom administration divided the purchase of all tires for 1948 among four companies. The company that received 70 percent of the purchase orders was the company that retained the used-car salesman W. Cleve Stokes as its sales representative. A *Birmingham News* reporter revealed that Folsom insisted that an out-of-state paint company make Wyatt Owens its Alabama representative. Owens was already a partner in a Birmingham firm that sold Caterpillar road machinery to the state. What made it seem worse was that a Birmingham widow lost her primary source of income when the paint manufacturer began paying sales commissions to Owens. At the end of the 1947–48 fiscal year, the chief examiner of public accounts, Ralph Eagerton, made the most detailed study of the administration's purchasing practices. His official report cited the Folsom administration for "gross inefficiency" and revealed that the governor had inflated the cost of all purchases by allowing all suppliers to pay 5 percent commissions to their politically connected sales representatives.[30]

Rumors of political favoritism in the operation of the ABC system abounded during 1947–48. Most of the suspicion stemmed from the rapid turnover of personnel on the ABC Board. In twenty-two months, Governor Folsom appointed fourteen different men to seats on the three-member ABC Board. During the same time, the ABC Board hired and fired the ABC administrator five times. The situation became even more suspicious in late 1947 and early 1948 as each new appointee ritualistically announced that he intended to conduct the state's liquor business in a way that would maximize profits. By implication, each new appointee was admitting that his predecessors had allowed distilleries with politically influential agents to sell the state less-popular brands of whiskey. However, as each new appointee took the same pledge, there seemed to be no end to the political favoritism.[31]

The Alabama Highway Department received closer public scrutiny than any other department. Trouble surfaced in March 1948 when the Highway Department could not meet its April payroll and match federal road construction funds. Experts predicted that the Highway Department would have a deficit of $2 million by the end of the fiscal year. While the Highway Department director, Ward McFarland, studied the alternatives, a Montgomery County grand jury and Chief Examiner Ralph Eagerton began investigations. In May, both the grand jury and Eagerton concluded that "gross inefficiency" plagued the department's operations and recommended that the Highway Department be placed under the supervision of "competent officials." The grand jury and Eagerton also cited four cases in which the Highway Department had overpaid or given special consideration to private construction companies. McFarland did not deny the citations, but he argued that they were an endorsement of his management. According to the highway director, his department had spent $30 million on construction in less than sixteen months. The fact that only four cases, involving less than $30,000, were found proved just how careful the Highway Department had been.[32]

Ed N. Rodgers, a former Highway Department director and head of the Alabama Road Builders Association, assessed the situation more objectively. The Highway Department had committed too much of its budget to the construction of farm-to-market roads, which could not qualify for federal matching money. These totally state-financed roads served the double function of fulfilling Folsom's campaign promise and winning the favor of local officials. In hope of earning their political support, the Folsom administration allowed local officials to designate the locations and priorities for local farm-to-market road construction. Usually, the construction projects that served political purposes best were also projects that could not qualify for federal matching funds. Thus, the Folsom administration faced a dilemma. It could eliminate the totally state-financed construction projects and risk losing political support among county government officials, or the Highway Department could continue to fund politically advantageous projects and be guilty of "gross inefficiency."[33]

Although Governor Folsom did not know how to resolve the Highway Department dilemma, he gave unequivocal support to his highway director. With a public pledge to correct any irregularity, Folsom asked Speaker William Beck, Senators Guy Hardwick and Robin Swift, and former Highway Department directors Ed Rodgers and Chris Sperlock to serve as a nonpartisan investigative committee. These five men possessed the technical expertise to investigate the Highway Department and the political independence from Folsom to give their report credibility. Although the grand jury, Ralph Eagerton, and Senator Bruce Henderson conducted their own investigations, the committee's report ended the controversy in August 1948. The report refuted the charges that Ward McFarland was guilty of "gross inefficiency" and demonstrated that the Highway Department had sufficient funds to meet its obligations until the legislature met in 1949. The committee recommended, however, that all road construction projects financed totally by the state be terminated. Despite this recommendation, the committee's findings succeeded in silencing criticisms of the Folsom administration.[34]

As the Democratic primary of 1948 approached, no political analyst in Alabama could confidently assess the fortunes of Governor Folsom and his administration. Folsom's success in opposing the self-starter amendment capped a series of successes for his leadership. However, Folsom's personal conduct and administrative actions also strengthened his opposition. Uninhibited personal behavior, patronage decisions, and administrative problems left Big Jim vulnerable to legitimate public criticism. Nevertheless, Folsom looked forward to the Democratic primary elections of 1948 as an opportunity to consolidate his political victories. At stake in the elections were nominations for one seat in the U.S. Senate, nine seats in the U.S. House, and eleven presidential electors. Alabama Democrats would also elect their delegates to the national convention in the 1948 primary. A Folsom-led faction in the elections had the potential for establishing the governor as Alabama's unquestioned political leader.

As far as most Alabamians were concerned, "Folsomism" was not the major issue to be decided in 1948. When the Alabama Democratic Executive Committee began accepting qualifying documents from candidates, President Truman had already endorsed a permanent Fair Employment Practices Committee and established a Civil Rights Commission to study racial discrimination. Closer to home, local chapters of the NAACP were challenging the Boswell amendment in federal court and were seeking guarantees of civil rights for Negroes. Most Alabama Democrats believed that the preservation of white supremacy was the central issue at stake in 1948.[35]

The issue of white supremacy divided leaders of the Alabama Democratic party into the two traditional factions. The more conservative faction was committed to secession from the national party if the party adopted a platform plank or nominated a presidential candidate sympathetic to civil rights. The Alabama Democratic Executive Committee chairman, Gessner McCorvey, who based his racism on social Darwinism assumptions, led the conservative faction with the support of former governor Frank Dixon, a staunch believer in the virtues of limited government. McCorvey and Dixon appealed to all Alabamians who feared that the extension of political rights to blacks would produce a chaotic social revolution.[36]

U.S. Senators Lister Hill and John Sparkman were the logical leaders of the progressive Democrats. While endorsing white supremacy, they were committed to maintaining the unity of the Democratic national party. With other southern Democrats, they had urged President Truman not to seek reelection for fear of endangering the Democratic majority in Congress. Although Truman ignored the advice, Hill and Sparkman remained committed to a united national party. While Sparkman ran for reelection in 1948, Hill offered himself as a candidate for delegate to the national convention.[37]

Governor Folsom could have strengthened the progressive faction by aligning himself with the position of Hill and Sparkman. Instead, he offered himself as a favorite-son candidate for president. Most Alabamians thought the idea was idiocy. John Temple Graves credited him with originality: "Men who get themselves into his state of hallucination generally imagine themselves Napoleon

Bonaparte. He says President of the United States." Folsom explained his candidacy as an alternative for southern Democrats who opposed Truman but did not wish to break with the national party. At the same time, if Folsom went to the Democratic National Convention with the solid support of the Alabama delegation, Truman's campaign leaders would have to appeal directly to him in order to win delegate votes for the president. Thus, Folsom stood to gain influence over the federal patronage which Truman distributed in Alabama.[38]

Governor Folsom challenged the leadership of Hill and Sparkman even more directly when he endorsed his own candidate for U.S. senator. Declaring that U.S. foreign policy was the primary issue of the campaign, Phillip Hamm resigned as revenue commissioner in order to qualify for the race. Both Hamm and Folsom insisted that Hamm was not Folsom's puppet in the race. However, no one believed either man after the governor gave an address on foreign policy at the opening rally of Hamm's campaign.[39]

When the field of candidates for the 1948 Democratic primary was complete, Alabama appeared ready for a three-cornered political fight. Then, Jim Folsom's personal life intruded into the campaign. On 2 March 1948, Christine Putman Johnston filed suit in the Eighth Judicial Circuit of Alabama to establish the legality of her common-law marriage to Folsom and the paternity of their son. Mrs. Johnston's suit claimed that she and Folsom were married in 1946 but that he had not recognized the union or the child for political reasons. When the news of the suit became public, Folsom was en route to testify before a congressional committee. In private his reaction was angry, but he betrayed no emotion in public. Without denying the allegations, Folsom reminded reporters that he was a public figure engaged in a political race. Considering the tactics of his opposition in the past, Folsom dismissed the suit as another attempt to embarrass him publicly. As if to substantiate his unconcern, Folsom posed for photographers in front of the Supreme Court building wearing a grin that proclaimed, "What? Me Worry?"[40]

Strangely, the first full account of the paternity suit appeared on the front page of the *New York Daily News*. After Mrs. Johnston agreed to settle with Folsom's agents in October 1946, she remained silent long enough to collect the second $5,000 of her compensation. Then, she took the story to William Bradford Huie of Hartselle, a locally prominent novelist and short-story writer. Huie wrote a first-person account of Mrs. Johnston's experiences and they agreed to seek a publisher. However, Alabama newspapers did not want to publish the story in 1948 for the same reason they had not published rumors of it earlier: the story reflected personally on the governor of Alabama, and it was based only on "off the record" comments and Mrs. Johnston's uncorroborated testimony. Therefore, Huie took the story out of the state. The *Daily News* agreed to buy it on the condition that Mrs. Johnston retain an attorney and file the paternity suit before they printed the article. The documents that Mrs. Johnston's lawyer filed in the circuit court at Cullman included all the information contained in Huie's account. Therefore, when the *Daily News* exposed the scandal on March 3, the story appeared to have been based on court documents, which were public records.[41]

Governor Folsom never denied that Christine's baby was his son, but he attempted to ignore the suit. Folsom hit the campaign trail, instead, promoting his candidacy for convention delegate and the candidacies of Phillip Hamm for U.S. senator and Broughton Lamberth for Democratic national committeeman. It was the same Folsom campaign style: plain-spoken talks, hillbilly music, jokes, and personal greetings. Throughout, Folsom ignored the civil rights debate and the paternity suit to harp on foreign policy. His position, closely akin to that of Henry Wallace, followed the logic of a radio speech he made in late 1947:

> Look what they're doing in the name of democracy in Washington. They're running all over the world dumping billions on top of billions. They're trying to bribe foreign leaders to vote a certain way. They're carrying bribes in one hand, and a sword of fear in the other. . . .
>
> But you can't bribe and threaten the world into peace. Here's the proof. Look at the countries where our agents have been handing out bribes and guns. The kings and dictators are getting stronger. But the Democrats are getting weaker.
>
> Real Democrats don't want to accept bribes and they don't want guns. They want freedom and bread. . . . All these billions we've been slushing out in bribes and guns haven't helped anybody but the Communists, the kings, the dictators, and the rotten aristocracy.[42]

While Folsom campaigned against Truman's foreign policies, the Alabama Democratic Executive Committee made the 1948 primary a referendum on white supremacy. Under Chairman McCorvey's leadership, the committee resolved that the Alabama delegation should bolt the national convention if the convention adopted a

platform with a strong civil rights plank. The committee also com-
mended twenty-one candidates for presidential elector who had
already pledged to vote against Truman or any other pro–civil
rights candidate in the electoral college. Then the executive committee decided to send out a questionnaire to determine which of
the candidates for convention delegate and presidential elector
supported the committee's resolutions. There was no place on the
questionnaire for the candidates to write more than yes or no. After
allowing time for the candidates to reply, the committee counted
refusals to return the questionnaire as opposition to its resolutions
and published the responses. In this way, the Alabama Democratic
Executive Committee forced every candidate to take a public position on the issue of civil rights.[43]

With the Democratic Executive Committee proclaiming that he
opposed white supremacy, Folsom and his friends encountered
stiffening opposition. Folsom, Hamm, Lamberth, and other pro-
Folsom candidates argued that the state government, and not the
federal government, should deal with all civil rights issues. Since
they did not return the questionnaire, however, this position did
nothing to defuse the issue. Instead, Folsom's opponents published
new evidence that his administration abused its powers. A
Montgomery Advertiser reporter found state employees using state-
owned office machines on state property (Room 101 of the capitol)
to promote Phillip Hamm's campaign. Meanwhile, W. LaRue Horn
worked full-time at Hamm's campaign headquarters in downtown
Montgomery while remaining on the "temporary clerk hire"
payroll. Editors of weekly newspapers complained that the Alabama Division of Records and Reports slanted its press releases to
favor Hamm and other pro-Folsom candidates. One week before
the Democratic primary, reporters revealed that Folsom had asked
state employees to vote for a slate of pro-Folsom candidates. The
existence of the slate convinced the *Advertiser* editor Grover Hall,
Jr., that Folsom's ultimate objective was political domination of the
state.[44]

The 311,929 Alabamians who voted on 4 May 1948 were deeply
divided on the issue of civil rights. Senator John Sparkman easily
won renomination to his senate seat and Senator Lister Hill received more votes for delegate-at-large than any other candidate.
However, candidates who had pledged to bolt the national convention were the three most popular vote-getters behind Hill, and the
convention delegation was divided between fourteen conservative

and twelve progressive Democrats. The voters also reelected Alabama's conservative national committeeman while nominating conservative candidates for every Alabama elector in the electoral college.[45]

The Alabama electorate spoke much more clearly on the issue of "Folsomism." Governor Folsom barely won enough votes on 4 May to qualify for the 2 June run-off. On 2 June he ran dead last among the eight candidates for convention delegate. Phillip Hamm, Broughton Lamberth, and almost every other candidate appearing on the Folsom slate experienced defeat. Only Attorney General A. A. Carmichael won a place in the convention delegation after receiving Folsom's endorsement. Clearly, the voters of Alabama had repudiated Folsom's political leadership. Grover Hall, Jr., wrote: "At least for the foreseeable future, Folsom is only a shell of a political figure. He is without force or effect in the affairs of Alabama."[46]

"Folsom is only a shell of a political figure" sounded much like Hall's observation in September 1947 that Folsom was a political "has-been." Although both comments were appropriate at the time Hall made them, neither represented political affairs in Alabama during the intervening months. With many administrative accomplishments and successful opposition to the self-starter amendment, Governor Folsom had proven his continuing political influence. Then, his personal conduct, the paternity suit, and rumors of corruption within his administration weakened his position. His attempts to divert attention from the issue of civil rights and to lead his own political faction to victory in the 1948 Democratic primary brought embarrassing defeat. In June 1948, Governor Folsom was still in the political situation that had existed eight months earlier: he was locked in political stalemate.

7

Getting Ready to Run Again

In the aftermath of the 1948 Democratic primary, Jim Folsom's analysis of the voting returns overlooked the impact of the civil rights issue. Folsom saw his defeat as a clear mandate concerning his administration. According to the governor, the people had voiced their support for the Marshall Plan and told him to lose interest in U.S. foreign policy. The people had also told him that he should never again offer a slate of candidates. Most of all, Folsom said, the people wanted him to settle down and become the hardest-working governor in Alabama history. Ever responsive to the popular will, Folsom promised to follow the people's instructions. He promised to concentrate on the administrative responsibilities of his office and to seek public notice only in support of his program or in defense of his administration.[1]

For the next six months or so, while the memory of defeat was fresh, Governor Folsom adhered to his promise. He reformed his public conduct drastically, played an insignificant role in the presidential politics of 1948, and attracted attention only when he defended the work of his appointees. Still, Big Jim was a young governor with a lifelong passion for politics. He soon grew restless with his passive administrative routine, especially when he saw how President Truman ignored predictions of defeat and snatched victory away from Tom Dewey. Even though the Alabama Constitution would not permit him to seek reelection in 1950, Folsom was planning for the 1954 campaign by the end of 1948. Because his opponents controlled the Alabama senate, Folsom sought to turn the senate's intransigence to his advantage. In the meantime, the governor cultivated the friendship of the organizations which represented Alabama's local politicians: the Association of County Commissioners and the League of Municipalities. Also, Folsom's loyalty to his appointees and his distribution of patronage advertised the tangible rewards that came from supporting his administration. Thus, although the legislature refused to enact any of his proposals during 1949 and 1950, Governor Folsom accepted the frustrations as temporary setbacks while he prepared for reelection in 1954.

By mid-1948, the paternity suit, stories of wild nights of carousing with "the boys," and rumors of the governor's sexual escapades had converted Folsom's bachelorhood into a political liability. Meanwhile, domestic tensions between the governor and First Lady Ruby Folsom Ellis frequently disrupted the tranquility of the governor's mansion. Folsom eliminated all these problems on 5 May 1948 when he married Jamelle Moore. Folsom first met his bride-to-be during a 1946 campaign swing through Fayette County. The nineteen-year-old Jamelle stood at the back of the audience, but her flowing black hair, radiant smile, and shapely figure attracted Folsom's attention. When he noticed her, Folsom broke off his campaign talk to exclaim, "That's the prettiest girl I've ever seen! I'm going to marry her!" After the inauguration, the state senator Fuller Kimbrell of Fayette County secured clerical work for Jamelle in Montgomery and encouraged a covert courtship. On 5 May 1948, Bill Lyerly chauffeured the bride and groom to Coosa County, where Judge Winston Stewart of probate court had prepared the marriage license and a local minister performed the wedding ceremony.[2]

After the wedding, Folsom settled into a more subdued lifestyle. He traveled less frequently after mid-1948. Big Jim no longer adorned the pages of *Life,* and he carefully kept his declamations on the relative virtues of beer and whiskey off the public record. "Kissin' Jim" became a character of the past. When Governor Folsom represented Alabama in President Truman's inaugural parade, spectators along the parade route called out, "Give us a kiss, Kissin' Jim!" Every time he heard them, Folsom leaned over to kiss Jamelle again.[3]

While the governor and the new first lady settled into married life at the mansion, Folsom's lawyers resolved his problem with Christine Putman Johnston. During April, his attorneys had filed demurrers to Mrs. Johnston's suit, claiming that she could not support her charges with admissible evidence and that she filed the suit to harass the governor. Since Folsom had introduced Christine as his wife to friends, and Alabama law recognized the marriage of any couple who announced their marriage to respectable people, the demurrers were not legally sound. However, the circuit judge in Cullman took them under advisement and scheduled the cases for hearings in October 1948. This six-month delay convinced Mrs. Johnston that she could not sustain her suits against Governor Folsom. Unwilling to endure the long, bitter court battles, Christine agreed to accept monetary compensation for another pledge of silence. Her decision angered the circuit judge in Cullman. As Mrs. Johnston formally withdrew her suits in July, the judge criticized the plaintiff for bringing suits "for the purpose of gaining notoriety, shallow publicity, or for personal reward." Governor Folsom was not affected politically by his affair with Christine Putman Johnston again.[4]

After 1 June 1948, Governor Folsom played a minor role in the presidential politics of that year. Fourteen of Alabama's twenty-six delegates to the Democratic National Convention honored their pledges to bolt if the party platform included a strong civil rights plank. Their leaders, Gessner McCorvey and former governor Frank Dixon, invited like-minded southerners to meet with them in Birmingham to consider their political alternatives. In Birmingham, southern Democrats who had bolted the national convention organized the States' Rights party and nominated Governor Strom Thurmond of South Carolina for president.[5]

The eleven Alabama Democrats who had won Democratic nominations as presidential electors were all allies of the Alabamians who led in the organization of the States' Rights party. As a result, every Democratic ballot cast in Alabama on 2 November supported the Dixiecrats' Strom Thurmond. Alabama's progressive Democrats and Governor Folsom resented the situation but had no power to alter it. Folsom might have called a special session of the legislature to place President Truman, the candidate of the national party, on the ballot. However, Folsom could not be certain that the legislature would follow his instructions. Folsom and other Democratic loyalists might have fielded an independent slate of electors pledged to support the national party. But, since the Dixiecrats controlled the leadership positions within the Alabama Democratic party, they could have expelled Democratic loyalists from the state party for such political independence.[6]

Folsom chose, instead, to endorse Truman publicly while supporting litigation to compel the Alabama Democratic electors to vote for the Democrats' national candidate. He delivered his endorsement of Truman at a rally in Montgomery to raise money for the court suits. First, Folsom bemoaned the fact that Alabama voters would not be able to vote for the candidate of the Democratic party, the party that had aided Alabama with "welfare, health, rural electrification, highways, social security, and many other humanitarian measures." The reason Alabamians could not vote for Truman, Folsom explained, was because a conspiratorial minority had put its will above the interests of the people. A small group of politicians had decided that the people could not vote for Truman regardless of recognized political tradition or majority opinion. "This small group of our democratic leaders are (sic) using every cunning device they can lay their hands on to force their out-moded prejudices and bigotry upon all the people. . . . We butted our heads against such vain-glory and bigotry in Berlin, Tokyo, Rome, and Moscow. We don't need any of it here in Alabama." As he concluded, Folsom announced that he would vote the straight Democratic ticket and said, "I hope it will be counted for President Truman."[7]

Whether they agreed with Folsom or not, three-fourths of the 225,000 Alabama voters on 2 November 1948 voted for the electors listed under the Alabama Democratic party's rooster. The plan to instigate court proceedings to compel the electors to vote for President Truman fizzled. Before 2 November, neither state nor federal courts would enjoin the electors to vote for the national Democratic candidate because no electors had been elected yet. After 2 November, Truman's reelection was assured, Folsom lost interest in the case, and the final decisions of the courts changed nothing.[8]

Except for his endorsement of Truman, Governor Folsom sought public attention in late 1948 only to defend the conduct of his administration. Folsom's detractors never ran short of scandals to expose. Finding fault with the Folsomites was a full-time occupation for columnists like Hugh Sparrow of the *Birmingham News*. Disgruntled state employees, disappointed contractors, and politicians out of favor routinely supplied reporters with graphic details of corruption and influence peddling. Most of the exposés dealt with unspectacular instances of political favoritism: legislators hired as "temporary clerks," political friends who received lucrative road construction contracts, lumber companies that won the privilege of harvesting lumber on state-owned land. Governor Folsom tried to minimize the significance of these reports by repeating, "Boys, you can write anything about me you want—just spell the name right." Occasionally, however, the critics leveled charges that Folsom could not ignore. During the second half of 1948, such accusations emerged from investigations of Alabama prisons and from the findings of the Department of Examiners of Public Accounts.

Alabama prison conditions drew criticism in 1947 when the prison director, Frank Boswell, reinstituted corporal punishment. One year later, Montgomery civic clubs invited Austin MacCormick, a New York penologist and director of the Osborne Foundation, to investigate the prison system. Most of the system's problems originated in the assumptions about prison management that Alabamians had adopted during the nineteenth century. Assuming that the best prisons were also the least expensive ones, the Alabama Legislature appropriated only a minimum of funds for the Department of Corrections. Prisons were outdated, overcrowded, and unsanitary because Alabamians expected prison farms and machine shops to supply practically all of the system's needs. This was the same attitude that had perpetuated the convict-lease system in Alabama until the 1920s. B. R. Reeves, the warden at Draper Prison, told a legislative committee in 1948 that the problems would not be solved without increasing the quality of prison personnel, improving working conditions, and upgrading physical facilities. In short, Alabama prisons needed more money.[9]

Although the problems of Alabama prisons were chronic, the criticisms that commanded the greatest public notice were politically partisan. Critics legitimately charged that Frank Boswell lacked the professional expertise to direct the Department of Corrections. Like most prison personnel, Boswell was a former guard who had advanced to higher positions through political loyalty. In 1948, Boswell administered the prison system with assumptions about penology that he learned from veteran prison guards during the 1920s. The critics were right when they accused Folsom and Boswell of using their authority to grant political favors. During 1948, the governor lent more than forty-five inmates to friends for use as housemaids, gardeners, and chauffeurs. Furthermore, Boswell regularly exceeded his authority and granted temporary paroles to inmates on holidays or in case of family crisis. Boswell even granted leaves of absence to inmates at the request of political friends. However, these abuses by the governor and the prison director were trivial when compared with the tragic condition of the entire prison system.[10]

Hugh Sparrow was primarily responsible for turning the problems of Alabama prisons into direct criticisms of the Folsom administration. Sparrow's *Birmingham News* column introduced Alabamians to an inmate assigned to highway work whose guards attempted to drown him and to convicts at the Atmore Prison Farm who harnessed themselves to plows in the place of mules. Sparrow told the story of Eugene Kah, a twenty-three-year-old inmate who was flogged "to the brink of insanity" for neglecting to clean his cell. One Negro convict, Sparrow reported, complained of chest pains one morning. His guard chained him to a radiator pipe for the rest of the day and forced a pint of mineral oil down his throat. Sparrow's lurid descriptions consistently attributed problems to the Folsom administration. The "hulking prison flogger" who whipped Eugene Kah was not an undertrained prison guard. Rather, he was one of the "Governor's sadistic bullies, who place their tempers above all concepts of humanity." Later, Sparrow would even claim that his writings had moved the people of Alabama to turn Folsom out of office in the gubernatorial election of 1950.[11]

Governor Folsom could not make a satisfactory answer to such emotional, partisan writing. Although he personally opposed flogging, he would neither dismiss Boswell nor ban corporal punishment while public controversy raged. Instead, Folsom announced the appointment of a three-man investigative committee, which included two pro-Folsom legislators, in August 1948. After three months of study, the committee reported that prison conditions were as good as could be expected and made several minor recommendations. The Folsom administration promptly implemented the recommendations and filed the report away as evidence that it was genuinely concerned about prison conditions.[12]

Governor Folsom also felt compelled to defend his administration from criticisms originating in the Department of Examiners of Public Accounts, which the legislature had created in 1947 with Folsom's approval. By mid-1948 the chief examiner, Ralph Eagerton, was making public the findings of the department's first audits. Conflict between the governor and the chief examiner was inevitable. It was Eagerton's job to ferret out every irregular use of public money, from slightly padded expense accounts to cases of wholesale fraud. Eagerton's work, Folsom felt, encouraged the news media to make picayune irregularities appear to be major cases of fraud.

The governor and the chief examiner fought their most intense battles over the operation of the Highway Department. Highway contracts were always politically sensitive because they were the most common form of political patronage. In early 1948, Eagerton helped expose irregular contracts between the Highway Department and four private contractors. Later in the year, he revealed that the state was constructing gutters, curbs, and sidewalks along an Oneonta street. Eagerton charged that the state could not finance such construction within an incorporated municipality. Folsom's response confused the issue and thereby diffused its political significance. He explained that the project in Oneonta lay along the route of a designated state highway. Furthermore, the construction was being funded by an "advice and aid" grant from the state to the local government. Of course, Folsom's answer did not satisfy the examiners of public accounts. However, it made the issue sufficiently complex so that the average citizen did not understand it well enough to censure Folsom.[13]

As the end of 1948 approached, Governor Folsom grew increasingly restless with his passive administrative routine. Despite the disastrous defeat in the Democratic primary, Folsom wanted to be at the focal point of Alabama politics again. His friends noticed that President Truman's "whistle-stop" campaign tour gave Folsom the greatest encouragement. Folsom perceived Truman as a leader who refused to concede defeat to overwhelming political opposition and who gamely fought to win reelection. With two years remaining in his term and the biennial session of the legislature scheduled for 1949, Governor Folsom determined to follow the president's example. He prepared to promote his 1946 campaign program aggressively. Even if the Alabama senate rejected his proposals and the political stalemate continued, Folsom believed his active leadership would contribute to his reelection in 1954 and the eventual implementation of the People's Program.[14]

Folsom unveiled his recommitment to active leadership with his "Two-Year Report to the People," a statewide radio broadcast in January 1949. The speech celebrated the accomplishments of the Folsom administration to date: pay raises for teachers, 1,408 miles of newly paved roads, higher old-age pensions, and record-breaking state revenues. Although he was proud of these achievements, Folsom reported that they seemed "only a drop in the bucket" when compared with "what we need." He reminded Alabamians of his 1946 campaign promises: old-age pensions, farm-to-market roads, poll tax repeal, legislative reapportionment, and constitutional revision. Folsom declared, "These are things I promised you when I ran for Governor, and I intend to carry on your fight to make them a reality."[15]

So saying, Governor Folsom looked ahead to the opening of the 1949 legislative session in May. At the same time, Alabama's four leading interest groups were also preparing for the biennial session. By February 1949, the Alabama Education Association and two other groups of educators had adopted their legislative recommendations. All agreed that in order to provide an "adequate" program of public education, the legislature should appropriate at least $60 million for fiscal 1949–50 and provide another $66 million for new school construction. The educators' requests exceeded the unprecedented appropriation for 1948–49 by more than $8 million. Meanwhile, the Alabama Farm Bureau readied its bill to rebate five-sixths of the gasoline tax paid on farm machinery fuel to the farmer. The Alabama League of Municipalities drafted legislation to make the state government pay for the construction and maintenance of designated state highways within the boundaries of incorporated municipalities. The Association of County Commissioners recommended a bill requiring the state to purchase all rights-of-way for the construction of new state highways. Both the League of Municipalities and the Association of County Commissioners endorsed an additional one-cent-per-gallon gasoline tax for use on local road construction.[16]

The Alabama senators who had rallied around James B. Allen and Bruce Henderson in the self-starter campaign also made plans for the 1949 biennial session. Allen and Henderson hosted a series of meetings in early 1949 to discuss major legislative issues and tactics for limiting the influence of Governor Folsom. By May, at least eighteen of the thirty-five senators had attended the meetings. They insisted that they were not organizing an anti-Folsom bloc and that if they voted alike in 1949, it was only because they shared similar views. Nevertheless, journalists dubbed them the "Economy Bloc," borrowing the label from a legislative group which had opposed Bibb Graves during his second administration.[17]

The Economy Bloc label fit the senators because they all agreed that Folsom's fiscal irresponsibility was Alabama's most serious problem. To protect the state treasury, the senators decided that the 1949–51 state budget could not be any larger than the budget for 1947–49. If any department needed additional funds, those funds would have to come from cuts in the budgets of other departments. The Economy Bloc also agreed that no new taxes or tax increases would be enacted and that all forms of waste in the state government would be eliminated. They readily identified "waste" with the existence of "open-ended" appropriations, provisions like "temporary clerk hire" that allowed state officials to spend money that the legislature had not specifically appropriated. Before the 1949 session began, the Economy Bloc senators drafted more than sixty "economy bills" to stop the "open-ended" appropriations.[18]

The Economy Bloc senators advertised their plans as statesmanlike proposals offered in the best interest of Alabama. Fiscal conservatism, however, was only a mask for political partisanship. While drafting the "economy bills," the senators also planned to oppose the confirmation of all Folsom appointees. The inclusion of Senator Albert Patterson in the Economy Bloc was further evidence of its inherent partisanship. The senator from Russell and Lee counties adhered to the dominant political faction in Russell County and maintained mutually beneficial ties with the owners of bars and gambling establishments in Phenix City. During 1947, Patterson had stood with Senators Fite and Kimbrell as a Folsom supporter. The governor had expressed his appreciation for Patterson's support by appointing Arch Ferrell to an unexpired term as Russell County solicitor. Early in 1949, however, Patterson had become angry with Folsom when the governor did not follow his recommendation in filling an unexpired term of the Lee County probate judge. Patterson was so angry that he severed all ties with Folsom and began attending the Economy Bloc meetings. By February 1949, Patterson had become an outspoken advocate of fiscal conservatism and a staunch opponent of the Folsom legislative program.[19]

While planning for the 1949 biennial session, Governor Folsom and the Economy Bloc traded insults. Folsom characterized the anti-Folsom senators as a rump session of legislators meeting in smoke-filled rooms to conduct secret business. He said their economy measures were aimed at minor expenses and would not reduce state expenditures significantly. Later, Folsom called his opponents cowards who evaded their responsibilities to the people. Senator George Quarles replied for the Economy Bloc by labeling Folsom an "amiable Newfoundland type" whose program was an attempt to "buy his way back" into public favor. According to

Quarles, Folsom would destroy Alabama's financial soundness in order to gain control over road construction money and enhance his political popularity. Taking up the cudgels, Senator Albert Boutwell denounced Folsom's promises as a "fantastic, multi-million dollar big-taxing and free-spending program" with "all the financial soundness of a pyramid club."[20]

Mercifully, the opening of the 1949 legislative session on 3 May ended the verbal abuse. By then, however, at least eighteen senators had joined the Economy Bloc, and Folsom could count on consistent support from only one-third of the representatives. Nevertheless, Governor Folsom renewed his familiar proposals in his opening-day address to the Alabama Legislature. Once again, Folsom asked the lawmakers to increase appropriations for old-age pensions and public education, repeal the poll tax, reapportion the legislature, and revise the Alabama Constitution. He recommended more than $60 million worth of new taxes and a road construction bond issue of $80 million. And he proposed it all with the apparent confidence that the legislators would give each recommendation serious consideration.[21]

Despite the governor's external confidence, the Folsom administration's plan for the session did not depend on the objective, statesmanlike conduct of the legislators. Instead, it depended on mastery of the legislature's rules of procedure. The Alabama Constitution limited the biennial session to a maximum of thirty-six legislative days. Any day on which either house conducted official business constituted a legislative day. No legislative day could begin before 12:01 A.M. or extend beyond 12:00 midnight. During the biennial session, only the biennial appropriations bills for the general fund and for public education had to be enacted.

Taking advantage of these rules, the pro-Folsom senators planned to waste as many legislative days as possible. By filibustering, they would hamper work on the "economy bills" and other partisan legislation. After the eighteenth legislative day, the senate would have to focus its attention on the biennial appropriation bills. By the time the budgets had been written and enacted, the mass of bills awaiting senate action would choke out partisan legislation and virtually prohibit the senate from overriding any gubernatorial veto. All legislation enacted during the final two days of the session would be subject to the governor's pocket veto. Simply put, Folsom's supporters had no expectation of winning the Economy Bloc's approval for any administration proposal. Therefore, they sought to frustrate the Economy Bloc by stalling from the beginning of the 1949 session until its conclusion.

The filibustering began on the first legislative day. The Economy Bloc proposed a rule change that would automatically send all recommendations from the governor to the Committee on Rules, where the Economy Bloc held a six-to-one majority. Folsom's supporters opposed the change, which would empower the Economy Bloc to defeat any of Folsom's proposals without action on the senate floor. After debating for two days, the senate finally adopted the change, but Folsom's men began a new filibuster on the third legislative day. This time they fought a rule change that would have made filibustering more difficult. As the change came to a vote, several Black Belt senators realized that the proposed rule might eliminate a tactic they used to avoid voting on reapportionment. With these unexpected allies, the Folsomites managed to defeat the change and waste the third and fourth legislative days.

On the fifth legislative day, the senate took up a bill to limit "temporary clerk hire," a bill which had already won by seventy-two to twenty-seven in the House. The administration's forces filibustered for five days before the senate approved the bill and sent it to the governor for his signature. In the meantime, however, the Folsomites had forced the senate to consume one-fourth of the 1949 biennial session.[22]

Long-winded debate on every piece of legislation obstructed the senate's proceedings throughout June 1949. On 17 June, the fourteenth legislative day, the Economy Bloc blundered when it brought a plan to build new highway bridges onto the floor for consideration. First, the bill was an obvious piece of pork-barrel legislation. Most of the 100 bridge sites were located in the senatorial districts of the cosponsors, while no bridges were planned for fifteen Alabama counties. After introducing the bridge-building bill, the Economy Bloc could no longer pretend to be a group of disinterested fiscal conservatives. In addition, the bill provoked a long, rancorous senate debate. Folsom's supporters unleashed a flood of amendments that increased the number of new bridges to 140 and added more than $3 million to the $17.2 million price tag. Not until the nineteenth legislative day did the Economy Bloc dam the flow of amendments. However, before the senate could enact the "bridge-building" bill, the pro-Folsom senators had wasted five more irreplaceable legislative days.[23]

With one-half of the biennial session gone, members of the house were becoming exasperated with their senate colleagues. In addition to defeating Folsom's tax proposals, the house had already enacted the "temporary clerk hire" bill; legislation sponsored by the Farm Bureau, the League of Municipalities, and the Association of County Commissioners; and reams of local legislation. In all, the house had passed fifty-two general bills and hundreds of local measures in the time the senate had approved one rule change, a handful of local bills, the "temporary clerk hire" bill, and the bridge-building bill. There were only eighteen legislative days remaining in the biennial session and neither the general fund nor the educational appropriation had been considered. The representatives knew that the senate's interminable delays doomed many bills in which they were directly interested.[24]

On 6 July, the nineteenth legislative day, the Economy Bloc broke the pro-Folsom filibuster; the day commenced at 1:00 A.M. and concluded at midnight. On the coattails of the bridge-building bill, the senate approved fifteen of the sixty "economy bills." Folsom's opponents managed to break the filibuster again on the twenty-fourth legislative day and enacted the Farm Bureau's tractor gasoline tax rebate. However, except for those two breaks, the Folsomites did not allow the senate to enact anything but local legislation between the twentieth and the thirtieth legislative days.[25]

While the senators wasted almost all of July, the house worked diligently and became even more impatient. The house defeated Folsom's road construction bond issue and enacted the fifteen "economy bills" that had originated in the senate. After detailed consideration, the house drafted and passed the biennial appropriation bills. The budget for public education appropriated $124 million, a $10 million increase over the 1947–49 budget. The house also appropriated $36 million for general fund expenditures. This represented a $6 million reduction from the preceding biennium with $2.4 million of the cut coming out of funds for the Department of Public Welfare. As the house completed this work and noticed the senate was still stalling, Governor Folsom returned all of the "economy bills" with his veto. The representatives were so upset with the senate's filibusters that they refused to override the governor's veto and allowed the "economy bills" to die.[26]

The Alabama senate considered the biennial appropriation bills for the first time with only six legislative days remaining in the session. In order to allow time for study and debate, the senate asked the house to permit a recess. The representatives had no sympathy for their senate colleagues and refused to recess, thereby forcing the senate to take immediate action on the budget proposals. With very little debate, the senate approved the general fund appropriation on the thirty-first legislative day and the educational budget on the thirty-second day.

Having dispensed with the biennial appropriations, the senate returned to the activity that dominated the 1949 session. With hundreds of bills awaiting senate action, the filibustering continued. In a fitting finale, Folsom's partisans—Senators Fite, Kimbrell, Lamberth, Langan, Howle, and Harvey—held the floor for twenty-three consecutive hours and wasted the senate's thirty-sixth and final legislative day.[27]

Governor Folsom emerged from the 1949 biennial session with more political influence than anyone expected him to have when the session began. His legislative supporters had thoroughly frustrated the Economy Bloc and had defeated every anti-Folsom measure except the "temporary clerk hire" bill and the reduction of the Department of Public Welfare's budget. In addition, Governor Folsom had taken advantage of the session to cement friendly relationships with the League of Municipalities and the Association of County Commissioners. Folsom attracted the support of these influential lobbying groups by advocating greater prerogatives for local government and by endorsing their 1949 bills to make the state responsible for the local costs of designated state highways. Ed Reid, the executive secretary of the League of Municipalities, and Coma Garrett, Jr., the probate judge of Clarke County and the president of the Association of County Commissioners, reciprocated by urging their legislative friends to support Folsom's road construction bond issue and sustain his vetoes. Since all legislators answered to their local constituents, the cooperation Folsom received from these two groups greatly enhanced his political influence.[28]

Governor Folsom derived a further political benefit from the legislature's failure to enact more than the essential legislation. Although Folsom's supporters had conducted the filibusters, Folsom effectively blamed the Economy Bloc. It was the Economy Bloc of senators who had agreed to defeat every administration bill and who authored the bridge-building bill. Here was proof that the senate was dominated by a "big-mule, tax-dodging bloc" that "wanted to do nothing and block everything." As he patterned his efforts after those of Harry Truman, Folsom appreciated the political advantage which the legislature's lack of accomplishment gave him.[29]

Ordinarily, the last fifteen months of an Alabama governor's term were uneventful. While political attention focused on the candidates who wished to succeed him, the governor remained a nonpartisan lame duck. Governor Folsom, however, did not intend to begin his political retirement. Instead, he wished to continue pursuing the goals of his administration and preparing for his 1954 reelection campaign.

The activity of the Folsom administration demonstrated the governor's vitality. In the fall of 1949 and again in the fall of 1950, Commissioner Hamm reassessed the property of thirty-one public utilities. As before, the reassessments valued the corporations' properties at 60 percent of market value and increased each firm's property taxes. The Department of Public Welfare struggled toward Folsom's goal of providing adequate old-age pensions. By January 1951, almost 90,000 elderly citizens were receiving average monthly checks of $22.46. At the Alabama State Docks, the Folsom administration planned a new grain elevator, new equipment for handling bulk materials, and an expansion of storage space. Still devoted to expanding the suffrage, Folsom appointed a "Governor's Committee on Voter Registration" to hear complaints from any citizen who had been denied the right to vote.[30]

In addition to his administrative vitality, Big Jim remained politically active. During October 1949, he embarked on his fourth statewide speaking tour since 1946, a series of "regional cabinet meetings." Meeting in a different section of the state each week, Governor Folsom and his department heads reported the progress of the administration and fielded questions from the local audience. Though Folsom advertised them as a means of informing voters about the work of their state government, the "regional cabinet meetings" predictably emphasized the accomplishments of the Folsom administration. As the 1950 Democratic primary approached, the meetings gradually evolved into political rallies at which the governor promoted his favorite candidates.[31]

Although Governor Folsom could not run for reelection in 1950, he viewed the gubernatorial campaign as an important opportunity to test the voters' continuing support for his political leadership. Thus, he ignored the advice of friends and searched for a candidate who would advocate the People's Program. First, he approached

Representative John Snodgrass, but Folsom's floor leader in the Alabama house did not want to be governor enough to expend the necessary money and effort. Two other men also declined Folsom's offers of support before the governor turned to his old friend Phillip Hamm.[32]

From the day he qualified to run for governor, Phillip Hamm insisted that he was not Folsom's puppet. As in 1948, however, Hamm's campaign rallies belied all such protestations. Each of Hamm's rallies began with music performed by the Strawberry Pickers, whose name had been changed to the Hog Scrapers. When Hamm made his appearance, the Hog Scrapers concluded their concert with a chorus of "Give Me That Old Time Religion." Hamm adapted Big Jim's campaign talk to fit his name and purpose. He explained that Big Jim had spent four years trying to wean the big, fat political hogs from the state government feeding trough. Big Jim had enjoyed some success, Hamm said, but the "Big Mules" of the Economy Bloc had balked at the People's Program, and all Folsom had won were some pickled pigs' feet for the people. Hamm promised to finish the job of weaning the political hogs and said that the people would eat "higher up on the hog" during the next four years. Hamm then began a demonstration of the proper method of dressing pork, using two barrels to show the scalding and scraping process. He concluded his analogy saying, "If the people do a good job of hog scraping" at the polls on 2 May, "you're going to have some good old country smoked Hamm up there in that Capitol." Hamm did all of this and still insisted that he was completely independent of Big Jim Folsom.[33]

The campaign may not have proven the popularity of Folsom's program, but it demonstrated the impact that Big Jim had made on Alabama politics. Virtually every candidate in the race employed some flamboyant gimmick in the hope of attracting crowds and votes. The Public Service Commissioner, Gordon Persons, traveled from one campaign appearance to the next in a two-man helicopter. Since few Alabamians had ever seen a helicopter in operation, Persons attracted great attention without grossly violating the bounds of good taste. Candidate Robert K. "Buster" Bell outfitted a truck with the body of a steam locomotive. At each of his campaign stops, Buster Bell's "Victory Train" offered free rides to children and drove through the streets blowing whistles, clanging bells, and advertising the candidate. The most inventive gimmick belonged to the probate judge Elbert Boozer, who built a replica of the state capitol on a truck trailer. At each rally, Boozer's aides attached a small platform to the side of the truck. From there, the conservative, middle-aged probate judge could deliver his somber address directly from the steps of the capitol. With such attention-getters, the candidates in 1950 hoped to duplicate Folsom's success with the mop and suds bucket.[34]

As the 1950 campaign wore on, Governor Folsom could not remain idle while everyone was having fun on the hustings. Not only had the "regional cabinet meetings" become weekly Hamm-for-governor rallies, but Folsom also threw the entire weight of his administration behind his friend's candidacy. Folsom gave his appointees the choice of supporting Hamm wholeheartedly or resigning. The governor used his patronage powers to encourage support for his former revenue commissioner. Then, from 14 April through the weekend before the Democratic primary, Governor Folsom conducted his own speaking tour on Hamm's behalf.[35]

Both the voters of Alabama and Phillip Hamm disappointed Governor Folsom. On 2 May 1950, the voters gave Gordon Persons a commanding lead in the gubernatorial primary. Persons's 137,055 votes more than doubled the votes which Hamm, his nearest competitor, received. However, Persons had fallen short of a simple majority, and Hamm was entitled to compete for the Democratic nomination in a run-off campaign. While Hamm considered the situation, Governor Folsom urged him to continue the race and delivered a statewide radio address for Hamm. Still, Persons needed only a few votes to win and many rural Alabamians remembered him as the head of the Public Service Commission at the time electricity and telephone service had reached their homes. Hamm was not confident that he could win support from rural voters who were grateful for Persons's past services. Thus, on 11 May, Hamm conceded the Democratic nomination to Gordon Persons.[36]

Hamm's concession angered Governor Folsom, but the results of other 1950 races gave him reason to celebrate. In the contests for seats on the Alabama Democratic Executive Committee, candidates who promised loyalty to the national party took control of the state party away from the States' Rights Democrats. In the legislative races, the returns were even more encouraging. Of the thirty incumbent legislators who had supported the Folsom administration, nineteen—56.66 percent—won reelection. Among the fifty-three incumbents who had opposed Folsom, thirty—56.60 percent—won reelection. Of course, legislative races in 1950 depended on many local issues over which Governor Folsom exercised little influence. However, the almost identical rate of success among pro-Folsom and anti-Folsom incumbents suggested that Hamm's defeat did not signal a popular repudiation of Big Jim Folsom or his People's Program.[37]

When the 1950 Democratic primary was finished, Governor Folsom started a new campaign, the last major attempt to enhance his administration's record before 1954. "Real progress can never come to our state and our people until the Legislature is reapportioned," Folsom declared on 8 May. On 4 June, Folsom ordered the Alabama Legislature to meet in special session beginning 19 June in order to consider reapportionment and constitutional revision. Folsom's proclamation stirred intense criticism. Lieutenant Governor Inzer and Senator Allen called the special session a waste of public revenue. Senators Henderson and Graham Wright announced that they would seek adjournment on the very first day. The *Montgomery Advertiser* editor Grover Hall, Jr., said Folsom was "truly pathetic." The legislature had defeated his proposals in 1947 and 1949, and he had suffered repeated electoral setbacks. "We had hoped that it wouldn't be necessary to mention his name again on this page," Hall editorialized, but Folsom did not know when to quit.[38]

The legislature convened as ordered on 19 June, but the legislators gave only perfunctory consideration to Folsom's proposals. On the fourth day of the session, reapportionment had only forty supporters in a house ballot, and constitutional revision fell victim to a vote of eleven to sixty-six. Having expressed themselves on the issues of reapportionment and constitutional revision, the legislators adjourned and returned to their homes.[39]

The news that the legislature had adjourned without reapportioning itself did not discourage Governor Folsom. At a press conference, he declared that the malapportioned legislature was illegal and unconstitutional. He even hinted that he would seek reapportionment through litigation.[40] Instead of filing suit, Folsom called the legislature back into session beginning on 5 July.[41]

The legislators were extremely annoyed by Folsom's proclamation when they reassembled on 5 July. Folsom's supporters managed to prolong the session for four days before the majority adopted an adjournment resolution. The governor resented the legislators' adjournment and ordered them to return for a third special session beginning 27 July. This session was the shortest of all, lasting only a few hours before the adjournment resolution was approved. The legislators barely had time to return home before Folsom announced a fourth special session. Again, pro-Folsom legislators prolonged the session artificially, but nothing was accomplished before the legislature adjourned on the third day. Enraged, Big Jim set 9 August as the date for the fifth special session and declared that he would continue calling sessions until reapportionment was achieved.[42]

At the beginning of the fifth special session, the legislators realized that they would have to act in order to stop Folsom's absurd summonses. Representative Earl McGowin proposed that they create an interim study committee on reapportionment. While the committee worked, the legislature would recess until October. With only a couple of weeks left before the general elections and the end of their terms, the legislators would meet again to receive the committee's report and recommendations. From November 1950 until January 1951, the problem of dealing with Folsom and reapportionment would belong to the members of the 1951–54 legislature. McGowin's plan sailed through both legislative houses without serious objection. The interim committee met several times during August and September. As planned, the legislators reassembled during October, received the committee report, and voted against reapportionment. This effectively killed the issue, because Folsom did not call another special session before the general election in early November.[43]

Even when McGowin's strategy had ended his reapportionment campaign, Big Jim Folsom was still unwilling to act like a retiring governor. Instead, he spent the final three months making patronage decisions that followed both his conception of the general welfare and his political self-interest. In one typical case, Folsom pressed the state's Banking Board to issue a new bank charter for several of his friends in Dothan. Representative Wallace Malone, president of Dothan's First National Bank, protested that the governor had interfered with the proceedings of a nonpartisan regulatory board. Malone's bank went on to file suit in the Fifteenth Judicial Circuit of Alabama, seeking an injunction against the chartering of the new bank. Governor Folsom claimed that his support for the new bank charter was not politically partisan. According to Folsom, his administration had always favored the operation of at least two banks in every county seat, a situation that would promote competition and ensure that local depositors received the best possible service. In the end, Judge Eugene Carter enjoined the Banking Board from issuing the new bank charter and cited the governor for attempting to influence the Banking Board improperly. Nevertheless, Governor Folsom still won the loyal support of those Dothan businessmen in future election campaigns.[44]

The Folsom administration also mixed public good with political self-interest in the management of the State Board of Pardons and Paroles. When Folsom appointed Bill Drinkard to the board in late 1949, his administration obtained a majority on the three-member panel for the first time. Almost immediately, Drinkard and Folsom appointee Glen Vinson suspended all rules for board proceedings, closed the board's records to public inspection, and instituted generous pardon and parole policies. In the first twelve months of their majority, Drinkard and Vinson released more inmates than the Pardon and Parole Board had released in any single year since its first year of operation. Then, between October 1950 and January 1951, Vinson and Drinkard acted with even greater dispatch. During that three-month period, the board granted 108 temporary paroles, 646 regular paroles, and 196 full pardons.[45]

In answer to critics, Governor Folsom equated the actions of his appointees with social justice. First, he claimed that Alabama prisons were unjustifiably crowded with inmates imprisoned by the "fee system." Under the fee system, many Alabama counties paid their sheriffs and other law enforcement officers according to the number of official actions—arrests made, warrants and subpoenas served, and so on—each had completed. Thus, it was in the financial interest of law enforcement officers to arrest and prosecute large numbers of people for dubious violations of the law. "I firmly believe," Folsom stated, "that the fee system accounts for half the people who are in prison today." Folsom also argued that Drinkard and Vinson were correcting a racial injustice. "I do not believe," Folsom said in December 1949, "that they have been given a fair deal at the hand of justice and jury in this state. There are sections of Alabama where a Negro doesn't stand a Chinaman's chance of getting fair and impartial justice on an equal footing with a white man."[46]

Nevertheless, evidence of political self-interest in the conduct of the Pardon and Parole Board undermined Folsom's arguments. Journalists wondered why Drinkard resigned his post as finance director to become a member of the Pardon and Parole Board, a job with a smaller salary and less prestige. Other reporters noticed the large number of political cronies who loitered around the offices of the Pardon and Parole Board. One inmate, the press learned, served only eighteen days of his four-year sentence for receiving stolen property. He won his release by reminding Folsom that he had supplied sound equipment for Folsom's 1946 election campaign. A legislator requested paroles for two Negroes who had been convicted of distilling spirituous beverages. All the legislator did was write a letter to Glen Vinson explaining how badly he needed the men to work on his farm, and the Pardon and Parole Board acted posthaste. A Tuscumbia attorney appealed to Folsom on behalf of a young client. The lawyer claimed that a Folsom aide had promised a parole if the client's family worked diligently for Phillip Hamm's election campaign. With cases such as these becoming public, there was no doubt that the Folsom administration used pardons and paroles as political patronage.[47]

Finally, Governor Folsom prepared to leave office. He collected resignations from all his appointees and delivered a farewell address to the organizational session of the new legislature. In that speech, Folsom emphasized the accomplishments of his administration: schoolteachers' salaries raised to more than $2,000, 3,165 miles of roads paved, the number of persons receiving old-age pensions more than doubled, a $10 million building program at the State Docks completed, and state revenue increased by almost one-third without new taxes or increased tax rates. However, Folsom's summary made no reference to the political work the governor completed during the second half of his term. After his disaster in the 1948 Democratic primary, Folsom had tamed his public image. With the help of the Economy Bloc, he had advertised himself as a democratic leader whose progressive proposals were rejected by selfish interest groups. During the 1949 legislative session, he had cultivated mutually beneficial ties between himself and the organizations that represented Alabama's local leaders. With patronage, Folsom had demonstrated that he was a politician who remembered his friends and rewarded them loyally. By the time Gordon Persons became the new governor, Big Jim Folsom was ready to run for reelection.

8

"Stickin' Up for Them What Sticks Up for Us"

Though he seemed politically isolated as a salesman for Emergency Aid Insurance Company and a private citizen of Cullman, Big Jim Folsom cast a long shadow over Alabama politics and government between 1951 and 1955. This was true even though Gordon Persons held the powers of the governor's office. During Persons's extended honeymoon with the Alabama Legislature, the state government addressed issues and problems that Folsom had introduced. At times, the Persons administration seemed preoccupied with efforts to discredit the former governor. Voters compared every action of the Persons administration with the promises of the People's Program. Although Folsom held no official powers, he utilized the four years of Persons's administration to prepare for his political future. By the end of 1954, Folsom had established himself as the undisputed master of Alabama state politics.

Ironically, Folsom contributed mightily to his successor's comfort and success before leaving office in 1951. During 1949, Folsom supported legislation, effective in January 1951, to raise the governor's salary from $6,000 to $12,000. The Persons family had the privilege of being the first occupants of Alabama's new governor's mansion. Folsom led the state to purchase the former Robert F. Ligon home in 1950 so that the First Family could live in one of Montgomery's finest residences. The contrast between the personalities of the two men also benefited Persons. In contrast to Folsom's apparent lack of sophistication, Governor Persons easily maintained an image of dignified, efficient, and competent leadership.[1]

120

The Folsom administration generously left Governor Persons with extraordinary power to direct the state government. In accord with his concept of Jacksonian democracy, Folsom required his appointees to resign their positions on state boards at the end of his term. Also, since the Alabama senate denied confirmation to Folsom's appointees during 1947 and 1949, Governor Persons was able to replace Folsom's nominees with his own men on the API Board of Trustees, the Board of Education, the Board of Pardons and Paroles, and many other state boards. This situation gave the new governor immediate control over practically every executive agency and the patronage which each agency dispensed.[2]

In the wake of Folsom's turbulent stalemate with the Alabama Legislature, Governor Persons won a reputation for harmonious, effective legislative leadership. Where Folsom had rarely given direction to the legislature's daily business, Governor Persons worked closely with his legislative leaders and supporters. Roberts Brown, the Speaker of the house; Noble Russell, the house floor leader; and Albert Boutwell, senate president pro tem, organized their colleagues effectively behind the administration's proposals. Furthermore, Persons did not publicly challenge legislators to enact proposals they opposed. Instead, the governor's legislative leaders polled their colleagues on each issue before Persons endorsed any measure. Because he did not challenge the legislators, Folsom's friends thought Persons a weak leader. However, journalists and politicians marveled at the ease with which each administration bill won enactment.[3]

Persons's legislative leadership contributed to the passage of several proposals which Folsom had proven to be popular. In 1951, the governor asked the legislature to provide a road construction bond issue. Although political considerations had blocked Folsom's road program, the legislature heeded Persons's request and approved a $25 million bond issue. Like Folsom, Persons endorsed increased appropriations for teacher salaries and new school construction. To achieve these goals, the legislature enacted an additional 1 percent sales tax and earmarked the new revenue for public education. Governor Persons realized that the cumulative poll tax was unpopular and endorsed legislation that reduced the cumulative feature to a maximum of two years. Persons won legislative support for poll tax reform by assuring the legislature that existing restrictions on voting remained strict enough to exclude Negroes.[4]

Persons not only took advantage of issues that Folsom had introduced, but he also attempted to capitalize on criticisms of the Folsom administration. Persons advertised his legislative proposals as remedies for waste, corruption, and fiscal irresponsibility. His leading remedy for waste involved public assistance for the elderly. Without advocating reductions of old-age pensions, the governor sponsored the "relative-responsibility" law. The act limited old-age assistance to those citizens who could prove that none of their relatives could support them adequately. The law and the confusion of reapplying for benefits reduced the number of recipients by one-third. Ignoring the hardships caused by the law, Persons claimed that his administration had provided adequate assistance for those elderly citizens who were most deserving of public aid.[5]

The new governor also encouraged investigations of every hint of scandal in the Folsom administration. In an examination of the Alabama State Docks, investigators found that just before Folsom left office, the State Docks had purchased ten thousand souvenir calendars proclaiming "James E. Folsom, Governor" and "E. S. Morgan, Director." The investigation found more substantial irregularities in the construction of the docks' new grain elevator. The state had paid a Mobile firm $23,453.30 for unspecified engineering services. The item seemed particularly suspicious because a member of the State Docks Advisory Board was a partner in the engineering firm.

When Persons's men examined the records of the Alabama Department of Corrections, they found records of prison floggings and evidence of fiscal mismanagement. Reacting to the corporal punishment, Governor Persons decreed an end to such "barbarity" and held a public ceremony to burn the prison's leather straps. Persons forwarded the evidence of fiscal mismanagement to Attorney General Si Garrett for prosecution. Garrett prepared a case against former prison director Frank Boswell in 1952, but the evidence did not convince the jury of Boswell's guilt. Having failed to win a judicial decision against Folsom's administration, the governor proposed legislative reform. At Persons's behest, the legislature vested control of both the state docks and the prison system in "nonpartisan" supervisory boards. These reforms, Persons believed, would prevent graft in the future.[6]

The Alabama Legislature, with Persons's blessing, conducted a more extensive investigation of the State Pardon and Parole Board during 1951. The five-member legislative committee reported that both Bill Drinkard and Glen Vinson had been incompetent. According to the report, Drinkard rarely gave more than one day a week to his full-time position. When he did visit his office, shotguns and fishing tackle were more prominent than the files of prospective parolees. Glen Vinson was more conscientious, but he suffered from alcoholism throughout 1950. On some days, Vinson could not forgo a drink long enough to sit through a meeting of the Pardon and Parole Board.[7]

The legislative committee found that Drinkard and Vinson had operated a racket in pardons and paroles. To secure a pardon or parole, an inmate or his family contacted a trusted friend of the Folsom administration. Frank Boswell, Broughton Lamberth, Rankin Fite, Ross Clark, and Fred Folsom were among the men who were most often contacted for inmates. Folsom's friends agreed to "represent" the inmates before the Pardon and Parole Board in return for attorney's "fees." The "fees" ranged from about $200 to $6,600. Once he collected his "fee," the inmate's "representative" notified Folsom, Drinkard, or Vinson, and the board acted promptly in the inmate's favor. Occasionally, an inmate's spouse obtained a pardon or parole by negotiating privately with Drinkard or Vinson in a hotel room or at a private residence. In a few cases, inmates gained freedom in compensation for political favors they had performed for Folsom.[8]

The investigation exposed a shocking abuse of power, but the committee's report was not an unequivocal censure of Jim Folsom. Since all five committee members had publicly opposed Folsom, his supporters effectively dismissed the investigation as a political attack. Folsom issued a nonchalant denial of complicity in the scandal, and nothing in the committee's report refuted his profession of innocence. The committee report did not show that Folsom, Drinkard, or Vinson had violated any law. Although no inmate needed to retain a representative, it was not illegal for attorneys to accept fees as compensation for their services. Once again, the exposure of wrongs in the Folsom administration led only to reform legislation. In the reformed system, the governor would appoint members to the Pardon and Parole Board from a list of nonpartisan persons compiled by three politically independent officials.[9]

Ironically, every act of the Persons administration seemed to be a boon for Big Jim Folsom. The investigations enhanced his popularity because they failed to produce evidence of guilt in any scandal. This lack of evidence lent credence to Big Jim's familiar attacks on the "lying newspapers." General Robert Steiner, a Montgomery lawyer with several "Big Mule" clients, claimed that he had never seen anyone harassed as much as Folsom without "a single damn conviction." The absence of evidence against Folsom persuaded Steiner to become a Folsom supporter.[10]

The changes in taxation and revenue laws and rumors of political favoritism in the Persons administration caused additional public resentment. The one-cent sales tax increase and the relative-responsibility law increased the financial burdens of Alabamians least able to bear them. At the same time, the Persons administration quietly reduced the property assessments of utility companies. While the Alabama Power Company's assessment fell from about $100 million to $66 million, Persons encouraged county tax assessors to replace the lost revenue by reassessing the property of farmers and cattlemen. Fulfilling a campaign promise, the governor proposed legislation that reduced the automobile license tax from $13 to $3. This initially popular idea became unpopular when the tax cut reduced the revenue available for local road construction. E. C. Boswell and LaRue Horn agreed that Persons was making himself an unpopular governor. Horn wrote Folsom, "I hear in the papers, your campaign manager (Gordon Persons) has started your re-election campaign mighty soon. . . . In these parts folks are already giving you the name of next Governor. They say he does not care for anyone but the blackbelters and the big mules and has already made the demonstration."[11]

While Folsom's political fortunes grew during the Persons administration, so did his family and his personal finances. During 1949, Jamelle had given birth to Folsom's first legitimate son, James E. Folsom, Jr. In early 1951, she gave birth to Andrew Jackson Folsom. Within two years, two daughters arrived at the Folsom home: Jamelle Alabama in 1952 and Thelma Ebelene in 1954. Because the second daughter was unhealthy at birth and seemed to fight for life, her father called her "Scrappy," a nickname that stuck for years. At the time of each child's birth, Folsom himself was admitted to the hospital because of a sore throat or some other minor ailment; actually he was suffering sympathetic labor pains.[12]

Meanwhile, Folsom converted the promise of his political future into dollars and cents. Taking a cue from Georgia's Talmadge family, Folsom invested in a line of hams and sausages which bore his signature on their labels. Later, he marketed a line of feeds bearing his name as a trademark. In 1954 his wife established the Jamelle Folsom Cosmetic Company. The one Folsom enterprise that consistently produced a profit was his automobile battery company, the Folsom-Nicholas Company. Businesses that desired Folsom's favor after 1954 readily purchased the Folsom Workall battery, and Folsom earned substantial profits until the mid-1960s. When he finally sold his interest in the firm, Folsom's share was worth more than $400,000.[13]

Although Governor Persons and the Alabama Legislature could not discredit Folsom, Big Jim almost discredited himself in 1952. One evening a highway patrol officer arrested Folsom near Birmingham for driving while intoxicated. Folsom spent the night in a Birmingham jail, but the arresting officer failed to secure a witness or collect evidence of Folsom's intoxication. At Folsom's trial, he won an easy acquittal when several friends testified that they had seen him sober a few minutes before the arrest. After regaining his freedom, Folsom explained his arrest as another example of political harassment. The Internal Revenue Service came even closer to embarrassing the former governor. The IRS found that Governor Folsom had failed to report $6,700 of income between 1948 and 1950. Folsom did not challenge the IRS and quietly paid back taxes of $974.28. His relatives were not so fortunate. Between 1947 and 1951, Fred Folsom, Cecil Folsom, and J. Ross Clark each evaded more than $5,500 of income taxes. None of the men challenged the IRS when they appeared in the U.S. District Court in Birmingham.[14]

As Folsom waited in Cullman for the end of the Persons administration, his reelection campaign began without him. Between 1951 and 1954, the trickle of encouragement became a surging flood of support. S. H. Moore wrote on behalf of a Negro political organization in Birmingham, "Those of my race join me in saying that we will be more than glad to support you in any political endeavor." Sam Jones, a Highway Department employee, estimated that 85 percent of the people he knew wanted Folsom back in the governor's office. Jones said that he was busy placing "Alabama Needs Big Jim Folsom" signs along the state's highways.[15]

The first real test of Folsom's popularity came in 1952. Before he left office, Folsom had appointed his legal adviser, Annie Lola Price, to an unexpired term on the Alabama Court of Appeals. When Miss Price sought election to her position, her service in the Folsom administration marked her indelibly as a Folsomite. Lest Folsom be tempted to campaign for his appointee, Joe Poole wrote to remind him that Alabama voters would resent any attempt to tell them how to vote. Instead, Poole encouraged Folsom to help Miss Price raise campaign funds without publicly endorsing her candidacy. Folsom accepted Poole's advice, and Price won by a narrow margin in the run-off primary. Her victory demonstrated that a Folsomite could still win the voters' confidence.[16]

Folsom drew increasing political strength from the influential Alabamians who became his supporters in 1952 and 1953. Ed Reid, executive secretary of the Alabama League of Municipalities, joined Folsom's camp in early 1953 and encouraged Folsom to make room in his councils for new friends. He explained that Ellis had forfeited many supporters in 1946 because he allowed his campaign organization to become a "closed corporation." The probate judge of Lamar County, S. G. Johnson, not only pledged his support but guaranteed that his county would give Folsom a big majority in 1954. Judge George C. Wallace of the circuit court wrote, "I am still spreading the Folsom gospel in these parts and looking forward to discussing politics with you." A leading Birmingham trial lawyer enlisted, in spite of opposing political interests of his corporate clients. When asked why he became a Folsomite, the attorney gave an answer that many others shared: "Since the son-of-a-bitch is going to be elected anyway, he might as well be my son-of-a-bitch."[17]

Even Grover C. Hall, Jr., recognized Folsom as the leading contender in the 1954 gubernatorial campaign. In a personal letter to Folsom, Hall conceded that Big Jim would win reelection in 1954, but he promised that he would have the last word. "Did you ever look at an Alabama history book and notice that they are largely written from the cited news stories and editorials? . . . In your case, my writings will undoubtedly be the chief source of future Alabama historians. So even if I fail to make the living agree with my estimates of you, I shall certainly have my way with posterity. Hell, ain't it?"[18]

As 1954 approached, the supporters who united behind Jim Folsom were more diverse than they had been in 1946. They included both ordinary citizens with no political experience and seasoned politicians. Some had backed Folsom before 1942 while others had become Folsomites since 1951. Many endorsed Folsom because they liked his program. Others worked for him and expected to benefit personally. A small minority supported Big Jim solely out of personal loyalty.

Of all his friends, Folsom prized the ones who came from the grass roots. Fred Gill, a steelworker and CIO union member, volunteered to collect campaign funds, distribute campaign literature, and erect billboards for the candidate. Gill spent his entire vacation in 1954 working for Folsom's reelection. Bill Watson, an employee in the Conservation Department, assured Folsom that 90 percent of his fellow workers would vote for Big Jim's reelection. In Talladega, automobile dealer Tom Cooley, Dr. J. L. Hardwick, and J. C. Monroe asked Folsom to recognize them as his local campaign leaders. While organizing their county for Folsom, Cooley, Hardwick, and Monroe did not allow any individual to contribute more than fifty dollars. Still, local support for Folsom was so broad that the Talladega County committee made large contributions to Folsom's statewide campaign.[19]

Of course, Jim Folsom did not reject the support of experienced political leaders. Eight probate judges, including Coma Garrett of the Alabama Association of County Commissioners, identified themselves as Folsom campaign leaders. In at least thirteen other counties, Folsom enjoyed the local support of circuit court judges, sheriffs, mayors, or other officials. In another seven counties, past members of the Alabama Legislature publicly endorsed Folsom's reelection. Folsom insisted, as he always had, that his local committees were groups of citizens who organized on their own initiative. However, the support he received from local leaders in 1954 distinguished his reelection campaign from the campaign of 1946.[20]

Where there had been virtually no campaign organization in 1946, a small inner circle supervised and coordinated Folsom's reelection campaign. Charles Pinkston, a former legislator, held the title of campaign chairman. Fuller Kimbrell managed the campaign in the northern half of the state while George Wallace supervised the campaign in the southern half. Legislative candidates Rankin Fite of Marion County and George Hawkins of Etowah County worked closely with the Folsom campaign but held no titles in the organization. As he had in 1946, Bill Drinkard organized Folsom's speaking tour, but Folsom's leaders kept Drinkard's work secret because of the Pardon and Parole Board scandal. Although Folsom never publicly recognized this group, his inner circle performed the essential work of uniting the diverse efforts of his many supporters. Throughout 1954, Folsom's campaign reflected the consensus of opinion within this small group of men.[21]

Considering the great diversity that existed among his supporters, Folsom's biggest challenge in 1954 was, as Charles Pinkston stated it, "to keep all factions happy and running smoothly without any jealousy arising between factions or personalities." LaRue Horn agreed. "The only real damage that may be done," he said, "will be by the supposed inner-Folsom crowd" as individuals sought to gain personal advantage during the campaign. For example, dissension erupted in Pike County between old Folsom loyalists and new-comers to the cause. The fight began when a newcomer signed a local campaign advertisement and made it appear that the old-timers had been ignored. In Mobile County, a squabble developed when a man of dubious loyalty became a member of the local cam-paign finance committee. Jim Buford, a Folsom supporter in Tuscaloosa County, distrusted Folsom's local leaders: "Certain of those men in whom you have placed a great amount of trust and confidence do not deserve it. Some of the executives of your admin-istration are double-crossing you, even now."[22]

A conflict that continued for several years developed over a legis-lative race in Geneva County. Senatorial candidate Neil Metcalf campaigned with the understanding that he had Folsom's support. E. C. Boswell, a leader in local politics and a Folsom adherent, supported Metcalf's opponent. Since local patronage was at stake, both Metcalf and Boswell questioned the other's loyalty to Folsom. Metcalf became so angry in 1954 that he wrote to O. H. Finney complaining that Boswell's "only contribution" to Folsom's cam-paign "was a refusal to steal his votes." Folsom prudently depended on his supporters to settle this and similar conflicts without his intervention.[23]

Six candidates challenged Jim Folsom in the campaign for the 1954 Democratic gubernatorial nomination. Political insiders rec-ognized three former Alabama senators—James B. Allen, Bruce Henderson, and Jimmy Faulkner—as serious contenders. Allen and Henderson had earned reputations for conservative leadership, while Faulkner, a Baldwin County newspaper publisher, was known as a political progressive. C. C. Owens, an incumbent on the Ala-bama Public Service Commission, entered the 1954 campaign as the protégé of Governor Persons, but Jimmy Faulkner won a share of Persons's supporters. Folsom's friends believed that Horace Wilkinson promoted the campaign of the former director of the Alabama State Docks, Henry Sweet, in order to discredit Big Jim. Rounding out the field of candidates, J. Winston Gullatte seemed to be running for the fun of it. His most memorable utterance during the heat of the campaign was, "If all my opponents are telling the truth about each other, I feel there is a very real possibility they will all be in jail by election day."[24]

At their kick-off rallies, each of Folsom's opponents outlined programs for improving public education, building more roads, and attracting new industries to Alabama. The various platforms differed only in detail. James Allen was unique as he asserted the state's ownership of offshore oil reserves in the Gulf of Mexico, but the tideland oil issue did not stir great popular interest. Bruce Henderson's program was unambiguously conservative with its opposition to Folsom's promises and its defense of racial segregation and restrictive labor laws. As the campaign developed, however, the issues addressed in campaign platforms had very little to do with the governor's race. Instead, Alabamians seemed most interested in who agreed with Folsom and who would oppose him in the run-off primary.[25]

Remembering 1946, each candidate sought a gimmick that would promote his candidacy. With organ and accordion, Judy and Terry Allen provided music for their uncle's campaign meetings. While "Hens for Henderson" appealed to female voters, "Heralds for Henderson," two horseback riders with banners proclaiming "Bruce Henderson is in town today," preceded the Wilcox County candidate to every campaign rally. Jimmy Faulkner staged talkathons. During twenty-four-hour talkathons in Birmingham, Mobile, and Montgomery, he answered unrehearsed questions from a live audience and telephone callers. In smaller county seats, Faulkner conducted talkathons of shorter duration. The format not only stirred curiosity, but it also allowed Faulkner to demonstrate his intelligence and candor in frank, thorough answers.[26]

Despite the effort the candidates put into their gimmicks, attacks on Jim Folsom commanded the greatest attention in 1954. Bruce Henderson told an audience in Dothan, "I may not be the darling of *Life* magazine; but I am for Alabama, and the dignity of Alabama, and the people of Alabama." Henderson went on to assert that he had done more to promote farm-to-market road construction during the legislature's 1943 session than Folsom had ever done.[27] Henry Sweet attacked Folsom more viciously than Henderson. Calling Folsom the representative of "organized evil," Sweet promised to present concrete evidence of Folsom's corruption. Several weeks later, Sweet produced photostats of bank deposit slips showing that Folsom had received $52,600 in excess of his salary between 1947 and 1951. Sweet claimed that Folsom had paid only $19.98 in state income tax during his four years as governor. Sweet also detailed Folsom's corruption in the administration of the ABC Board and the purchase of insurance on state property.[28]

At the official opening of his campaign, former governor Folsom appeared to be the same candidate that he had been in 1946. That appearance disguised the network of supporters throughout the state and the organizational work of Folsom's inner circle. Except for a new promise to promote Alabama's industrialization, Folsom's program issued the familiar calls for farm-to-market roads, better schools, and old-age pensions. Big Jim had consolidated his proposed political reforms into a single campaign promise. Now he urged the voters to endorse a "Fair Vote Convention," a constitutional convention that would reapportion the legislature. Folsom spoke to specific groups within the electorate with his promise to include women on Alabama juries and his opposition to antilabor legislation.[29]

Big Jim Folsom followed his proven formula as he embarked on his speaking tour of the state. As before, the Cullman office mailed thousands of campaign circulars to rural families; an ensemble of musicians entertained Folsom's audiences with country music; and Folsom involved the voters in his campaign by asking them for small contributions. Big Jim was a more dignified candidate in 1954 than he had been in 1946. He now wore conservative suits, argyle socks, and loafers, and he never kissed ladies or took naps on sidewalks. Folsom changed the name of the original Strawberry Pickers to the Corn Grinders and explained the name's significance in his campaign talk. Back in the old days, he began, farmers took their grain to a local miller for grinding. Since currency was scarce, each farmer paid the miller by leaving a portion of his corn in the miller's toll bucket. Holding up a bucket labeled "Toll Bucket," Folsom said that politics worked the same way. "Somebody has got to pay the toll in this campaign if I'm going to grind out the pensions, the Fair Vote Convention, and the mail box roads." As the Corn Grinders played, Folsom passed the "toll bucket" to collect the contributions.[30]

Still a master of communication, Folsom introduced new expressions and stories in the 1954 campaign. His theme song and greeting, "Y'all Come!" invited the people to the polls on election day and to the capital for his inauguration. Before each appearance, Folsom's aides searched for a local road on which the pavement extended only as far as it had in 1951. Then during his talk, Big Jim would ask, "Do you know where the pavement on that road ends?" And then he would answer, "It ends right where my administration went out of office." When discussing reapportionment, Folsom used two short sections of pipe. One pipe, only one inch in diameter, represented an underapportioned county with one seat in the Alabama house. The other, three inches in diameter, symbolized Dallas County with its three seats in the house. Using the pipes, Folsom demonstrated that Dallas County not only had more influence in Montgomery, but it also had a greater ability to funnel state money back to Dallas County. Folsom regularly personalized his plans for education and road construction by declaring, "I'm not going to have your children walking muddy roads to get to school. I'm going to put them on a paved road in a school bus with a heater."[31]

Big Jim was at his best as he dismissed the attacks of Henderson and Sweet. When he was a boy, Folsom said, his mother had taught him how to keep his white shirts clean. "If they throw mud at you, don't try to wipe it off or it'll smear. Just wait until it dries and it'll fall off by itself." Comparing his opponents' accusations to those clods of mud, Folsom said he would ignore them until they fell away by themselves. With another anecdote, Big Jim reminded voters that none of the recent investigations had proven him guilty of any illegal act. When he was a boy and plowed the fields on his family's farm, Folsom claimed, he often looked to the skies for rain-bearing clouds. On many afternoons, each puff of cloud seemed to promise a downpour and the young Folsom would turn the mules toward the barn. Inevitably, his father intercepted him and asked why he had stopped plowing. After Folsom predicted rain, his father would send him back to the field with the admonition, "Son, it may cloud up, but it ain't gonna rain." Big Jim compared the investigations and accusations to those imaginary rain clouds. He assured everyone, "It may cloud up on ole Big Jim, but it ain't gonna rain."[32]

Folsom borrowed his favorite response to charges of corruption from Eugene Talmadge of Georgia. When Sweet accused him of stealing, Folsom replied, "Sure I stole, but I stole it for you and you and you!" Expanding Talmadge's answer, Folsom explained that selfish interest groups and professional politicians had made his first administration a "four year filibuster." The Economy Bloc had thwarted every effort to give the average Alabamian a better standard of living between 1947 and 1951. "Sure, I'll admit that I did some stealing when I was your governor," Folsom confessed. "But the crowd I worked with, the only way you could get it was to steal it."[33]

With Big Jim's genius on the campaign trail and the organizational support of his inner circle, his reelection campaign gained momentum. The excitement peaked on 1 May 1954, the Saturday on which Folsom supporters from every county gathered in Montgomery. Early that morning, cars plastered with Folsom banners began the trek toward the capital. In every county seat along the way, more cars joined the caravans as they headed for Montgomery. That evening everyone parked at the Alabama State Coliseum for the largest political rally ever held in Alabama. More than 10,000 supporters heard Big Jim rehearse the contents of his program and fulminate against the "lying newspapers," the "monopolists and monied interests," and the "government snoopers" that had tried to discredit "the little man's big friend." As he spoke, Folsom radiated absolute confidence in his reelection.[34]

Almost 600,000 people voted in the Alabama Democratic primary on 4 May 1954, and more than 305,000 of them cast ballots for Big Jim Folsom. In forty-one counties, Folsom won clear majorities. In twenty others, he received a plurality of the votes. Of the six counties in which Folsom did not lead the field, he trailed Jimmy Faulkner in five and Bruce Henderson in one. Altogether, Folsom garnered 50.7 percent of the votes and won the Democratic nomination without a run-off. It was the most dramatic victory for any gubernatorial candidate in recent Alabama history.[35]

The voting returns in other races appeared to be equally favorable for Big Jim. Although he had not offered a slate, candidates who had supported Folsom loyally in the past won significant victories. Among candidates for the Alabama senate, approximately fourteen who sympathized with Folsom and fourteen who opposed him won nominations. This configuration of partisans greatly improved Folsom's chances of winning support for his proposals during his second administration.

In the run-off primaries for attorney general, secretary of state, superintendent of education, and associate justice on the Alabama Supreme Court, Folsom favored the nominations of Lee Porter, Mary Texas Hurt, Austin Meadows, and James Mayfield, respectively. He endorsed them indirectly by asking voters to support the candidates who lived farthest north. On 1 June, the voters followed Folsom's wishes in three of the four races. Lee Porter lost the nomination for attorney general to Albert Patterson by a vote of 191,766 to 190,912.[36]

Political analysts could attribute Folsom's success to a wide variety of factors: the effectiveness of his organization, the attractiveness of his program, his expertise as a campaigner, his record of rewarding loyal supporters, the reaction against the old Economy Bloc. None of the analysts assessed Folsom's success any more accurately than a writer who called himself "Earl Nunn of Bangor":

> I shore do feel sorry for that pore man in Bessemer (Henry Sweet). I reckon them Folsomite varmits dang nigh ruined him, goin' by the way he talks. If I could sling them two-dollar words around like he does, I'd run for govner myself. 'Course if I tried I'd wind up getting choked on one of 'em. Now me and the wife's got 80 acres, three kids, and 14 hounds. Ain't no Folsomite ever come around tryin' to take none of 'em yet. I reckon it's just like the feller said. They just don't bother us little fellers with the strong backs and weak minds. It's a shame there's so many of us scattered around Alabama. If it wasn't for that, ye all could just about have things your way. Don't blame us for stickin' up for them what sticks up for us.[37]

James E. Folsom won reelection in 1954 because the ordinary folks, the people who lived out on the Buttermilk Road, still knew him as "the little man's big friend."

The men who had organized the reelection campaign interpreted Folsom's victory as the beginning of their work. Almost unnoticed by Big Jim, they had constructed a political organization around him. During the months following his nomination, they were determined that he would not neglect to organize the Alabama Legislature, prepare his legislative program, or consolidate his leadership on the Alabama Democratic Executive Committee. Their preparations began before the returns of the 4 May Democratic primary became official.

With Folsom's approval his leaders reorganized themselves into planning committees. Committees of three to five men planned for every function of the governor's office. There were committees for finances, education, road construction, state purchasing, the ABC Board, and many other functions. Folsom appreciated the work of these committees because they developed detailed legislative proposals for each of his campaign promises and because they allowed him to answer questions about his preparations for taking office by responding that he had committees working on it. The committees also served to enhance the influence of the inner circle over Folsom. Members of Folsom's inner circle—Fuller Kimbrell, Rankin Fite, George Hawkins, George Wallace, and Charles Pinkston—held a majority on each committee. As the committees made recommendations to the nominee for governor, these men increased their ability to shape each of Folsom's decisions.[38]

Evidence of Folsom's planning became public on the Friday after the Democratic primary. On that day, Folsom designated Rankin Fite as his candidate for Speaker of the house and asked George Hawkins to be his house floor leader. Fite was an excellent choice because of his proven loyalty to Folsom and his unsurpassed knowledge of legislative rules. Although Hawkins coveted the Speaker's gavel, the young Gadsden attorney agreed to serve as floor leader because service in the Folsom administration seemed the best way to gain statewide political prominence. One week later, Folsom recommended that the Alabama senate select Broughton Lamberth as its president pro tem. Lamberth was the logical choice for president pro tem because he had supported Big Jim longer than any of his senate colleagues.[39]

Folsom designated his legislative leaders just in time to prevent the organization of another anti-Folsom legislative bloc. During the weeks after the primary, senatorial nominees Walter Givhan of Dallas County and E. O. Eddins of Marengo County discussed the formation of a new Economy Bloc with Jimmy Lawson of the Agricultural Extension Service. The three men appealed for the support of industrial leaders in a meeting with I. W. Rouser of the Coal Mining Institute and Hubert Baughan, editor of *Alabama*. Speaking for the "Big Mules", however, Rouser and Baughan scotched the scheme. They explained that organizing an opposition bloc before Folsom's inauguration would be foolhardy, especially while Folsom's great popularity made it possible for him to organize strong majorities in both legislative houses.[40]

The preparations for his second administration proceeded as Folsom conferred with legislative nominees. Beginning on 10 May, Folsom and his advisers met with future senators to seek pledges of support for the Folsom program and the election of Broughton Lamberth as senate president pro tem. In later meetings with the future representatives, Folsom and his men promoted Rankin Fite for Speaker of the house. Each of these meetings followed a similar format. After Folsom asked some general questions, Kimbrell, Fite, and Wallace engaged each legislator in a detailed discussion of patronage, committee assignments, and areas of legislative interest. O. H. Finney, Ralph Hammond, and Bill Lyerly also participated and kept records of the discussions. By the time they had held meetings with all of the legislators, the Folsom administration had identified its legislative friends and prepared its legislative strategies.[41]

While making legislative plans, Folsom and his advisers distributed prominent positions within the administration. For his office staff, Folsom chose O. H. Finney as his executive secretary, Myra Leak Porter as his corresponding secretary, and Ralph Hammond as his press secretary. For finance director, the single most important department head, Folsom selected Fuller Kimbrell. Recognizing their long-term loyalty, Folsom made LaRue Horn his commissioner of revenue, Bill Drinkard his conservation director, Bill Lyerly his public safety director, and Charles Pinkston his chief of staff. As he had in 1947, Folsom required his appointees to sign undated letters of resignation.[42]

One key appointment went to a man who had never supported Folsom actively. Folsom asked Herman Nelson to direct the Highway Department. Nelson had maintained political nonpartisanship throughout his twenty-eight-year career in the Alabama Highway Department. As a division engineer in the Highway Department, he understood every detail of highway construction and maintenance. While his administrative competence was unquestioned, Nelson also understood the significance of political loyalty. He had not worked in past election campaigns, but neither had he betrayed any political trust. As a member of the Folsom administration, Nelson was an ideal Highway Department director.[43]

Conspicuously absent from Folsom's cabinet were Phillip Hamm, Ward McFarland, and Frank Boswell. Hamm had fallen out of Folsom's favor in 1950 when he withdrew from the gubernatorial run-off with Gordon Persons. He had further displeased Big Jim in 1954 by sponsoring a senatorial candidate in opposition to a candidate supported by Folsom. Folsom helped Hamm obtain a job with the Alabama Trucking Association, but he did not include him in the cabinet. It took Folsom a year to find a position for Ward McFarland. After the legislature met in 1955, Folsom made McFarland the director of the Alabama State Docks. Because the legislature had removed the prison system from the governor's control, there was no convenient niche for Boswell in 1954. Instead,

Folsom used Boswell to coordinate the patronage requests of legislators and local supporters.[44]

Frank Boswell dealt with the most politically sensitive challenge of 1954. Dozens of disgruntled supporters complained that they were unappreciated when patronage went to men who were not as loyal to Folsom as they. Typical complaints came from supporters in Montgomery. On 3 June, Folsom's campaign leaders celebrated their victory at a party in the capital. The affair spotlighted Montgomery County campaign leader Pleas Looney as well as Charles Pinkston, Fuller Kimbrell, and George Wallace. The next day, the Montgomery city commissioner, Dave Birmingham, addressed an irritated letter to Folsom. He listed nine Montgomerians who had worked in Folsom's campaign but who were not invited to the party. Birmingham warned Folsom, "There are (sic) a group of men here in Montgomery who are trying to run the show for you and who seemingly don't appreciate the fact that it took more than that little handful to elect you." Birmingham asked no recognition for himself, but he insisted that Folsom appropriately recognize the men who had been overlooked.[45]

The patronage disputes notwithstanding, Folsom was a more potent political leader in 1954 than he had ever been before. The nominee for the governorship flexed his political muscles during the 1954 meetings of the Alabama Democratic Executive Committee. On 13 July, the Democratic nominee for commissioner of agriculture and industries died. Instead of holding a special primary, the Executive Committee decided to nominate a new candidate at its July meeting. Ordinarily, the runner-up in the recent Democratic primary, R. C. Bamburg of Marengo County in this case, would have been the committee's choice. However, Folsom intervened on behalf of A. W. Todd of Franklin County. Folsom's associates held meetings with committee members, made promises, and twisted arms until Todd received the nomination. The episode provided early proof that Jim Folsom and his advisers could exert substantial influence over state political affairs.[46]

With the advice of Kimbrell, Fite, Wallace, Pinkston, and other friends, Folsom laid the foundation for a successful second administration. However, while Folsom made his plans, events totally beyond his control created situations that would limit his success. The first event occurred thirteen days after Folsom's renomination. On 17 May 1954, the United States Supreme Court issued its decision of *Brown v. Board of Education of Topeka, Kansas.* The second event came approximately one month later, when an unknown assailant murdered A. L. Patterson, the Democratic nominee for attorney general. During the next four years, both of these events helped expose Governor Folsom's political weaknesses.

The Supreme Court's decision of *Brown v. Board of Education* shook Alabama, as it shook all of the southern states, with its pronouncement that racially segregated public education was inherently unequal and therefore unconstitutional. Litigation and public debate since the 1930s had foreshadowed the decision, but after 17 May 1954 white southerners knew that "resist though the South may, eventual desegregation is inevitable." Although the decision did not incite public rioting in Alabama, white responses to the decision were overwhelmingly negative. Grover Hall counseled his readers to remain calm. Technically, the landmark decision did not involve Alabama. Besides, Hall emphasized, the Court had not yet specified how it would enforce its ruling. Even before the decision was issued, Governor Persons announced that he would not call a special session of the legislature to protect segregation in Alabama public schools. Instead, he recommended careful assessment of the situation before the legislature took any action. Birmingham's Albert Boutwell, a state senator and Democratic nominee for lieutenant governor, was more aggressive. Boutwell proposed the establishment of state-subsidized private schools. Parents wishing to avoid "race-mixing" could place their children in the private schools, while the public schools would be open to anyone who did not mind integration.[47]

Jim Folsom attempted to avoid controversy over the *Brown* decision. During the campaign, he had ambiguously promised that he would not force Negro children to attend school with whites. This statement suggested respect for the dignity of Negroes without actually advocating desegregation. As the nominee for governor, Folsom did not comment on the issue directly. His advisers hinted that he would not support Boutwell's plan to establish state-subsidized private schools. They also indicated that Folsom was considering a large school-construction program in order to make Negro school facilities equal to those of white schools. Another clue came from the Southern Governor's Conference when Folsom refused to join other governors in a pledge of resistance to court-ordered desegregation. Still, Folsom withheld candid statements throughout 1954 that might endanger the implementation of his campaign program.[48]

The murder of Albert Patterson affected the second Folsom administration indirectly. The murder fit into a long tradition of crime and violence in Phenix City that stretched back beyond 1819. Just across the Chattahoochee River from Fort Benning, Georgia, local gangsters thrived on the town's gambling joints and brothels. Bribery, intimidation, and voter fraud were common in local elections and allowed the criminals to protect themselves from zealous law enforcement. With their control of local elections, the Phenix City bosses had regularly traded huge majorities in state elections for the acquiescence of state officials. In spite of the protests of local citizens, neither local nor state officials attempted to curb the corruption.

Albert Patterson began his political career in Phenix City. When he won election to the Alabama senate in 1946, most politicians assumed that he won with the support of the Phenix City gangsters. Having declared his independence from the bosses, however, Patterson sought the office of attorney general in 1954 and promised to eradicate vice all over the state. Eighteen days after his nomination, Albert Patterson was murdered. The crime attracted national attention and created pressure for thorough investigation. However, for five days after the crime, Attorney General Si Garrett and the Russell County solicitor Arch Ferrell—both of whom were later accused of cooperation with the murderer—supervised the investigation. By the time Governor Persons declared martial law and sent the Alabama National Guard to Phenix City, virtually all incriminating evidence had been destroyed.[49]

Patterson's murder affected Jim Folsom by catapulting Patterson's son into prominence. When the Alabama Democratic Executive Committee named John Patterson to succeed his father as the nominee for attorney general, he became Alabama's premier advocate of clean government and a prime gubernatorial candidate for 1958. Patterson's loyalty to his martyred father and his political ambitions made him a natural enemy of the Folsom administration. Folsom and Albert Patterson had ended their political friendship in 1949 when the senator joined the Economy Bloc. During the 1954 run-off campaign, Folsom had endorsed Lee Porter for attorney general. Even after the murder, Folsom maintained political friendships with leaders in Phenix City and with the probate court judge Coma Garrett, the father of Attorney General Si Garrett. John Patterson may have even suspected that Folsom had ties with his father's killers. Thus, for four years the governor and the attorney general were to be political and personal enemies. From 1955 through 1959, the attorney general used the resources of his office to expose every irregularity within the Folsom administration. Throughout his second term, Governor Folsom's administration was disrupted by the evidence of corruption that Patterson publicized.

As Jim Folsom's second inauguration approached, the difficulties created by the *Brown* decision and the political rise of John Patterson still lay in the future. Less than four years earlier, Folsom had left the governor's office under a cloud of suspicion. Now he was the political champion of Alabama returning to the governor's office with realistic plans for implementing his campaign program. That work commanded his immediate attention. The time for worrying about civil rights and corruption would come later.

9

"Grinding the Corn"

During the 1954 campaign, Big Jim said "Y'all come!" On May 4 1954, Alabama voters had responded by giving Jim Folsom more votes than any candidate had ever won in a state election. On 17 January 1955, Alabamians responded again by flooding the capital to witness Folsom's second inauguration. Grover Hall anticipated the scene with a vivid description of Folsom's constituency.

> The Folsom host in the one-lick primary victory brought whale-tailed Cadillacs parked beside high-cabbed pickup trucks with banging tail gates; calico rubbing against mink; overalls and tobacco juice seated with Brooks Bros. flannel and filter tips; unified applause from card-carrying C.I.O. organizers, and open shop operators; sin-hating fundamentalists cheek-by-jowl with liquor agents.
>
> But much more remarkable—and we believe unique in the line of Southern mob spellbinders—is the appeal of Folsom to both the "nigger hater" element and the Negro himself.[1]

The celebration of Folsom's second inauguration easily surpassed the scale of the festivities in 1946. The inaugural parade, with high school bands and floats from every county, took four hours to pass in front of the capitol. The most memorable float represented the effect of the Folsom administration on rural roads. On the float's first half, a rickety wagon stuck axle-deep in mud represented the years before Folsom. On the other half, a late model automobile seemed to speed over a smooth, asphalt surface. After the parade, a radio and television network broadcast Folsom's oath of office and inaugural address. The afternoon passed with an open house at the capitol and a tea at the governor's mansion. During the evening, celebrants attended one of two inaugural balls: white Alabamians partied at the Alabama State Coliseum while Negroes attended a "separate but equal" ball at Alabama State College.[2]

In addition to greeting Alabamians with "Y'all come!" during 1954, Big Jim had likened the political process to a transaction between a farmer and a miller in a barter economy. In this metaphor, the farmer's corn symbolized the progressive state services and political reforms proposed in the People's Program. Folsom had said that someone had to pay the toll for his election before he could go to Montgomery and grind the people's corn. His audiences had paid the toll during the campaign with money dropped into the toll bucket, and they paid it again when they voted for his election. As 1955 began, Folsom assumed responsibility for grinding the corn. His overwhelming victory in the Democratic primary and the careful preparations of his advisers certainly increased the prospects for the implementation of his proposals. Folsom would need these advantages because the task of securing legislative approval for his proposals—"grinding the corn"—remained to test Folsom's skill as a public servant and political leader.

Just before the inauguration, the governor-elect demonstrated that his second administration would not be as politically inept as his first. During the legislature's organizational session, the house elected Rankin Fite as its Speaker and recognized George Hawkins as the administration's floor leader without a fight. In the senate, Broughton Lamberth easily became president pro tem. The distribution of committee assignments consolidated the administration's power. Pro-Folsom majorities controlled the three most important committees in each house: the Rules, Ways and Means, and Judiciary committees in the house and the Rules, Finance and Taxation, and Judiciary committees in the senate. Folsom supporters also served as the chairmen and the vice-chairmen of the committees on Education, Roads, Public Welfare, and Conservation. As long as his supporters remained loyal, their control over these key legislative positions eliminated the possibility of organized opposition.[3]

On Inauguration Day, the Folsomites also took control of the Alabama Democratic Executive Committee. At the committee's first meeting, it followed Folsom's recommendation and elected the circuit judge Roy Mayhall of Jasper as its chairman. Fuller Kimbrell and other Folsom aides then persuaded the Executive Committee to fill a vacancy with Charles Pinkston and to elect Pinkston as the committee's vice-chairman. Folsom's cadre on the committee was even strong enough to elect Mrs. Ralph Hammond, the wife of Folsom's press secretary, as the vice-chairman for the women's division. With its control of the executive committee, the Folsom administration ensured that the state party leaders would not be able to organize opposition to the governor as Gessner McCorvey had done in 1948.[4]

Governor Folsom wasted no time in proving that he was a better legislative leader in 1955 than he had been in 1947. Four days after his inauguration, the governor called a special session of the legislature for the purpose of enacting his farm-to-market road program. The special session, scheduled to begin on 25 January, was the first phase of the legislative strategy he and his advisers had devised during 1954. Folsom called the session with the assurance that county commissioners and municipal officials would press their representatives and senators to enact a road construction program. After the legislators approved the road construction program, the Folsom administration planned to call additional special sessions to deal with old-age pensions and legislative reapportionment. In each of these single-issue sessions, the legislators would be compelled to take unequivocal, public positions while Folsom's control of road construction funds commanded the support of local politicians. Similarly, the special sessions would encourage private interest groups to work for Folsom's proposals at a time when no other issue cluttered the legislature's agenda. By beginning 1955 with single-issue legislative sessions, Governor Folsom also fulfilled major campaign promises without risking wasteful filibusters during the legislature's biennial session. When compared with his mismanagement of the 1947 controversy over the API Board of Trustees, this legislative strategy for 1955 demonstrated how much Jim Folsom had learned from his experiences and his circle of advisers.[5]

Folsom's road construction program combined a proposal for building farm-to-market roads with a plan to augment the governor's political power. On the first day of their special session, Folsom asked the legislators to increase the state gasoline tax by two cents per gallon, and to designate one cent of the increase for the Highway Department's operating expenses. The other cent, Folsom said, should be earmarked for revenue bonds to fund road construction. In recommending revenue bonds, Folsom sought funding for bonds that could be issued without competitive bids and without additional legislative action. Governor Folsom also requested that the legislature restructure the Alabama Highway Corporation, a semipublic corporation which borrowed money for the Highway Department without violating the Alabama Constitution's prohibition on governmental debt. Folsom proposed to reorganize the corporation's board of directors so that his appointees would constitute a majority. Altogether, Folsom was seeking new money for road construction projects, projects that would enhance the administration's appeal to local political leaders, and seeking the greatest possible discretion as to which investors would benefit from the new road construction bond issues.[6]

Since the legislative success of his administration hinged on Folsom's road program, he and his advisers devoted themselves to the work of winning votes. Recognizing that legislators were politicians with local constituencies to please, Folsom's administration offered them a variety of local favors. First, legislators were offered their preferred committee assignments and a chance to promote their favorite legislative proposals. Later, the administration sought legislators' recommendations in the appointment of jury commissioners, boards of tax equalization, and voter registrars. Periodically, Folsom's men consulted with legislators concerning local road construction priorities. Within the bounds of such friendly relationships, the governor hoped that the legislators would remember his favors when they considered his legislative program.[7]

Folsom's administration also sought to cultivate friendships with legislators through personal courtesies. The most common, although secret, of these in 1955 was the appearance of the "mystery whiskey." While the legislature was in session, most legislators drove to Montgomery on the first legislative day of the week, stayed in a hotel during the week, and returned to their homes on the weekend. Each week after the legislators had arrived, several Folsom aides located their hotel rooms and left a fifth of whiskey on each lawmaker's dressing table. Occasionally, Folsom's men returned on the last day of the week to leave another bottle. No bottle was accompanied by evidence of its donor's identity, but the legislators quickly deduced that the liquor came from Folsom, who received the bottles as "free samples" from distillers who did business with the ABC Board. Both friends and foes of the administration received the mystery whiskey until Hugh Sparrow wrote about it in his *Birmingham News* column. Then constituent pressure forced a reluctant legislature to ask that the anonymous benefactor withhold his gifts.[8]

Since the direct trading of patronage favors for legislative votes resembled bribes and depleted the administration's patronage stores, Folsom discouraged such bargaining. However, the Folsom administration was ready to provide such inducements when absolutely necessary. In early 1955, O. H. Finney instructed all department heads to supply Senator Lamberth and Representative Hawkins with regular information about state job openings. Lamberth and Hawkins would use the information "to trade with members of the Legislature . . . from time to time." While the senate considered the farm-to-market road program, one northern Alabama senator complained that a friend had lost his job as a physician at a convict road construction camp. Folsom restored the friend to his former position and secured a vote for his road program. One Calhoun County legislator said he could not vote for the Folsom road program because he did not understand it. A member of Folsom's cabinet promptly contacted the legislator and explained that if he voted for the program, the Highway Department would widen and pave Anniston's Quintard Avenue over a distance of seven miles. However, if the legislator voted against the administration, the Highway Department would postpone the Quintard Avenue project for at least four years. Enlightened, the Calhoun County legislator supported each of Folsom's proposals.[9]

If the administration could not trade patronage for votes, it appealed to local politicians for help. While the legislature considered Folsom's road program, Herman Nelson, director of the Highway Department, requested that every county commissioner submit a list of local projects that could be begun immediately if the legislature provided funding. Meanwhile, Ed Pepper of Clay County, the executive assistant to the finance director, Fuller Kimbrell, maintained a record of each legislator's votes. Whenever town or county officials sought state aid for local projects, either Folsom or Kimbrell consulted Pepper's record before giving the officials an answer. The Folsom administration could apply even more local pressure to legislators from counties in which large state institutions were located. The University of Alabama, API, the Highway Department's eight divisional offices, the state hospitals, and similar institutions made major economic contributions to their communities. No legislator could afford to oppose the Folsom administration as long as the governor's supporters could reduce the appropriations to a state institution in his county. Folsom's willingness to pressure legislators through local officials inspired a rhyme among members of the house:

Hawkins, Dawkins, and Rankin Fite;
If you want a road, you'd better vote right![10]

When Folsom considered an issue vital to his success and no other inducement won votes, his administration resorted to direct threats and monetary payoffs. While the legislature studied the farm-to-market road program, Herman Nelson halted all state highway maintenance and claimed that the Highway Department had run out of funds. During the same period, the governor instructed his department heads to deprive uncooperative legislators of every form of patronage. "Don't give them as much as one gem clip 'till you see how they're going to vote." Folsom aimed his most extreme threat at Senator Sam Engelhardt of Macon County, a Black Belt County in which the majority of the population was Negro. When the senator fought the road program, Folsom blurted, "I'm going to get a new board of registrars in Macon County and register every damn nigger in the county." The finance director, Fuller Kimbrell, normally allowed only the administration's political friends to profit from selling merchandise to the state government. However, when one Black Belt senator blocked the road program in the Finance and Taxation Committee, Kimbrell agreed to purchase several new state vehicles from the senator's automobile dealership. Miraculously, the senator's objections to Folsom's proposal vanished.[11]

With all of the incentives that the Folsom administration offered, the house of representatives acted promptly on the farm-to-market road program. During the first week of the special session, the representatives approved the two-cent-per-gallon tax increase. While the tax bill went on to the senate, the house amended Folsom's bond issue proposal and his restructuring of the Alabama Highway Corporation. The amendments limited the bond issue to a maximum of $100 million, required competitive bids in the sale of the bonds, and allowed the governor to appoint only three of the highway corporation's five directors. Having made these changes, the house passed the road program by a vote of seventy-three to twenty-five.[12]

The Folsom road program encountered stiff political opposition in the Alabama senate. In the Finance and Taxation Committee, anti-Folsom and nonpartisan senators barely outnumbered the seven Folsomites. Unwilling to give Folsom all the patronage power he requested, the committee's majority, led by Senators Albert Boutwell of Birmingham and E. O. Eddins of Marengo County, refused to endorse the administration's road program. Folsom's men could have forced the committee to report the administration's bills, but they did not want to provoke an anti-Folsom filibuster on the senate floor. For two weeks, the farm-to-market road program remained bottled up in committee, until Folsom asked Lieutenant Governor Guy Hardwick to help work out a compromise. Hardwick consulted with Boutwell and Eddins and secured their endorsement of either a one cent gasoline tax increase with a $50 million bond issue or a two cent tax increase with a $25 million bond issue.[13]

Fuller Kimbrell, the finance director, was the first of Folsom's advisers to learn the terms of the compromise. He quickly met with several other advisers, including Herman Nelson and the budget officer, Jake Jordan, to calculate which of the alternatives would be most advantageous. Kimbrell was surprised to learn that the two cent gasoline tax increase and the $25 million bond issue would provide more revenue for highway construction and more patronage for the Folsom administration. Explaining that the two cent tax increase would boost the Highway Department's general operating funds substantially, Kimbrell advised Folsom to accept the larger tax increase and the smaller bond issue. However, Governor Folsom had already decided that his administration would have the largest road construction bond issue in Alabama history, and Kimbrell could not change his mind.[14]

After Governor Folsom made his decision, his legislative leaders gave the compromise package their full support. The Finance and Taxation Committee sent the road program to the senate floor, where only three senators voted against it. With only six representatives opposing, the house concurred with the senate and forwarded the compromise road program to Folsom for his signature. Thus, by the end of February, the Folsom administration had secured a road construction program, and the first special session of 1955 adjourned sine die.[15]

As politicians are wont to do, both Folsom and his opposition claimed victory. The governor boasted that his administration had gained the largest road construction bond issue in Alabama history. Folsom not only welcomed the additional patronage which the new road construction funds afforded his administration, but he was also pleased that the legislature had given him control of the Alabama Highway Corporation and had not required that the Highway Department take competitive bids in the letting of road contracts. Folsom's opponents also celebrated. In spite of his impressive electoral victory in 1954 and the concentration of his administration on the road program, they had tied his proposals up in committee and forced him to accept a compromise. Their opposition had provoked Folsom into an uncharacteristic public expression of frustration as he threatened to "register every damn nigger in Macon County." Most significantly, Folsom's opponents had shown that Folsom would not exercise uncontested control over the legislature.[16]

On the last day of the first special session, Governor Folsom announced that the second special session of 1955 would convene eight days later and consider old-age pension legislation. The governor's official proclamation recommended the repeal of the relative-responsibility law of 1951 and instructed the legislators to enact revenue measures that would provide monthly pensions of fifty dollars for every elderly Alabamian.[17]

Legislative action on the relative-responsibility law was quick. On 4 March, the first day of the second special session, Representative Charles Adams and Senator Joe Davis introduced identical bills to make 138,000 people eligible for public assistance by dropping the requirement that pensioners have no relatives capable of providing financial support. Since fifty-two representatives and nineteen senators cosponsored the legislation, its enactment was ensured. One week later, the legislature placed the relative-responsibility repeal on Folsom's desk for his signature.[18]

The process of enacting new revenue measures to fund old-age pensions proved to be more complex. Representative George Hawkins headed a four-member committee that drafted and introduced the administration's revenue bills. They included tax increases on beer, liquor, cigarettes, cigars and corporate capital invested in the state; new taxes on cosmetics, jewelry, furs, and luggage; a surcharge on all taxes already levied in Alabama; and a graduated tax on insurance premiums. Altogether, Hawkins introduced tax legislation that would increase state revenues by $50 million each year. Since only $10 million worth of new taxes was needed for old-age pensions, Folsom wanted the legislature to choose which of the tax bills should be enacted. The process of elimination began in the house Ways and Means Committee.[19]

Although the administration's revenue bills did not encounter stiff legislative opposition, the house worked on them for most of March 1955. Lobbyists for the insurance industry attended the public hearings conducted by the Ways and Means Committee and argued that the tax on premiums would cripple their business. Governor Folsom, in spite of his own background as an insurance salesman, minimized the lobbyists' testimony in a conversation with one legislator: "Now, don't you feel sorry for those damn insurance companies. They've got a mortgage on the world." Lobbyists against new taxes, however, could scarcely be heard above the voices of old-age pension advocates. The Alabama Old-Age Pension Association reminded its members of Folsom's invitation, "Y'all come!" and elderly citizens descended on the capitol by the hundreds. Even if they did not speak during the committee's hearing, the old men in their worn overalls and tobacco-stained shirts made a forceful statement in favor of the administration's proposals. On 23 March the house Ways and Means Committee recommended five revenue bills to the house. Four of them proposed increased taxes on beer, liquor, cigarettes, and the operating capital that foreign corporations employed in Alabama. The fifth bill contained a graduated tax on the premiums Alabamians paid to out-of-state insurance companies. Within one week, the house approved the revenue package and sent it to the senate.[20]

In spite of majority support for old-age pensions, the tax package met determined opposition in the Finance and Taxation Committee. Claiming to be uneasy over the administration's piecemeal tax program, opposition senators wanted to postpone the old-age pension taxes while they conducted a comprehensive study of the state tax structure. Although no such study was made and the committee gave favorable reports to four of the tax bills, the opposition mustered enough strength to postpone the increase of the corporate franchise tax indefinitely. Folsom responded in anger, "Any man who was a Christian would never have voted against the old folks program." He announced his intention to pack the Finance and Taxation Committee with Folsomites in order to win a favorable report for the entire tax package. Folsom's threat provoked an opposition filibuster that slowed the senate's action on the other four revenue bills. Two days later, the governor agreed to forget about packing the senate committee and his opponents promised to report the tax on corporate capital favorably.[21]

Once the Finance and Taxation Committee reported all five revenue bills, the senate completed its work quickly. All five won the senate's approval on 7 and 8 April. The administration expected the new laws to raise $10 million per year for old-age pensions. Naturally, Folsom was well pleased with the legislators' work when they adjourned sine die.[22]

After his success in the first two special sessions, Folsom planned to capitalize on his administration's momentum. Calling constitutional revision "the next great step forward for our people," the governor convened a third special session on 13 April. This time, however, Folsom overestimated the goodwill of weary legislators. After eleven weeks of deliberations, most legislators wanted to rest and attend to personal business before the 1955 biennial session began on 3 May. On the first day of the special session, the legislators rebelled. They met just long enough to appropriate money for their salaries and then recessed the session until 21 July. On 21 July, the legislators adjourned sine die without giving serious consideration to the calling of a constitutional convention.[23]

In spite of the rebellion, Governor Folsom had confidence that the legislature would continue to follow his leadership during the biennial session. On the opening day of the session, he presented new issues for legislative action. Folsom gave his strongest recommendation to bills that would restore to the governor control over the Alabama State Docks and that would establish a department to promote industrial development. As in the past, Folsom supported public education, but in 1955 he relied on the strong education lobby to fight the legislative battles on that issue. Fulfilling a campaign promise, the governor gave verbal support to the repeal of Alabama's right-to-work law. Although still committed to legislative reapportionment and constitutional revision, Folsom deferred these issues until a time when debate would not threaten to defeat other important legislation.[24]

Folsom's plan for industrial development consisted of two proposals. First, he asked the legislature to create a Department of Industrial Development with a director and advisory board appointed by the governor. The department would work with local governments to compile information about natural resources, transportation, labor supplies, and potential plant sites. The department would then make the information available to any firm interested in constructing a new plant. While the firm constructed its new plant and began operations, the department would continue to offer counsel and assistance to the company officials. The gover-

nor also sought to encourage investments in Alabama industries.
His proposal, patterned after a Texas law, required all insurance
companies doing business in Alabama to invest a percentage of
their assets within the state. The exact proportion of assets so invested, Folsom believed, should equal the proportion of total premiums each company collected from Alabamians. Folsom hoped
that the investment of insurance assets would provide ample capital for industrial development.

The creation of a Department of Industrial Development proved
to be very popular with the legislature. It complemented similar
efforts already being made by the Committee of 100 in Birmingham, the Alabama Chamber of Commerce, and the Alabama
Power Company. The idea was so popular that the Alabama house
approved it in a vote of one hundred to zero. The senate was equally
enthusiastic, and Folsom signed the legislation into law. In choosing
the department's director and advisory board, the governor went
outside his circle of friends. Major General Lewis A. Pick, the retired head of the U.S. Army Corps of Engineers, agreed to become
the first director of industrial development. General Pick not only
had the technical expertise to direct an industry-hunting campaign,
but his national reputation gave Alabama's search instant credibility among corporate executives. Asking for no pledges of political loyalty, Folsom filled the department's advisory board with
prominent business leaders from every congressional district.[25]

Although the legislature did not require insurance companies to
invest their assets in Alabama, Governor Folsom became the state's
most enthusiastic industry hunter, frequently accompanying General Pick on out-of-state junkets. Before the Marathon Corporation
built a $30 million pulpwood plant in Choctaw County, Folsom led
the negotiations with company officials in Wisconsin. He forthrightly declared that Alabama wanted the new Marathon plant and
would offer incentives to persuade the company to choose an Alabama plant site. When the Coosa River Newsprint Company decided to build a $36 million paper mill in Talladega County, Folsom
authorized the temporary exemptions from state income and property taxes that persuaded the firm to invest in the new plant.
Folsom's contact with Louis Reynolds helped secure complemen-
tary investments by Reynolds Aluminum and Ford Motors in the
Muscle Shoals area. By the end of 1955, the new Department of
Industrial Development had contributed to the attraction of thirty-
one new industries to Alabama. These new plants created more

than eight thousand new jobs while thirty-two Alabama firms were also expanding their plants and their payrolls.[26]

Folsom's effort to return the Alabama State Docks to executive control provoked a mild controversy. On the fifth day of the biennial session, the entire Mobile County delegation cosponsored the administration's bill. Since the legislature had made the docks independent of the chief executive after an investigation of corruption in 1951, Folsom's opposition claimed that he intended to make the docks a political plum. The *Mobile Register* protested most vigorously: "Of all the governors holding office during the more than a quarter of a century of docks history, only Mr. Folsom has sought to invade the docks with spoils politics." The Mobile legislators defended their bill with the argument that politics determined docks policies even while the department was technically independent of the governor's office. Governor Folsom ignored the critics publicly and promoted the bill as a reform that would make the docks responsive to the will of the people.[27]

While the public controversy raged, Folsom's supporters quietly fashioned a compromise with their opponents. According to the gentlemen's agreement, the opposition supported the bill in exchange for Folsom's promise to retain Jerrold P. Turner as general manager of the Alabama State Docks. Since Turner supervised the daily operations of the docks, the compromise assured skeptics that the Folsom administration would not radically alter the docks' business practices. On the basis of this agreement, the legislature promptly enacted the State Docks bill and the governor proudly signed it into law.[28]

When he had regained control over the Alabama State Docks, Governor Folsom directed new expansion and development of the port facilities. The State Docks deepened the shipping canal, enlarged its warehouse space, constructed three new shipping berths, began construction of a terminal for river barges, and promoted property adjacent to the docks as industrial plant sites. The improvements led to an immediate increase in shipping traffic. In 1954, the docks had moved almost 5 million tons of cargo from 1,770 ships to 112,038 railroad cars. By 1957 the docks were handling 6.7 million tons of cargo, 1,853 ships, and 153,738 railroad cars each year.[29]

In addition to improvements in Mobile, Governor Folsom and the director of the State Docks, Ward McFarland, initiated a program for constructing inland docks. Folsom envisioned a series of river ports offering shippers water transportation routes between Mobile and towns on Alabama's navigable rivers and making industrial sites in Alabama more attractive to corporate investors. With its income, the State Docks Department drew up plans and secured property for inland docks at Columbia on the Chattahoochee River and at Florence, Huntsville, and Decatur on the Tennessee River. In 1957 the Folsom administration supported a $10 million general obligation bond issue for the inland docks system. The bond issue financed the construction of docks already under way and at Eufaula, Phenix City, and Demopolis.[30]

While working for industrial development and state docks expansion, Governor Folsom became interested in the construction of a canal between the Tennessee and the Tombigbee rivers. Though he was not the first to see its potential, Major General Lewis Pick saw the canal as a means of connecting the Tennessee River valley with the port of Mobile. Before Pick died in late 1956, Folsom began work with the governor of Mississippi, J. P. Coleman, to plan for the waterway. Coleman and Folsom first asked their states' congressional delegations to introduce federal legislation for the creation of an interstate compact. Originally, the governors' plan was for the compact to include construction of the canal. However, when Congress enacted and President Eisenhower signed the bill creating the compact, the law allowed the compact only to receive appropriations from member states, to conduct surveys and draft plans, and to lobby Congress for funds to construct the canal. By the end of the Folsom administration, Mississippi and Alabama were actively supporting the organization that eventually persuaded Congress to construct the Tennessee-Tombigbee Waterway.[31]

With the Folsom administration concentrating on its development projects during 1955, proponents of public education waged their own campaign for larger appropriations. Governor Folsom agreed with most Alabamians that a good educational system prepared young people for responsible citizenship, increased the value of the labor force, and provided a higher standard of living for everyone. But Folsom also knew that the superintendent of education, Austin Meadows, and the Alabama Education Association would knowledgeably and forcefully present education's needs to the Alabama Legislature. Thus, he depended on them to assume leadership in the effort to improve Alabama schools.

As the house Ways and Means Committee studied public education in 1955, it discovered difficult problems. The annual appropriations that Alabama's public schools and colleges requested totaled $123 million, a sum that exceeded the previous annual appropriation by more than $42 million. The educators' requests were thoroughly documented and politically popular. Existing taxes produced no more than $87 million annually for education, and the state constitution specifically prohibited deficit financing. Plainly, the Ways and Means Committee needed to recommend new tax legislation. However, the legislature had already raised taxes in 1955 for road construction and old-age pensions. It seemed that the legislators would either have to offend educators with budget cuts or offend the voters with another tax increase. On the horns of this dilemma, the educational appropriation bill bogged down in the Ways and Means Committee.[32]

Superintendent Meadows and the leaders of AEA grew impatient as committee meetings and public hearings failed to produce an acceptable solution to the dilemma. With the educational appropriation stuck in committee at the end of June, the educators quietly planned a dramatic demonstration. On Wednesday, 29 June, more than 1,800 teachers converged on Montgomery from every county in Alabama. The teachers' unexpected appearance startled Folsom and moved him to make the appropriation bills his number one legislative priority for the second half of the biennial session. The Ways and Means Committee responded to the demonstration on 7 July by hammering out an appropriation bill and eight new revenue bills during thirteen hours of uninterrupted deliberation.[33]

Both the house and the senate accepted the Ways and Means Committee's recommendation and appropriated $114.3 million for public education during each year of the 1955–57 biennium. The legislators were not as enthusiastic about the committee's eight revenue bills. Of the eight proposals, two were generally unpopular: a reduction of personal exemptions for state income tax and the elimination of federal income taxes as a deduction on state tax returns. Two other bills, an increase of corporate income taxes and the ending of several sales tax exemptions, kindled the ire of businessmen. The legislature finally enacted two of the bills—a tax on motel room rentals and the establishment of a withholding system for state income taxes.

Instead of passing the other six revenue bills, the legislature enacted a hastily devised graduated tax on the adjusted gross incomes of individuals and corporations. The Goodwyn tax bill, a constitutional amendment authored by Representative O. J. Goodwyn, earmarked the proceeds of the new tax for education. It presented a perfect political solution to the legislators' dilemma, promising to generate enough revenue to fund the 1955 educational appropriation. However, as a constitutional amendment, it would become law only if the voters ratified it. Thus, no one could accuse the legislators of failing to provide adequately for public education or of enacting onerous new taxes. The legislators were so relieved to dispose of the problem that few calculated the prospects for the Goodwyn tax bill's ratification.[34]

Governor Folsom was extremely proud of the legislative achievements of 1955. He counted paved rural roads, increased old-age pensions, industrial development, administration control of the Alabama State Docks, and unprecedented appropriations for public education as triumphs of his administration. It seemed to Folsom that the legislature had enacted most of the major parts of his campaign program. In spite of these general successes, certain legislative goals eluded the Folsom administration. Several goals, of which the repeal of the right-to-work law was typical, fell victim to disunity within Folsom's ranks. Others, like legislative reapportionment and constitutional revision, required more political power than the Folsom administration would ever have.[35]

Jim Folsom probably sympathized with organized workers more strongly than had any previous Alabama governor. His support for unions went deeper than glib campaign promises and the appointment of labor leaders to token positions in his cabinet. During strikes against the L&N Railroad and the Southern Bell Telephone Company in 1955, company officials appealed to Folsom for the assistance of the Alabama National Guard. The governor not only refused to use the National Guard for strike duty, but he also complained that the companies were not interested in settling the strikes fairly. Commenting on the telephone strike, Folsom said, "They are trying to run over the workers and make them work for low wages and I resent it." When someone argued that Southern Bell suffered more during the strike than the employees, Folsom was sarcastic: "I feel sorry for the little fifteen billion dollar telephone company. I am solid worried about them and my heart bleeds for them. . . . If this telephone strike isn't settled before long, I intend to ask the Legislature to pass a seizure law . . . whereby the State takes over a public utility if it is on strike."[36]

Governor Folsom's personal support for the rights of organized labor led him to recommend the repeal of Alabama's right-to-work law. In accordance with the Taft-Hartley Act of 1947, the law prohibited labor unions from requiring that employers hire only union members. Folsom believed that the prohibition of the "closed shop" worked to the detriment of laborers and contributed to labor-management disputes. Faithful legislative supporters like floor leader George Hawkins, assistant floor leader Joe Dawkins, Senator E. L. Roberts, and Representative A. K. Callahan agreed with Folsom. However, Folsom could not make the repeal of the right-to-work law a test of loyalty because the Speaker of the house, Fite; the executive secretary, Finney; the legal adviser, Battles; and the senate president pro tem, Broughton Lamberth, favored the existing law. The administration's internal differences frustrated Folsom's desire to see the law repealed.[37]

The momentum of Folsom's legislative success vanished when he placed legislative reapportionment on the legislature's agenda. In spite of accomplishing nothing during the five special sessions of 1950, Folsom began his second administration just as committed to reapportionment as ever. He did not ask the legislature to enact his political reforms during the 1955 biennial session because he knew the debates over political reform would detract from the other major parts of his programs. Nevertheless, Folsom predicted that either the legislature would enact reapportionment or he would keep it in session for four years. The latter was more likely than the former.

During the third special session of 1955, Folsom had focused all his political influence on the reapportionment battle. He informed the legislature that it was long overdue: the Alabama Constitution called for it, the people had endorsed it repeatedly, and he had waited eight years to see it accomplished. He ordered his cabinet to make all patronage conditional on legislative support for reapportionment: "I don't want any man in the Legislature to get any gravy if he doesn't vote for reapportionment." Because one Lowndes County legislator doggedly opposed reapportionment, Folsom asked the chairman of the ABC Board, Harrell Hammonds, also from Lowndes County, to keep the legislator away from the capitol. When Representative J. W. Stokes of Elba voted against the administration, Folsom canceled a road construction project in his own county. Folsom told his Highway Department director, "Herman, you call anyone who has roads on docket for plans—call them and tell them to get down here and vote." Still, the legislators adjourned the third special session of 1955 without enacting reapportionment.[38]

Governor Folsom allowed the reapportionment issue to rest until the last day of November 1955, when he announced that a special session for reapportionment and constitutional revision would begin on 3 January 1956. Two days before Christmas, 1955, Folsom made a quick tour of Alabama in support of reapportionment. Early that morning, he and several aides boarded a state plane and began hopping from one county to the next. While Folsom was airborne, highway patrol officers escorted legislators to the nearest landing strip in time to meet the governor's plane. As his plane touched down in each county, Folsom disembarked carrying bottles of whiskey. Placing two bottles in the hands of each legislator, Folsom wished everyone present "Merry Christmas!" and "Y'all come!"[39]

Governor Folsom greeted the legislators again on 3 January 1956 as he addressed the first special session of the new year. Folsom argued that reapportionment was not a partisan political issue and that he would be satisfied with any form of reapportionment the legislature proposed. To legislators who were unhappy to be attending another special session, Folsom said, "I would remind you that this (reapportionment) is indeed an old refrain." However, he continued, "if you do not finish the task in this deliberation, there shall be other singings of that old refrain." He concluded his address with a stern warning: "Knowing the temper of the voters on this subject, I make this observation: those voting against some form of reapportionment just do not have any future state-wide political ambitions."[40]

For the first three weeks of 1956, Folsom's supporters had no more success than they had had during the summer of 1950. The strongest opponents of reapportionment were legislators from overrepresented Black Belt counties who would not accept the reduction of their own legislative influence. The legislators from small, rural counties in every section of the state supported the Black Belt representatives and senators. Their counties benefited because the state government divided highway revenue, ABC system profits, and other state funds equally among the sixty-seven counties. Reapportionment threatened to alter this basis for distributing state monies.

Luckily for reapportionment's enemies, many other issues demanded legislative attention. With the Montgomery bus boycott in progress just outside the capitol and the desegregation of the University of Alabama scheduled for 31 January, the preservation of racial segregation seemed much more important than reapportionment. In December 1955, Alabama voters had rejected the Goodwyn tax bill, and public education now faced a financial crisis. Some legislators demanded investigations of reports that Folsom's political friends were denuding two state parks of timber with the Conservation Department's permission. With all these distractions, it was easy for opponents of reapportionment to ignore the primary issue of the special session.[41]

After three weeks of frustration, Folsom's legislative leaders despaired of achieving their objective. On 19 January, the senate rejected a constitutional convention resolution in an eighteen-to-fifteen vote. On 20 January, the house defeated a similar resolution by a vote of sixty-three to twenty-three. With no chance of winning reapportionment, the administration decided to end the session before the legislators initiated embarrassing investigations or enacted inflammatory segregationist legislation. Wielding a speedy gavel, Speaker Fite put an adjournment motion to a voice vote on 20 January. Ignoring the overwhelming "nays," Fite declared that the house had adjourned sine die and ducked out of the house chamber through a back door. Other Folsom leaders also left the chamber, but sixty-one representatives remained in protest of Fite's high-handedness. Obviously, the house had not adjourned. Fite returned to the capitol on the following legislative day, apologized profusely for his strong-arm tactic, and promised to put every future motion to a roll-call vote.[42]

While Fite reconciled himself to the house, Senator James Coleman of Greene County wrote a compromise reapportionment bill that satisfied both his fellow Black Belt legislators and Folsom's legislative leaders. He proposed a senate of 67 members, one senator for each county. By expanding the house to 152 representatives, the bill would not reduce the number of seats held by any county but would increase the power of underrepresented counties. Although they would remain underrepresented, the three most urbanized counties—Jefferson, Mobile, and Montgomery—would have at least twice as many representatives as before. Coleman and other supporters of the plan admitted that it did not provide reapportionment according to population. They supported it, instead, as a plan that had a chance of legislative enactment. With large majorities in both houses, the legislature endorsed Coleman's work and scheduled a state referendum on reapportionment to coincide with the presidential election on 6 November 1956.[43]

Governor Folsom greeted the legislature's action with unabashed enthusiasm. "I'm mighty happy," he told reporters. "I've been working on this so long that now that it's passed I feel like I'm ready to retire." It was not the true apportionment that Folsom had consistently promised, reapportionment according to population. The governor explained that he could still support the legislature's proposal because it provided for the reapportionment of the house after the 1960 census and would erase any inequities in representation then. Folsom was also enthusiastic about the proposal because it offered him a face-saving way to retire the reapportionment issue. By 1956 even Jim Folsom knew that the legislature would never enact his political reforms. But he had promised reapportionment in each of his election campaigns and had threatened to keep calling special sessions until reapportionment was accomplished. With Coleman's reapportionment measure, Folsom could claim that he had fulfilled his campaign pledge and that it was up to the voters to accept or reject the bill. Even if the voters rejected it, Folsom could say that the people had spoken on the issue and that his administration would honor the popular will by proposing no more political reforms.[44]

Before making these rationalizations, however, Governor Folsom worked hard to promote a victory for reapportionment on 6 November. Realizing that voter interest in the amendment was low, Folsom conducted an anonymous campaign for reapportionment during the fall of 1956. His men printed and distributed advertisements proclaiming, "Keep Alabama segregated! Vote Yes for Amendment No. 1!" The advertisements explained that Black Belt counties whose populations were predominantly Negro held power in the malapportioned legislature. When federal courts eliminated discriminatory suffrage restrictions, as they would inevitably do, the Black Belt Negroes would be able to dominate state government. As the date of the referendum approached, Folsom instructed his men to replace the segregationist appeal with constructive arguments for reapportionment. Neither phase of the administration's campaign stirred voter interest until newspaper reporters and one of Attorney General Patterson's assistants caught a Folsom appointee using state-owned office equipment and supplies to print the campaign advertisements. The voters turned out in moderate numbers on 6 November and defeated the reapportionment plan by a vote of almost two to one. Folsom concluded that the people did not want reapportionment, and he did not ask the legislature to consider political reforms again.[45]

Although the voters rejected the reapportionment amendment, Jim Folsom believed that he had honored every one of his 1954 campaign promises by the spring of 1956. Between January 1955 and February 1956, he had obtained a $50 million bond issue for farm-to-market roads and approximately $10 million in additional annual revenue for old-age pensions. His administration had regained control of the Alabama State Docks, had begun expansion of dock facilities in Mobile and at river ports throughout the state, and had initiated planning for the Tennessee-Tombigbee Waterway. Folsom and the legislature had created the Department of Industrial Development, which attracted several hundred million dollars worth of industrial investment to Alabama in less than two years. Folsom had supported the largest appropriation of funds for public education in Alabama history. Even without the Goodwyn tax bill, the appropriations raised Alabama teacher salaries to $3,386, or equal to 81.5 percent of the national average. According to Governor Folsom, it had been "the most successful year of accomplishments" of his public career.[46]

Folsom's legislative successes of 1955 and 1956 stood in stark contrast to the frustrations of his first administration. Many factors, including Folsom's own maturation as a political leader, contributed to the difference in the administration's legislative record. Folsom's victory in the 1954 Democratic primary gave him a mandate that no elected official could ignore. Folsom's advisers—Kimbrell, Fite, Wallace, Hawkins, and Pinkston—skillfully translated his campaign promises into legislative action. They drafted the bills, supervised daily political business, directed the distribution of patronage, and utilized the rules of both legislative houses on Folsom's behalf. Most important, Folsom's advisers helped him formulate an effective legislative strategy. They worked first for legislation that every local political leader favored—road construction and old-age pensions. During the 1955 biennial session, the administration recommended action on issues—industrial development, the State Docks, and public education—for which a legislative consensus was easily achieved. In the meantime, Folsom dealt with reapportionment and constitutional revision in special sessions. In those legislative sessions, the administration devoted itself to political reform knowing that the implacable opposition of Black Belt and rural county legislators would not defeat other portions of the governor's program. Because it took account of local political leaders and their interests, Folsom's legislative strategy allowed him to stand before the Alabama Legislature in 1956 and say, "My program presented to the people has practically been completed and I humbly thank you for your help."[47]

10

"Let's Start Talking Fellowship and Brotherly Love"

During his 1954 reelection campaign, Big Jim's itinerary included an appearance at Clayton, the seat of Barbour County. Since George C. Wallace was a native of Barbour County, he briefed Folsom on local political affairs as they rode to the campaign rally. After listing all the local politicians toward whom Folsom should be especially friendly, Wallace reminded Folsom that the probate judge planned to meet Folsom in Clayton and emphasized that Folsom should greet him before greeting anyone else. When they arrived in Clayton, Folsom's driver parked so that Folsom's door opened onto the street and Wallace's opened onto the sidewalk. Wallace stepped out and immediately greeted the probate judge on the sidewalk. Folsom stepped out into the street and proceeded to walk around the car. Before he reached the curb, Folsom noticed two black men standing near his car. Without hesitation, he hailed both of them heartily, shook their hands, and asked for their support. He then joined a chagrined Wallace on the sidewalk and met the probate judge.[1]

The incident in Clayton demonstrated that Jim Folsom's attitudes toward Negroes deviated from the attitudes of most white Alabamians. At the time when the fight for Negro rights emerged as a mass movement and alarmed most white southerners, Governor Folsom made many such demonstrations. Instead of adopting the politically popular rhetoric of segregationists, Folsom chose to respect the dignity of Negroes and to defend their rights as citizens. During his first administration, Folsom's deviation won him the loyalty of racial liberals without provoking the anger of other white Alabam-

161

ians. After the decision of *Brown v. Board of Education,* the civil rights movement gained momentum in Alabama while Folsom promoted his legislative program. By 1956, the civil rights movement had inspired whites to defend their social institutions from desegregation and to regard Governor Folsom as a traitor. Popular censure of Folsom's stand on racial issues rose to a crescendo that culminated in the 1956 Democratic primary. His attempts to dismiss criticism with ridicule or compromise failed to erase the notion that Big Jim was "soft" on the racial issue.[2]

When Folsom discussed his stand on racial issues in later years, he related family stories to prove that his own attitudes conformed to the traditions of his family. According to Folsom, his maternal grandfather and his grandfather's five brothers opposed secession in 1861 and refused to fight for the preservation of slavery. Because the Dunnevants were all tall, physically powerful men, none of their neighbors dared to argue the issue with them. The heritage of dissent resurfaced in Folsom's family during the 1890s. Folsom's father supported the Populist movement in Coffee County and won county office in the process. As did many small farmers in the Alabama Wiregrass, the Coffee County Populists emphasized agricultural and economic issues and regarded racial traditions as a matter of lesser importance. Although Folsom's stories may have been apocryphal, he told them often and with pride as he attributed his racial attitudes to the legacy he had inherited.[3]

The experiences and environs of Folsom's early life reinforced family traditions. Like several of his friends, Folsom learned from his mother to regard Negroes in the spirit of noblesse oblige. While Negroes deserved respect as human beings and children of God, they were less fortunate than most whites and deserved to be treated with sympathy. Folsom had relatively few contacts with blacks that might have challenged his mother's admonitions. In Coffee County, Negroes composed a small minority of the population and rarely entered into public life. Folsom was further isolated from blacks because his family worked their farm with their own labor. The few contacts Folsom made with Negroes as a teenager tended to complement, rather than challenge, the concepts he learned at home. One man who impressed the young Folsom was a Negro who worked at a lumberyard in Elba. The man was an amputee who had learned to stack lumber with only one hand. For a time, Folsom worked alongside the Negro and learned that no one in town was stronger or could stack lumber more rapidly than the black amputee.[4]

By the time Folsom ran for governor, his ideas concerning racial issues had taken shape. He simply assumed that Negroes were citizens and entitled to all the rights of citizenship. This meant that blacks were entitled to a ballot, to equal justice before the law, and to the educational and economic opportunities that whites enjoyed. In holding these views, Big Jim did not seek a fundamental shift of political power or a revolution in social mores. He did not even view segregation as an inherent violation of the Negro's civil rights. But he was confident that the federal courts would guarantee the civil rights of all citizens in the near future, and he believed that all Alabamians should be prepared for that day. Still, when Jim Folsom became governor in 1947, his attitude toward racial relations seemed radical to most white Alabamians.

As a candidate in 1946, Big Jim Folsom clearly expressed his concern for civil rights. His campaign program called for the abolition of the cumulative poll tax. He considered this reform as important as reapportionment and constitutional revision because the tax kept thousands of working citizens from voting. Publicly opposing the poll tax because it discriminated against Alabama's poor whites, he rarely complained that the poll tax was unfair to Negroes. The issue identified Folsom as a racial liberal anyway because several national civil rights groups had made poll tax repeal a primary goal of their post–World War II work. After winning the Democratic gubernatorial nomination, Folsom again endorsed the rights of Negroes by opposing the ratification of the Boswell amendment. Folsom argued that the amendment granted arbitrary power to the registrars. Without mentioning racial discrimination, Folsom warned that unscrupulous registrars could abuse such power for partisan purposes.[5]

Symbolic gestures at his inauguration communicated Folsom's goodwill to Alabama blacks. In the inaugural parade, the Alabama State Teachers College Band and a unit of black soldiers marched between white groups. This broke with the tradition of segregating black marching groups at the very end of the procession. At Folsom's direction, Charles Long of the Alabama Newspaper Association was admitted to the press section and allowed to photograph Folsom at close range. In one shot, Long caught Folsom applauding as the Alabama State Teachers College Band passed in front of the reviewing stand. No one attempted to segregate the people who stayed to hear Folsom's inaugural address. The inaugural committee extended every courtesy to blacks who accepted Folsom's invitation to visit the capitol after the inaugural ceremonies. These gestures convinced the *Birmingham World* editor Emory Jackson that Folsom intended to be "the faithful servant of all." Jackson editorialized, "The little people, decent people, the big people, the people of goodwill had a big day in Montgomery, January 20. It was inaugural day for Honorable James E. Folsom as Governor of Alabama. . . . He communicated to the people in his personality, speech, behavior . . . that he would try to be the governor of all the people."[6]

Governor Folsom gave substance to his gestures as he appointed voter registrars during the fall of 1947. Working on a committee with the commissioner of agriculture, Haygood Patterson, and the state auditor, Dan Thomas, Folsom used his prerogative to appoint one registrar in each county who would implement his voter registration policies. His selection of men such as W. H. Bentley of Tuskegee and E. J. Gonzales of Mobile won him the faithful support of black voters in all subsequent campaigns. These men not only cooperated with Negroes who attempted to register, but they also protected black voters when the registrars purged the county voting lists every other year. Folsom knew that few white appointees would be willing to register blacks in large numbers, but he asked his appointees to give identical consideration to the applications of all prospective voters and to approve the applications of all World War II veterans who attempted to register.[7]

Although the Alabama Legislature blocked his program and the Alabama Democratic Executive Committee challenged his leadership, Governor Folsom consistently worked for the interests of Alabama Negroes. He and the superintendent of education, Austin Meadows, cooperated to equalize the salaries of black and white schoolteachers. After the 1947 legislative session, Folsom pocket vetoed a resolution authorizing a study of new ways to restrict Negro voting. In 1948, when every other Alabama politician criticized President Truman's civil rights policies, Folsom attacked only Truman's foreign policies. Even after the 1948 Democratic primary demonstrated the popularity of racism, Folsom did not stoop to race baiting. In January 1949, the United States Supreme Court declared the Boswell amendment unconstitutional and void. Whereas other state leaders lamented the decision, Folsom welcomed it and reminded Alabamians that he had originally opposed the amendment in 1946.[8]

Jim Folsom did not hesitate to point out racial discrimination in the enforcement of state law. Soon after Bill Drinkard joined Glen Vinson on the Alabama Pardon and Parole Board, critics began to scream about the large number of paroles and pardons they granted. Folsom defended his appointees in a statewide radio address in December 1949. He observed that although Negroes constituted only 35 percent of Alabama's population, they composed 65 percent of the prison population. According to Folsom, the fee system was responsible for the disproportionate number of Negroes in prison because local officials arrested and prosecuted Negroes for minor offenses in order to collect the fees for each judicial procedure. Folsom went on to accuse Alabama courts of racial discrimination:

> While I realize that Negroes, due to lack of economic opportunity, education, and life in general do not have the same chances as do the rest of our people, I do not believe on the other hand that they have been given a fair deal at the hand of justice and jury in this state. There are sections of Alabama where a Negro doesn't stand a Chinaman's chance of getting fair and impartial justice on an equal footing with white men.[9]

Less than two weeks after he defended the Pardon and Parole Board, Governor Folsom broadcast a more extensive critique of racial discrimination. On Christmas Day, 1949, Folsom noted the prosperity of America and reminded Alabamians that their good fortune gave them a moral obligation to provide "a human, decent way of life for all our people." The governor mentioned the need for old-age pensions and rural hospitals before moving to the heart of his message:

> Our Negroes, who constitute thirty-five percent of our population in Alabama, are they getting thirty-five per cent of the fair share of living? . . . Are they getting adequate medical care? . . . Are they provided with sufficient professional training? . . . Are the Negroes being given their share of democracy, the same opportunity of having a voice in the government under which they live?

Assuming that the answers to his rhetorical questions were negative, Folsom warned that poor white people would also suffer as long as Negroes were denied equal opportunities for educational, economic, and political development. Folsom admonished his listeners, "It is time for us to adopt a *positive* attitude toward our fellow man. Let's start talking fellowship and brotherly love and doing-unto-others, and let's do more than talk about it, let's start living it."[10]

Throughout his first administration, Folsom made his sympathy for blacks a matter of public record, and his forthright respect for Negroes did not provoke racist attacks. Grover Hall, Jr., accused Folsom of demagoguery, but he noted with appreciation that Big Jim never relied on racial slurs to win popular support. Among the legislators, Folsom's unorthodoxy concerning race did not stir up opposition. Legislative opponents labeled him a political simpleton who had been duped by a radical coalition of Henry Wallace, Aubrey Williams, and Gould Beech; but such criticism did not specify that respect for Negroes was a part of Folsom's alleged radicalism. Instead, the anti-Folsom legislators seemed to accept Folsom's racial ideas with good humor. Folsom and Representative Walter Givhan of Dallas County repeatedly laughed at a standing joke. It began with one of them predicting that the federal courts would soon extend the franchise to Alabama Negroes. Folsom would then tease Givhan that when the courts finally acted, "you'll be serving with more niggers in the Legislature than you've ever seen on your farm."[11]

The electorate was surprisingly tolerant of Folsom's racial views. Several factors appeared to contribute to the absence of racist agitation against him. During the late 1940s, civil rights for Negroes was not a major issue in state politics. President Truman's policies and the 1948 Democratic platform threatened the racial status quo; but these threats had not yet developed to the point that the state government could act. While no social revolution impended, the stalemate between Folsom and the Alabama senate provided adequate protection. Folsom's eccentric personality also helped Alabamians minimize the import of his racial views. Jim Folsom was the undignified governor who kissed girls with wild abandon, stripped off his shoes and socks in public, drank beer for breakfast, and posed for *Life* while taking a bath. He was no radical intent on overturning the South's social system. He was just a clever country boy who had talked his way into the governor's office once and whose words lacked credibility. As long as the legislators frustrated Folsom's program, white Alabamians were secure in the belief that his sympathy for blacks was only the harmless rhetoric of an eccentric politician.

The manner in which Folsom spoke for civil rights further assuaged the anxieties of whites. In both of his December 1949 addresses, Folsom criticized racial discrimination in the language of paternalism. The problem with the prison system was that Negroes had not been given a fair deal by Alabama's judicial system. On Christmas Day, Folsom had declared that "our Negroes" had not received adequate medical care, professional training, or political rights. Certainly Folsom criticized the status quo more boldly than any other Alabama politician. But he did not advise Negroes to take action to correct these injustices. Governor Folsom recommended only that white Alabamians who exercised social and political power adopt a more humanitarian attitude toward the Negroes with whom they dealt. Humanitarianism of this kind might eventually alter the distribution of social and political power, but it was not Folsom's purpose to foster such basic change. The governor's words did not provoke strong racist reaction because his humanitarianism did not challenge the racial prejudices of most white Alabamians.

Even though Jim Folsom did not transcend the racial assumptions of the culture in which he lived, his support for civil rights was genuine. Folsom was equally sincere in his desire to win black votes in 1954. Deferring to racial customs, Folsom did not appeal to black voters in his campaign addresses. Instead, he discreetly solicited the support of the minority of Negroes who voted. The key figure in Folsom's campaign for Negro votes was Winston Craig, a merit system employee who acted as chauffeur for the governor of Alabama. Although driving the governor's limousine was Craig's primary responsibility, Folsom utilized him as a valet, messenger, bodyguard, and adviser. And because Craig had chauffeured every governor since Bibb Graves, Folsom frequently asked for his advice. Observing the racial and status differences between himself and his chauffeur, Folsom would ask for Craig's opinion by saying, "Winston, what would Governor Graves have done about . . . ?" and then name the issue. Craig understood the rules of etiquette and phrased his own opinion as if it had come from Governor Graves.[12]

During the reelection campaign, Craig worked as Folsom's primary liaison with Alabama's Negro leaders. At the direction of Folsom's campaign advisers, Craig contacted leading Negroes and informed the campaign office if a particular black needed Folsom's personal attention. In one case, Craig reported that a clergyman in Florence wanted a personal letter from Folsom before he would make a public endorsement. Folsom promptly signed a letter to the minister, asking for help in winning the support of the League of Negro Voters in Florence. Craig also supervised the political trading necessary to win the support of other blacks. Before the end of the campaign, Folsom promised to appoint several Negroes to state jobs, support Negro voter registration, and make Negro schools as good as white schools. Folsom also pledged to offer no resistance to the desegregation of the University of Alabama.[13]

With Craig's help, Folsom received enthusiastic support from leading Alabama Negroes. A Birmingham businessman, A. G. Gaston, wrote during 1954 and offered help if Folsom ever needed his services. Gaston said that Negroes all over the state had "expressed gratitude for your interest in their behalf, enabling many of them to register and qualify to vote." After the 1954 Democratic primary, a Negro high school principal sent his congratulations and reported, "Just like for you to know that the Negro teachers in Butler County voted for you one hundred per cent." A similar letter came from C. G. Gomillion of Tuskegee Institute. Gomillion attributed the solid support which Tuskegee blacks gave Folsom to the fact that Folsom's first administration had supported the registration of Negro voters.[14]

Big Jim Folsom did not hide his racial views from Alabama voters in 1954. Though shaking hands with a Negro was a symbolic violation of the racial caste system, Folsom publicly greeted the two Negro men he met in Clayton. At campaign rallies in Selma and Union Springs, blacks and whites had equally good seats on opposite sides of the auditoriums in which Folsom spoke. After campaign talks in many Black Belt counties, Big Jim went into the black half of his audience greeting voters and shaking hands before he greeted any of the whites who attended the rally.[15] These expressions of respect for Negroes did not disturb most Alabama voters, however. Farm-to-market roads, old-age pensions, public schools, and political reforms appeared to be more important to the voters in 1954 than misgivings about Big Jim's racial attitudes.

Between the Democratic primary of 1954 and the end of 1955, popular tolerance for Folsom's violations of racial customs disappeared. As Alabama Negroes joined the mass movement to secure their civil rights, whites perceived the protests as direct attacks on the racial caste system that lent stability to southern society. Whites expected all of their leaders to forget political differences and rally to the defense of racial segregation. When Jim Folsom chose not to speak the language of segregationists and continued to express respect for the dignity of blacks, white Alabamians regarded him as a renegade. Even though his opinions did not change significantly during 1954 and 1955, Jim Folsom became the enemy of Alabama's white supremacists.

When, two weeks after the 1954 Democratic primary, the United States Supreme Court issued its decision on *Brown v. Board of Education,* the Court did not immediately prescribe the procedures for implementing the decision and waited for a year to issue the supplemental decision. The interim between 17 May 1954 and 31 May 1955 allowed white Alabamians to condemn the Court's action verbally while postponing more vigorous resistance until the Supreme Court ordered the decision's implementation. Governor Persons used the interim as a rationale for ignoring demands that he call a special session of the legislature to protect segregation in Alabama schools. The delay also served Folsom well. By the time the Supreme Court instructed inferior courts to enforce the *Brown* decision with "all deliberate speed," the Folsom administration had perfected its legislative organization and was pushing its legislative program through the 1955 biennial session.

Newspaper reporters pressed Folsom for a reaction to the *Brown* decision as soon as it became public knowledge. Prudently, Folsom asked to be "included out" of any trouble over segregation and announced that he would withhold comment while he reviewed the decision and consulted his advisers. E. C. Boswell advised Folsom to do nothing until the Supreme Court issued its implementation order. Then, Boswell suggested, Folsom should introduce legislation that gave local school boards the authority to preserve segregation by assigning students to particular schools according to nonracial psychological and sociological criteria. Attorney Vincent Kilborn, a Folsom supporter in Mobile, offered advice that was more in line with Folsom's previous statements. Kilborn warned, "There is no use in kidding ourselves into thinking that we can buck the Supreme Court." Kilborn suggested the repeal of all laws making segregation mandatory and the enactment of a single statute to protect students from being compelled to attend any particular school. Kilborn assumed that only a few Negroes wanted to attend white schools. He believed that if Alabama complied with the *Brown* decision in apparent good faith, "Nothing more will come of it except a few isolated instances of where a few colored people try to push themselves into white institutions."[16]

Folsom avoided public comment on the *Brown* decision for as long as possible. In the spring of 1955, he repeated portions of his campaign program that touched the issue of desegregation tangentially and claimed that he had already made his position "plain, simple, and clear." He frequently repeated his pledge that he would not force black children to go to school with white children. It was an ambiguous promise that sounded like the words of a segregationist without specifically opposing segregation. Speaking to the Alabama Education Association in 1955, the governor recommended a school construction bond issue and implied that the money would help prolong segregation by improving the physical facilities of Negro schools. Governor Folsom did not issue a more definite statement of his views until the fall of 1955. When a reporter asked him where he would send his children to school if the public schools were desegregated, Folsom responded, "It's not what I want or would like. It's what's the law." With that statement, Folsom signaled his determination to honor his oath of office, an oath in which he pledged to uphold the United States Constitution.[17]

The anxieties generated by the *Brown* decision did not compel Big Jim to treat Negroes as less than full-fledged citizens. In planning his second inauguration, Folsom insisted that "Y'all come!" applied to blacks as well as to whites. Just as in 1947, inaugural officials made no racial distinctions among people who marched in the inaugural parade, listened to Folsom's inaugural address, and visited the governor's office in the capitol. In his inaugural address, Folsom attempted profundity by issuing his list of the six "freedoms" that all Alabamians should enjoy. His fifth "freedom," "freedom for you to walk among your own—upright with dignity, fearless, and proud," summarized Folsom's concept of the ideal: racial relations in which Negroes enjoyed all the rights of citizenship, dignity, and security without challenging racial segregation.[18]

Folsom decided to honor all of his Negro supporters by giving the first inaugural ball for Negroes in Alabama history. He felt that blacks deserved recognition for their contributions to his reelection and assumed that they would prefer to be recognized at a party attended only by Negroes. Folsom and his white aides were shocked by black responses to the idea. Negro leaders protested that the ball insulted them by reminding blacks of their inequality with whites. "Jim Crow in tuxedoes is no different than Jim Crow in overalls" was the theme of the protests. The *Birmingham World* editor Emory Jackson wrote that the protests were not criticisms of Folsom himself but that the governor-elect should not invite Negroes to a ball until they could attend the same ball as whites. Folsom did not acknowledge the protests publicly and sponsored the ball as planned. He was careful, however, to give the Negro ball as much attention as he gave the white ball. Folsom and all his cabinet members attended the ball at Alabama State Teachers College for about an hour, shook hands with the celebrants, and acted as though they enjoyed themselves immensely. Folsom gave the party to honor his supporters who were black, and he hoped Negroes would accept his expression in the spirit in which he offered it.[19]

Governor Folsom's actions proved that he intended Alabama Negroes to exercise all the rights of citizenship. Hosting the Southern Governor's Conference in 1955, Folsom told reporters that blacks "came here as slaves, but they're not slaves now—they're voters. And I'm doing all I can to get the vote for them." Folsom's plan to extend the franchise to more Negroes involved the state auditor, Agnes Baggett, and the commissioner of agriculture and industries, A. W. Todd, both of whom served with Folsom as the committee to appoint county voter registrars. Customarily, each official independently selected one of the three registrars for each county. But in 1954, Folsom had supported Baggett's election campaign, and his aides had persuaded the Alabama Democratic Executive Committee to nominate Todd as commissioner of agriculture. Therefore, Folsom expected no difficulty in appointing voter registrars who would allow Negroes to register to vote.[20]

Feeling confident that Baggett and Todd would follow his leadership, Folsom ruined his strategy by discussing it with a *New York Herald Tribune* reporter. Almost five months before Folsom, Baggett, and Todd actually appointed the registrars, the *Herald Tribune* published the news that Alabama's next voter registrars would register Negro voters. The news motivated politically influential groups, identified only as "Big Mules" in the press, to pressure Baggett and Todd to oppose Folsom's policies. The political pressure succeeded by mid-summer 1955, and both Baggett and Todd announced their independence from Folsom. The governor failed to regain their loyalty with counterpressure. When the voter registrars were appointed in October 1955, Folsom once again made certain that one of the three registrars in each county favored the registration of blacks. However, since neither Baggett nor Todd followed Folsom's example, most Alabama registrars were still opposed to the registration of Negro voters.[21]

Paradoxically, Folsom's most successful year of legislative leadership was also the year during which the Alabama Legislature enacted a host of new laws to preserve segregation. Throughout the 1955 biennial session, the defense of segregated public education was uppermost in the minds of most legislators. Their concern reflected the widespread fear that desegregation would begin the disintegration of southern civilization and the realization that during their careers the fortunes of each Alabama politician would be determined by his record on racial issues. Senator Albert Boutwell of Jefferson County, who chaired a 1953 legislative study committee on segregation, was prepared to lead the lawmakers in massive resistance but postponed the introduction of major proposals until after the Supreme Court completed its work on the *Brown* case. In the meantime, Senator Albert Davis drafted a resolution calling for the impeachment of all nine Supreme Court Justices. Another senator wrote a resolution which urged Congress to investigate communist influence in the Court's desegregation decisions. Then, after 31 May 1955, the floodgates which had held back the segregationist bills swung wide open.[22]

The student-placement bill, the Alabama Legislature's primary bulwark against the desegregation of public schools, followed the general outline of E. C. Boswell's advice to Folsom just after the *Brown* decision. It granted local school systems the authority to assign students to schools on the basis of psychological and sociological factors. The bill also established an intricate procedure through which families could appeal the placement decisions of local school officials. The legislators intended the appeal procedure to be so difficult that a student's parents would become discouraged before they exhausted all appeals and filed suit in federal court. The student-placement bill seemed to be a perfect evasion of the *Brown* decision. Grover Hall, Jr., called it "the most resourceful ruse yet devised" because it used the same social science concepts to defend segregation as Chief Justice Earl Warren had cited in his *Brown* opinion. The student-placement bill sailed through the legislature with only three members of the house daring to vote against it.[23]

Governor Folsom detested the student-placement bill because it was an obviously unconstitutional evasion of a United States Supreme Court decision. However, Folsom did not ask his legislative supporters to oppose it. He was not certain that his partisans would follow his instructions, and he feared that a fight against the bill might jeopardize the enactment of his legislative proposals. Because the bill received overwhelming support in both the house and the senate, Folsom's veto would have been futile. Therefore, Folsom allowed the student-placement bill to become law without his signature and contented himself with a verbal attack against segregationist legislation. He told reporters at a news conference, "I just never did get all excited about our colored brothers. We have had them here for three hundred years and we will have them for another three hundred years. I have found them to be good citizens and if they had been making a living for me like they have for the Black Belt, I'd be proud of them instead of kicking them and cussing them all of the time."[24]

Dozens of other segregationist bills were introduced during the biennial session, but most legislators felt that the student-placement law adequately protected segregated public schools. A few lawmakers, however, wanted to protect segregation further by restricting the activities of civil rights workers, or "racial agitators." Lacking majority support, they utilized the legislative courtesy on local bills to establish restrictions that applied only to specific counties. The legislative delegations from Macon and Wilcox counties proposed local legislation which gave their county school boards the authority to dismiss without a hearing or prior notice any teacher who advocated desegregation. The Wilcox County legislators also dredged up an old antilabor bill and fashioned it into a bill aimed at restricting the NAACP. This bill required any organization that recruited new members in Wilcox County to pay a large license fee, another license fee for each recruiter, and a membership fee for each new member. All three bills passed the house and senate as local legislation and without serious opposition.[25]

Governor Folsom found all three local bills more offensive than the student-placement law. On the last day of the 1955 biennial session, he vetoed one of the two bills that authorized local school boards to dismiss teachers. The other fell victim to his pocket veto after the session adjourned. Since the bill that was aimed at the NAACP passed early in the session, Folsom could not kill it. Nevertheless, he returned it to the legislature with a veto message that called the bill "unfair, unjust, and undemocratic" and "an instrument to undermine the broad rights and privileges . . . of freedom and the pursuit of opportunity." After sending the bill back to the house, Folsom heard that his veto angered the senator from Wilcox County. Folsom's reaction to this news expressed his antipathy to all segregationist legislation: "Hell, he's crazy if he thinks he can rape the Constitution every thirty days and expect me to sign it." Despite Folsom's objections, the legislature overrode his veto.[26]

Even as the anxieties of Alabama voters intensified after the *Brown* decision, Governor Folsom did not shy away from expressing public opposition to die-hard segregationists or their vigilantism. During June 1955, Southern Union College in Wadley, a small college supported by the Congregational Christian Church, sponsored an institute on international relations. Since the denomination was integrated, both black and white members attended the institute and stayed in the college's only dormitory. Local whites objected to the institute's housing arrangements. An armed and hooded delegation interrupted the meeting and threatened to "blow the place up" if the college president did not "get these niggers out of here." Governor Folsom reacted to news of the incident by ordering the Alabama Highway Patrol and all other law-enforcement officers to enforce Alabama's antimasking law strictly. In a public statement, Folsom declared, "So long as I am governor, I will not tolerate hoodlums interfering with the assembly of the people."[27]

Neither did Folsom mince words concerning white citizens' councils in Alabama. The movement to establish "law abiding" groups to resist the *Brown* decision originated in Indianola, Mississippi, during July 1954. White supremacists in Selma organized the first council in Alabama during November and helped their compatriots in four other Black Belt counties to establish councils by early 1955. Prominent among the initial citizens' council leaders were Senators Walter Givhan and Sam Engelhardt. After the movement dropped "white" from its name and formed a statewide organization, Engelhardt became the executive secretary of the Citizens' Councils of Alabama. Governor Folsom opposed the organization from its beginning. He predicted that it would be short-lived, because nothing based on hate and prejudice could flourish in a democratic society. Among his friends he joked about the reason "white" was deleted from the group's name. "They took 'white' off Citizens' Council because they sleep all night with Negro gals but they run downtown the next morning and holler, 'white, white!'"
When the Citizens' Councils of Alabama surveyed the racial views of

candidates in the 1956 Democratic primary, Folsom refused to cooperate, "I answer only to the people and not to haters and baiters."[28]

Governor Folsom used his office in 1955 to extend the rights of citizenship to Negroes, to assure Alabamians that the Supreme Court's decisions were not the beginning of social catastrophe, and to discourage whites from openly defying the United States Constitution. But judging from the actions of the Alabama Legislature, Folsom's cool, dispassionate leadership failed to reduce racial tensions. Instead, the events of late 1955 and 1956 intensified the fears of whites. During those months, Congressman Adam Clayton Powell visited Montgomery, the Montgomery bus boycott began, and Autherine Lucy enrolled at the University of Alabama. These events not only frustrated Folsom's continuing efforts to diffuse popular anxieties, but they also undermined his popularity among the folks at "the brush arbors and the forks of the creeks."

Adam Clayton Powell's visit to Montgomery on 3 November 1955 was the first dramatic blow to Big Jim's popularity among white voters. During that fall Montgomery's Negro leaders conducted Operation 5000, a campaign to register five thousand local black voters. Operation 5000 had received favorable notice nationally in the black press, and the New York congressman came to Montgomery to make an appearance with the campaign's leaders. Although Powell personified Negro arrogance in the eyes of most southern whites, the governor of Alabama extended official courtesies to the representative from the Empire State. Winston Craig met Powell's plane at Maxwell Field, acted as his chauffeur for the day, and drove him to a meeting with Folsom at the governor's mansion. During their meeting, the governor and the congressman chatted informally about race relations over cocktails.

After meeting with Governor Folsom, Congressman Powell addressed an Operation 5000 rally at Alabama State Teachers College. Powell used the speech to thank Folsom publicly for his warm hospitality. The congressman professed satisfaction with the knowledge that a southern governor would welcome a Negro into his home and treat him as a social equal. Powell mentioned that he and Folsom had conversed freely while sipping scotch and soda. They had laughed, Powell said, when Folsom quipped that the Alabama Baptists would be upset if they knew he was drinking. According to Powell, Folsom had admitted, "Integration in Alabama is not only inevitable, but is already here." Powell even implied that Governor

Folsom endorsed the efforts of Negroes to secure civil rights and to end racial segregation in the state. Before leaving Montgomery the following day, Powell repeated the gist of his comments to white news reporters.[29]

Congressman Powell's account of his meeting with Folsom shook Alabamians like an underground explosion. Already apprehensive about the coming social revolution, whites interpreted Folsom's conduct as blatantly disgraceful. Not only had the governor welcomed the New York congressman to Alabama, but he had entertained the obnoxious black politician in his home. Folsom had insulted white southerners by treating Powell as an equal and sharing cocktails of scotch and soda with him. Folsom had degraded his office when he placed the governor's own limousine and chauffeur at Powell's disposal. Folsom sank to the depth of degradation, whites believed, when he conceded that desegregation was an accomplished fact. Throughout Alabama and neighboring states, white people were enraged at Governor Folsom's brazen violations of southern racial conventions.[30]

Jim Folsom deeply resented Congressman Powell's public remarks. Surrounded by trusted advisers, he declared, "Adam Clayton Powell is one son of a bitch I wish I'd never seen!" and complained that Powell had deliberately violated his confidence in order to grab publicity. Folsom also knew that the incident had undermined his political influence. As a result, he avoided direct, public dealings with Negro leaders. When white hoodlums assaulted the singer Nat King Cole in Birmingham during 1956, the Folsom administration did not dare issue a public apology to Cole. Instead, a message of regret went to the singer through the Birmingham businessman A. G. Gaston. Folsom also began to hedge on his commitment to promote Negro voter registration. In public statements, he inserted warnings that Negro leaders were pressing their demands for civil rights too hard. All the while, Folsom groped for an explanation of his conduct that would quiet the protests of whites.[31]

In vain Folsom attempted to justify his hospitality. First, he tried to discredit Powell's account of their meeting. According to Folsom, he assigned the governor's limousine to Powell because it was the only state car with a black driver; he met Powell only at the visitor's request; he had not received Powell in his home but in the official quarters at the governor's mansion; he did not treat Powell as a social equal but made him enter through the back door; and he did not drink scotch with his guest. Most important, Powell had misquoted his comment concerning integration. Folsom had observed, he insisted, that integration was happening within the nation but not in Alabama. When Folsom's account of his meeting with Powell failed to quiet the outrage, the governor argued that his behavior had been absolutely proper. To one journalist, Folsom wrote, "I have always made it a practice to extend the hospitality of the State to visiting governors, congressmen, and senators. Their title deserves that courtesy regardless of . . . what race they might be." However, critics did not accept protocol as a sufficient explanation of Folsom's conduct, and he adopted a more segregationist view of the infamous meeting. Since the decisions of federal courts carried the weight of law, Folsom explained, the most effective way to fight desegregation was to resolve problems before Negro leaders filed any suits. His meeting with Powell, Folsom claimed, was simply a conference in which he sought to avoid litigation by communicating directly with a black leader.[32]

Folsom's efforts to explain what happened on 3 November 1955 might have succeeded if the relentless parade of events had not inflamed Alabama whites even further. On Thursday, 1 December 1955, Montgomery police arrested Rosa Parks for violating the city's segregation ordinance on a city bus. In protest of Mrs. Parks's arrest, Montgomery's black leaders called for a boycott of the city bus lines on Monday, 5 December. Practically all Montgomery blacks, who constituted the overwhelming majority of bus passengers, honored the boycott. Celebrating their solidarity at a mass meeting on Monday evening, the blacks decided to continue the boycott as a protest of Mrs. Parks's arrest and as a means of seeking redress for accumulated grievances. In their list of grievances, the Negroes demanded that the city bus line hire some Negro drivers, instruct all drivers to treat all passengers courteously, and replace the movable line between white and black passengers on each bus with a fixed line that established a constant number of seats for each race. Participants in the mass meeting also established the Montgomery Improvement Association as the organization that would direct the bus boycott, coordinate a network of car pools, and hold frequent mass meetings. By the end of the evening, Montgomery's black community was united behind the leadership of the labor leader E. D. Nixon; the mortician Rufus Lewis; the attorney Fred Gray; the pastor of the black First Baptist Church, Ralph Abernathy; and the pastor of the Dexter Avenue Baptist Church, Martin Luther King, Jr.[33]

Because the boycott occurred within the city of Montgomery,

Governor Folsom was not directly responsible for dealing with the conflict. Folsom announced that he would use his authority to maintain order and to protect life and property if local authorities failed to do so. However, Montgomery officials never called for assistance from the State of Alabama. Personally, Folsom sympathized with the aims of the Montgomery Improvement Association and respected Montgomery's Negro leaders. Although segregationists in Montgomery and throughout the state pressed him to intervene in opposition to the boycott, Folsom made certain that the State of Alabama remained completely neutral. Through friends and supporters in Montgomery, Folsom kept himself informed of daily events without becoming directly involved.[34]

In spite of the embarrassment he suffered after Powell's visit, Folsom utilized Winston Craig to open lines of communication with the boycott leaders. On at least three occasions, Craig arranged confidential meetings between Folsom and the Negro leaders. At one of these, Folsom asked the blacks to explain the reasons for the protest. As the leaders recited their list of formal grievances, they emphasized the need for a fixed line on each bus separating white and black passengers. According to one account, Folsom told the Negro leaders that their objectives were too limited: "Segregation don't make no sense no way. What you ought to do is try to get segregation completely abolished. The Supreme Court has already spoken about it. Why go after a few crumbs when you can have the whole loaf?" The third meeting between Folsom and the boycott leaders took place on 31 January 1956, one day after a bomb destroyed part of Dr. King's home and one day before the attorney Fred Gray filed suits in the U.S. District Court in Montgomery challenging segregation on Montgomery buses. The federal court rulings on the suits, which were known as *Browder v. Gayle,* eventually overturned the segregation ordinance and brought the boycott to an end. Undoubtedly the Montgomery Improvement Association wanted to fight segregation long before Jim Folsom offered his advice. However, the timing of Folsom's advice and the filing of the suits suggest that Folsom's words may have encouraged the blacks to make the Montgomery bus boycott an open fight against segregation.[35]

While Montgomery Negroes maintained their boycott for 380 days, whites used every judicial tactic to preserve segregation and quell the threat to white supremacy. In the third month of the boycott, another racial crisis erupted in Tuscaloosa as Autherine Lucy became the first Negro to enroll in classes at the University of Alabama. Lucy had earned an undergraduate degree at a black college before she and another black woman applied to the university for admission to the graduate school. Since neither woman disclosed her race on the application for admission, school officials admitted both of them and accepted a dormitory room deposit from each. On the day they attempted to register, university officials reversed their decision, refunded the room deposits, and advised the two women to seek admission at a black college. Lucy retained the Birmingham attorney Arthur Shores and initiated a three-year-long court battle to gain readmission to the University of Alabama. While the case moved slowly through state and federal courts, Lucy had the support of Negroes throughout Alabama, and her attorney received assistance from the NAACP lawyer Thurgood Marshall. In the fall of 1955, the U.S. District Court judge H. H. Grooms ordered the University of Alabama to admit Autherine Lucy to classes during the spring semester of 1956.

Judge Grooms's decision allowed ample time for everyone to prepare for the desegregation of the University of Alabama. In good faith, the dean of women arranged for room and board for the new student. To avoid conflict in the dormitory, she assigned Lucy to a room surrounded by the rooms of tolerant white girls. However, university officials did not communicate with Lucy and did little else to prepare for the registration of the first black student. Lucy and her advisers assumed that she would not be safe in the dormitory and planned for her to commute to classes every day from Birmingham. No one considered the problem of registering Lucy for classes without provoking violence. On the day of registration, she arrived in a late-model Buick wearing a fashionable suit, hat, and high-heel shoes. School officials and newsmen met Lucy and her attorneys at the edge of the campus and accompanied them to the site of registration. While thousands of white students waited in long lines to register, the officials whisked the new student to the front of the lines for registering and paying tuition. One of Lucy's attorneys paid her fees with a crisp one hundred dollar bill that had been a gift from A. G. Gaston. The proceedings displayed a great lack of forethought as university officials and lawyers gave special treatment to the first Negro student in front of a student body already unhappy about her presence.[36]

The University of Alabama was similarly unprepared for the disturbances that followed Autherine Lucy's registration. On the evening of the first day of classes, white students joined in a spontaneous protest demonstration. Gathering on the university campus, they walked to downtown Tuscaloosa singing "Dixie" and harassing any hapless Negro who mistakenly crossed their path. Once downtown, the students heard impromptu harangues delivered by militantly segregationist students. Except for the cruel scare they gave to a few blacks, however, the students simply expressed their dislike for desegregation and their boredom on an otherwise quiet Friday night. The next evening produced a second, and slightly less spontaneous, demonstration. It followed the same format as the first and culminated with about a dozen white supremacist students delivering speeches in downtown Tuscaloosa. A third and more frightening demonstration occurred on Monday morning. This time the sign-carrying, slogan-shouting mob included both students and industrial workers from industrial plants around Tuscaloosa. The crowd gathered in front of the building where Lucy was attending class and waited for her to emerge. Fearing for her safety, Lucy waited inside with several school officials until a car arrived to drive her away. Then, in a dramatic moment, the school officials and Autherine Lucy slipped out a back door and into the waiting automobile. The mob quickly realized what was happening and surged toward the getaway car as Lucy made a narrow escape through a barrage of rocks and other projectiles. Later on that day, 6 February 1956, the university's Board of Trustees announced that the university could not ensure the Negro student's safety and suspended her from classes for her own protection.[37]

Although the president of the University of Alabama, Oliver Carmichael, insisted that Autherine Lucy's safety had been the sole reason for her suspension, the Board of Trustees looked for a way to expel her permanently. Lucy's attorneys asked Judge Grooms to find the university in contempt of his original court order. In the hearing on the attorneys' motion, Lucy testified that the University of Alabama permitted the protest demonstrations and conspired to defy the order of the U.S. District Court. In spite of the testimony, Judge Grooms decided that the university had not acted in contempt by failing to anticipate the protests against Lucy's admission. Therefore, the judge ruled only that Autherine Lucy should be readmitted to classes by 5 March 1956. After Judge Grooms refused to cite the University of Alabama for contempt of court, the Board of Trustees expelled Lucy from the university. Referring to statements she made in court, the trustees cited Lucy for making public accusations against the university that were "false, defamatory, impertinent, and scandalous." When Lucy returned to U.S. District Court to contest the expulsion, Judge Grooms upheld the trustees because they had not expelled her for reasons of race. The judge indicated that Autherine Lucy could challenge the expulsion through appropriate legal channels. But Miss Lucy resigned herself to defeat rather than renew the long court battle which had already consumed more than three years of her life.[38]

As in the case of the Montgomery bus boycott, Folsom's office did not involve him directly in Autherine Lucy's ordeal. The authority to establish policies and supervise personnel at the university belonged to a self-perpetuating board of trustees. Although the governor and the superintendent of education were ex-officio members, the board was a homogeneous, conservative group of white men over whom Folsom had little influence. Folsom had so little influence over the trustees' decisions that he rarely attended their meetings. The only authority Folsom possessed was the authority to maintain law and order if local officials could not protect life and property. As usual, Folsom claimed that he was ready to exercise his authority if necessary.[39]

Instead of becoming involved, Folsom isolated himself from Autherine Lucy's enrollment and the disorder that followed. On Friday, 3 February, the day of the first demonstration, Governor Folsom left Montgomery for a weekend fishing trip without giving Ralph Hammond instructions for responding in case of an emergency. The governor was completely ignorant of the demonstrations against Lucy until he heard a radio news broadcast at the end of the weekend and decided to phone university officials from a country store in southeastern Alabama. At the time the mob threatened Lucy on Monday morning, an Alabama National Guard Unit awaited the governor's instructions in an armory less than two miles from the university campus. Folsom did not call the unit to active duty but relied instead on a few highway patrol officers to help campus police maintain order. Representative George Hawkins was instrumental in restoring sanity on campus after the mob almost caught Autherine Lucy coming out of class. Hawkins's activity, however, did not represent an attempt by Folsom to exercise leadership during the crisis.[40]

Only after the danger of violence passed did Folsom react to the protest demonstrations. He declared that he stood "ready at all times to meet any situation properly." He had taken no action,

Folsom explained, because the unrest in Tuscaloosa did not seem serious to him. "It is perfectly normal," he said, "for all races not to be overly fond of each other. . . . We are not excited, we're not alarmists." Just before Judge Grooms ordered the university to end Lucy's suspension, Folsom criticized "outside agitators" for causing turmoil in Tuscaloosa. "They're pushing this one too hard and it's causing a reaction." Paradoxically, Folsom welcomed later news that the university trustees had expelled ten students for leading the protest demonstrations. Sharing the news with his cabinet, Folsom rejoiced, "The Board of Trustees of Alabama declared against mobocracy!" It was almost seven months later when Folsom publicly acknowledged that the highway patrol officers in Tuscaloosa had been unable to maintain order and that his response to the crisis had been inadequate.[41]

The Montgomery bus boycott and Autherine Lucy's enrollment at the University of Alabama became milestones in the long history of the American Negro's struggle for civil rights. Even though Jim Folsom avoided direct involvement in either, the boycott and Autherine Lucy altered his political career dramatically as they made race relations the primary issue in Alabama politics. The spread of citizens' councils during 1955 and 1956 illustrated the effect that the boycott and the desegregation of the University of Alabama had on white Alabamians. The *Brown* decision in 1954 was upsetting because most whites strongly opposed desegregation. However, Alabama whites had remained relatively calm as they waited to learn how the Supreme Court would implement its ruling. As if the decision were a cause for concern but not for panic, only five citizens' councils were established in Alabama before the end of 1955. Then the Montgomery bus boycott and the crisis in Tuscaloosa alarmed whites. By the end of February 1956, twenty-six citizens' councils in seventeen counties boasted a membership of 40,000 Alabamians. The Montgomery Citizens' Council alone drew 15,000 people to a public rally against desegregation after Autherine Lucy entered the University of Alabama. The overnight spread of the citizens' councils in Alabama reflected the rapid polarization of opinion on racial issues between mid-1955 and the spring of 1956.[42]

Governor Folsom lost political influence as white opinions crystallized. He had not quieted the furor over Adam Clayton Powell's visit to the governor's mansion before the Montgomery bus boycott began. After the disorders in Tuscaloosa, whites saw him as a traitor to southern racial values. The mere mention of his name at citizens' council rallies provoked thunderous jeers.[43] The Alabama Legislature, which followed his leadership during 1955, rebelled in 1956. The legislators listened politely when the governor addressed each of their sessions, but they ignored his proposals and overrode his vetoes. Alabama voters turned against "the little man's big friend." In the Democratic primary of 1956 and in referendums on constitutional amendments, the voters repeatedly defeated candidates and amendments identified with Governor Folsom.

The two special sessions that Folsom called during early 1956 demonstrated how the civil rights movement had weakened and isolated him politically. The session that began in January, the second month of the Montgomery bus boycott, was the session Folsom convened to consider legislative reapportionment and constitutional revision. The legislators were not interested in the political reforms Folsom endorsed and crowded their agenda with segregationist bills instead. The most important of these was Senator Albert Boutwell's "freedom-of-choice" plan, a proposal that paralleled segregationist strategies in other southern states. Boutwell's plan was a constitutional amendment that authorized the Alabama Legislature and local school systems to support education in private schools with public funds and properties designated for educational purposes. The bill also authorized the attorney general to represent any school official who became involved in civil rights litigation. Boutwell called it "freedom of choice" because the bill gave students and their parents the freedom to choose an integrated or segregated school. Governor Folsom protested that his usual opponents, the "Big Mules" and the Black Belt planters, were using the race issue to dodge the reapportionment issue. Folsom's protests fell on deaf ears. While Senator Jamie Coleman worked out his bogus reapportionment plan, only one legislator voted against the freedom-of-choice amendment as it zoomed through both the house and the senate.[44]

As the first special session of 1956 continued, Governor Folsom did not have enough power in the legislature to kill discriminatory legislation with his veto. The only thing Folsom could do was to offend the racial sensibilities of Alabama voters. He accomplished this when Representative Charles McKay of Talladega County introduced a resolution that declared the *Brown* decision "null, void, and of no effect" in Alabama. Only four legislators voted against the "nullification resolution" as it won overwhelming approval. Governor Folsom could not veto the measure because it was a resolution, but he called a press conference to tell the public that he resented the legislators' neglect of constitutional revision and their preoccupation with racial issues. The nullification resolution, Folsom said, was a "two-bit resolution" and "just a bunch of hogwash." "All this clap-trap about the resolution is just like a hound dog baying at the moon and claiming it's got the moon treed." Folsom argued that the Alabama Constitution required the state government to uphold the United States Constitution. Therefore, "that resolution doesn't mean a thing; the one thing to do about it is to have a constitutional convention and let the delegates consider such things as 'Nullification.'" Although Folsom accurately summarized the significance of the nullification resolution, his fulminations shocked white voters and further eroded his shrinking political base.[45]

Governor Folsom called a second special session in March 1956 to deal with the financial crisis that the Alabama Department of Education confronted after voters rejected the Goodwyn tax bill. With the Montgomery bus boycott continuing just outside the legislative chambers, Folsom also urged the legislators to create a state commission of black and white leaders who would work together to resolve racial problems in Alabama. Folsom's Bi-Racial Commission drowned in a deluge of segregationist legislation. After the legislators trimmed three million dollars from the annual budget for education and raised corporate income taxes to provide additional revenue, they concentrated on racial concerns. The house adopted a resolution calling for an investigation of communist influence in chapters of the NAACP. A senate resolution asked the U.S. Congress to distribute the Negro population of the South evenly among all forty-eight states. Both houses approved a resolution requesting that the U.S. Supreme Court change its decision of Brown v. Board of Education. The house considered a bill authorizing the state to dismiss any employee who belonged to or sympathized with the NAACP. Meanwhile, Folsom's Bi-Racial Commission never received formal consideration on the floor of either legislative house.[46]

Perhaps Folsom's Bi-Racial Commission best reflected the political isolation that the civil rights movement created for him. He presented his idea to 175 Alabama newspaper editors and publishers during February 1956 while passions were most inflamed over the events in Montgomery and Tuscaloosa. Although the journalists endorsed the concept of a commission that would seek solutions to racial problems, there was no political support for the Bi-

Racial Commission. Few Alabamians were willing to submit racial concerns to bi-racial examination and observation. Negroes were not willing to cooperate after Folsom made it clear that the commission would not challenge racial segregation. "Anybody with any sense," he told the editors, "knows that Negro children and white children are not going to school together in Alabama any time in the near future." White supremacists objected to a Bi-Racial Commission that would propose compromises for racial disputes. Southern racial customs, they believed, were the basis of peace and stability within southern society and could not be compromised. By February 1956, the civil rights movement had polarized Alabamians to the point that Folsom's effort to reduce racial tensions succeeded in alienating him from both Alabama Negroes and whites.[47]

Apparently, Governor Folsom did not realize how severely the civil rights movement had eroded his support at "the brush arbors and the forks of the creeks." After enduring the insults of segregationist legislators during two special sessions, Folsom announced that he would run for the office of Democratic national committeeman in 1956. Remembering the self-starter amendment referendum of 1948, Folsom entered the race seeking a popular mandate for his leadership in the continuing racial controversy. He also entered the race with hopes that his candidacy would divert partisan opposition away from his political friends in other campaigns.[48]

When Big Jim hit the campaign trail in March 1956, he spoke forthrightly in defense of his approach to racial problems. In northern Alabama, Folsom sounded like the Georgia Populist Tom Watson as he argued that the Black Belt politicians and the "Big Mules" were using the racial issue as a tactic to defeat the People's Program. In Folsom's words, "When the politicians start hollering 'Whip the Nigger!' then you know damn well they are trying to cover up dirty tracks." Folsom did not apologize for criticizing the nullification resolution. In mid-March, he declared that southern officials were obligated to comply with the *Brown* decision: "You can call the Supreme Court justices s.o.b.'s if you want to, but that doesn't relieve Southern officials sworn to uphold the Constitution of their responsibility." Folsom publicly ridiculed the resolutions that Black Belt legislators authored in resistance to segregation. Referring to the senate, Folsom said:

Why, you know what that crowd did last month? They passed a resolution asking the federal government to move all the Negroes out of the

South. Why, if all the Negroes were moved away, every last one of those folks who have been raising so much sand would starve to death. They wouldn't work. I know that because I know every one of them. . . . Most of these fellows . . . live with Negroes, work with Negroes, and get their living made by Negroes.[49]

Folsom's opponent in the 1956 Democratic primary, Representative Charles McKay, gladly cooperated in making the campaign a referendum on racial issues. The author of the nullification resolution viciously attacked Folsom as the friend of the Negro and of the NAACP. McKay's campaign advertisements boosted him as "Alabama's Fighting Champion for Segregation," and blasted Folsom as the "Darling of the N.A.A.C.P. and host of Adam Clayton Powell, the whiskey-drinking Negro Congressman from Harlem." McKay had no statewide organization, but the citizens' councils provided all the support he needed. The events of the preceding winter had swollen council memberships, and council leaders used the membership to influence state politics. The Montgomery County Citizens' Council surveyed the racial views of all candidates in the 1956 Democratic primary, just as the Alabama Democratic Executive Committee had done in 1948. Governor Folsom and other members of his administration earned the council's automatic censure because they refused to complete the questionnaire.[50]

Alabama Democrats demonstrated that they were as upset about Adam Clayton Powell, the Montgomery bus boycott, and Autherine Lucy as the legislators had been. On 1 May 1956, Charles McKay overwhelmed Folsom in the contest for Democratic national committeeman by a vote of 232,751 to 79,644. In races for positions on the Alabama Supreme Court, the Alabama Court of Appeals, and the Alabama Public Service Commission, candidates identified with Folsom fell victim to the voters' antipathy for the governor. The rout was statewide as McKay rolled up majorities in sixty-four of the sixty-seven counties. The worst defeat of Folsom's political career was an unmistakable indication of the damage that the civil rights movement had done to his popularity.[51]

After the 1956 Democratic primary, every Alabama politician understood that support for segregation was the prerequistite for political success. The legislators acted on this understanding during their 1957 biennial session. Early in the session, Speaker Rankin Fite supported a long resolution that opposed the enactment of civil rights legislation by the U.S. Congress. When the time came to vote on the resolution, Fite was annoyed because only a few legisla-tors were paying attention. He leaned over the microphone on his desk and said, "Boys, this resolution has the word segregation in it." There was a rush in the house chamber as each legislator ran to his desk and lit the green light beside his name on the electronic voting scoreboard.[52]

In the wake of McKay's upsetting victory, Governor Folsom did not know how to react. As a political leader, he gave appearances of conforming to the mandate of the 1956 Democratic primary. In 1957 he selected E. C. Boswell to be his legal adviser and allowed rumors to circulate that he would endorse segregationist legislation in the 1957 regular session. Personally, he resigned himself to pe-rennial frustration. In 1956, Folsom was philosophical about his defeat in a letter to the U.S. senator Estes Kefauver. Though he was proud to have opposed die-hard segregationists, Folsom wrote, "I guess I will always be on the short end of that issue." While discuss-ing his defeat with Jim Battles, Folsom explained: "It is our kind of people that prejudices upset the most. That is the reason that prej-udice is always used to beat down those in public affairs who be-lieve in democracy for all the people."[53]

Despite the defeat and the political concessions he made to white supremacy, Jim Folsom remained a supporter of Negro rights. After six racially motivated bombings in Montgomery on 10 January 1957, Folsom posted a $2,000 reward for the arrest of the guilty parties and volunteered to cooperate with federal investigators. In July 1957, Attorney General John Patterson tried to crush a civil rights boycott of white merchants in Tuskegee by raiding the offices of the Tuskegee Civic Association. Folsom protested, "There is no room for Gestapo methods in Alabama. I want it publicly known that what happened in Tuskegee yesterday was without my knowl-edge." At the end of the 1957 legislative session, Folsom had an opportunity to pocket veto seven segregationist bills. He did so happily, explaining, "I have tried to soft-pedal racial legislation throughout my administration. All I want is for everyone to get along together without trouble." Folsom continued to recognize rac-ism in Alabama's judicial system. Of the nineteen death sentences Folsom commuted to sentences of life imprisonment, seventeen had been pronounced against Negroes. Grover Hall marveled at Folsom's steadfast respect for the rights of Negroes: "Folsom was almost consumed in the blaze over his having had . . . Adam Clayton Powell . . . around to the mansion for a snort. But he keeps boring back in a fashion that would not seem advisable for a man who wants to be the first governor to serve a third term."[54]

One of Folsom's cabinet members remembers a time during the second administration when the governor and several aides retired to a hotel room one afternoon in between appointments. As was his custom, Folsom stretched out across the bed for a brief nap. Lying there about half asleep, Folsom moaned, "What in the world am I ever going to do with the Niggers?" It was a lament that Folsom might have uttered at any time after mid-1955. He was trapped. He was attempting to respond to racial problems calmly and rationally at a time when opinions about racial issues were polarized. Big Jim Folsom could take pride in the conviction that he was right, but he had to learn to tolerate the political frustration that being right produced for him.[55]

11

No "Shining Knight in Armor"

When he won his second Democratic gubernatorial nomination in 1954, Jim Folsom amazed political experts with his apparent invulnerability to personal or political embarrassment. During his first administration, Folsom's uninhibited behavior repeatedly shocked respectable citizens and led Hartselle author William Bradford Huie to refer to him as "Old Kissin' Jim, the Guckenheimer Kid, multiplying his kind behind every barn door." By the end of his first term, journalists and political opponents had good reason to suspect Folsom and his appointees of corruption in their administration of the ABC Board, the Department of Prisons and Institutions, the Alabama State Docks, the Highway Department, and the Pardon and Parole Board. Incredibly, Big Jim Folsom did not incur public censure and won more votes in the 1954 Democratic primary than any previous candidate for state office. Although veteran newsmen could not explain the resilience of Folsom's popularity, a voter from Tuscaloosa County revealed the key to Big Jim's success in a letter to the editor of the *Birmingham News*:

> Admittedly, Governor Folsom does not have all the virtues of a "Shining Knight in Armor," nor does he reveal the tact and discretion of a Black Belt or Big Business aristocrat. However, his shortcomings and mistakes, which are so widely publicized, are insignificant compared with his theory and the program he advocates behind it for democratic government giving the common man a break.

The "common man," it seemed, was not alarmed by Big Jim's personal behavior or by stories of graft within his administration.[1]

Still, popular tolerance for Folsom's foibles was not unlimited. Before Folsom's second administration was two years old, Grover Hall's editorials in the *Montgomery Advertiser* marked the decline of public confidence in Governor Folsom. Hall speculated that the truth of the Folsom administration had finally awakened the "common man" from his previous "pleasing vision." More likely, Big Jim's unwillingness to resist the civil rights movement changed public opinion toward him. Many white Alabamians may have shared the view of the voter who wrote Folsom to declare that he had tolerated all of Folsom's "shabby doings" until the day Folsom shared cocktails with Adam Clayton Powell. Unhappy with a governor who would not fight desegregation, Alabamians lost patience with his eccentric behavior and the graft that his administration was unable or unwilling to curb.[2]

Political circumstances, especially the emergence of the civil rights movement, helped Folsom's opponents exploit his weaknesses; but flaws within Jim Folsom's character made him vulnerable to those attacks. He enjoyed the luxuries and the social life that being governor afforded him so much that critics successfully portrayed him as an extravagant, self-indulgent governor who had isolated himself from the people. Like every other successful political leader, Folsom depended on the loyalty of his supporters and rewarded that loyalty whenever possible. Loyalty bordered on venality, however, when it involved expensive state contracts or when it prevented Folsom from dismissing associates who placed personal gain ahead of the state's welfare. Throughout his adult life, Jim Folsom consumed alcoholic beverages. Done in private and in moderation, Folsom's drinking was not politically significant. It became important when Folsom made public appearances while intoxicated or when inebriation incapacitated him for several days at a time. In the midst of the popular anxieties of the mid-1950s, the flaws within Folsom's character became too obvious for voters to overlook.

Jim Folsom took great pleasure in what he called the "emoluments of office." Because he was the governor, his family lived in one of Montgomery's finest houses and were attended by a full complement of servants at all hours of the day. The state budget appropriated funds for "official entertaining"; and since guests dined with the governor regularly, the Mansion Fund paid for the majority of the Folsom family's groceries. The governor rode in a chauffeur-driven limousine in Montgomery or on short trips within the state. For longer trips, he could call for a state-owned aircraft and charge the travel expenses of everyone who accompanied him to the account of the state government. Because the governor influenced the decisions of the ABC Board, liquor distillers kept the mansion's liquor cabinet well stocked at all times. For relaxation, Folsom could reserve one of the two sporting boats owned by the Alabama State Docks.

As far as Governor Folsom was concerned, all of these advantages were his by right. In the first six months of his second administration, he used the Mansion Fund to redecorate the mansion even though Mrs. Persons had furnished the house completely only four years earlier. Out in the yard, Folsom had a tennis court constructed and the garage remodeled into a guest cottage. The State of Alabama paid for a pony for Folsom's children and a new custom-built Cadillac limousine for Folsom. Late in the summer of 1955, Grover Hall, Jr., estimated that Folsom was spending the Mansion Fund's $60,000 annual appropriation at the rate of $122,000 annually. He could continue to do this by periodically replenishing the Mansion Fund with transfers from the Governor's Emergency Fund. According to one Folsom legend, a newsman once quizzed Folsom about the purchase of a new state yacht. Folsom's reply, "Well, somebody's going to have it and I'm the Governor, ain't I?" indicated his attitude toward all the perquisites of his office.[3]

Recreational junkets constituted Folsom's most dubious use of his gubernatorial privileges. When he traveled, Folsom often invited half a dozen friends and their wives to accompany him. In September 1955, Folsom and a party of fifteen flew in a National Guard airplane to Houston for a University of Alabama football game. Later that fall, Folsom used a National Guard plane to transport friends from their hometowns to the Alabama-Auburn football game in Birmingham. When the U.S. Air Force criticized his recreational use of National Guard planes, Governor Folsom evaded the warnings. In December 1955, he announced that the Alabama Air National Guard would test the runway facilities and conduct "weather inspections" in Jacksonville, Florida, on the day API's football team played in the Gator Bowl. During 1956, Governor Folsom used the planes of the Department of Industrial Development to take large parties to a meeting of the Young Democrats of New York and to the Veterans of Foreign Wars convention in Miami. On each trip, Folsom assumed that he and his friends were representing the State of Alabama and charged their expenses to the state government.[4]

The Alabama press focused critical attention on the governor's lifestyle and what it cost the state. The *Montgomery Advertiser* reported expenditures from the Mansion Fund until Folsom ordered his executive secretary to quit recording how the money was being spent. Grover Hall concentrated on the cost of the new tennis court. After Governor Folsom tried to justify the expenditure by saying that the court was open for public use, Hall christened it the "People's Court." Folsom became so annoyed by the criticisms in the fall of 1955 that he refused to reveal the names of his guests at out-of-state football games. Thereafter, sportswriters trained their binoculars on the stands to discover who was sitting with the governor. The scrutiny of the press motivated Folsom to close the governor's mansion for six weeks and move his family to a cabin on Lake Guntersville during the summer of 1956.[5]

The criticisms of Folsom not only annoyed the governor, but they also attracted the official interest of the chief examiner of public accounts, Ralph Eagerton. In October 1956, Eagerton formally requested that Folsom deliver the Mansion Fund records to the Department of Public Examiners for an audit. Protesting that this would violate the constitutional separation of powers, Folsom removed the records from the capitol to prevent Eagerton from seizing them. While Eagerton prepared to subpoena the records, a bitter battle in the state courts seemed inevitable. Actually, Folsom did not know whether or not he had spent public money illegally and had asked a private accounting firm to audit the records. Stalling for time while his accountants worked, the governor left Montgomery for a week in October to keep Eagerton from serving him with a subpoena. On 30 October, Folsom met with the Committee on Public Accounts, the legislative committee that supervised the Department of Public Examiners, and worked out a compromise. He promised to deliver the records to Eagerton no later than 27 November. Folsom delivered the records as promised after his accountants advised him that he had misspent $5,180. By the time the Department of Public Examiners completed the official audit in January 1957 and declared that the governor had spent only $4,689 illegally, Folsom had already repaid half of the money and thus avoided additional embarrassment.[6]

In light of the abundant opportunities for graft that existed within state government, Folsom's abuse of the Mansion Fund and other perquisites held more symbolic than substantive significance. He violated the public's trust, though not the law, more seriously as a result of his loyalty to supporters. Folsom believed that loyalty was the chief of all political virtues. He believed that an elected official had a moral and political obligation to reward the people who worked to elect him. When Folsom occupied the governor's office, the Alabama civil service system limited his freedom to place supporters in public jobs. Nevertheless, the absence of regulations on the awarding of most state contracts allowed Folsom to divert state funds legally into the pockets of his political friends. As expressions of loyalty exceeded the bounds of public ethics, they worked with his proclivity toward self-indulgence to undermine public confidence in him further.

The Folsom administration took full advantage of its few opportunities to reward political friends with public jobs. During 1955 and 1956, the Department of Conservation hired a man to be caretaker and concessionaire at each of three new state fishing lakes. The three jobs went to Folsom's father-in-law, E. H. Moore; the Conservation director's brother, E. L. Drinkard; and Folsom's boyhood friend, William Prescott. The jobs proved to be lucrative: Moore earned a $6,000 profit from the sale of concessions during nine weeks of 1956. Governor Folsom did not forget the friends who helped him when he was arrested for driving while intoxicated in 1952. Under the Persons administration, Officer Felton Yates had lost his job after he testified on Folsom's behalf. Folsom reinstated Yates to the highway patrol and arranged a promotion for him. C. G. Boner, the judge who presided over Folsom's trial, was unemployed in 1955. When the probate judge of Jefferson County vacated his office, Folsom appointed Boner to complete the unexpired term.[7]

Folsom's most humane expression of loyalty was his regard for Dr. J. S. Snoddy of Haleyville. Dr. Snoddy had pioneered the use of X-ray technology in Alabama while the technology was still crude. As a result, Snoddy had almost completely lost the use of his hands. Unable to practice medicine any longer, Snoddy became involved in politics as an advocate for old-age pensions. Folsom rewarded him by arranging for the Alabama Board of Welfare to select Dr. Snoddy as commissioner of public welfare in 1955. Although Dr. Snoddy could not perform the duties of his office, Folsom kept Snoddy in that job throughout the four years of his administration.[8]

The Folsom administration found ad hoc methods for getting friends on the state payroll. The most common of these was the practice of hiring the professional services of political friends for specific jobs. Charles Pinkston collected $15,000 in legal fees from the state in September 1955 for assisting the Highway Department in the sale of $15 million worth of road construction bonds. During 1957, Senator Neil Metcalf collected a $300 legal fee for unspecified legal services he performed for the Revenue Department in October. Also during 1957, the Highway Department retained fifteen pro-Folsom legislators who were also licensed attorneys to help secure property for highway right-of-way. One of the legislators, Representative George Hawkins, received $1,325 for his services.[9]

The Folsom administration made other arrangements for friends without professional skills. Several supporters received incomes as the representatives of distillers who sold liquor to the ABC Board. A few of the liquor agents directed their companies' advertising efforts in Alabama, but most relaxed and collected the sales commissions on liquor that the ABC Board purchased. Among the liquor agents during Folsom's second administration, two were relatives of pro-Folsom legislators, one was a personal friend of Bill Lyerly, and one was the business manager for Jamelle Folsom Cosmetics. The liquor agent Roy Grimmett had been a Bibb Graves partisan before becoming a Folsom supporter in 1942. Johnny Steifelmeyer accompanied Folsom on his election campaigns in 1946 and 1954, and Jerry Hilliard had worked as Folsom's 1954 campaign leader in Lee County. The Folsom administration also made arrangements for the state government to lease office space from other political friends. As a result, Folsom's supporters frequently leased property from a third party at one rate and then subleased the same property to the state at a higher rate. Among the Folsom supporters who enjoyed this privilege were Clarence Evans, Folsom's 1954 campaign leader in Mobile County; Dr. Louis Friedman, a generous campaign contributor from Birmingham; Joe Wells, a wealthy supporter from Montgomery; and Senator Herman Vann, a pro-Folsom senator from Huntsville.[10]

Among friends and supporters who qualified as insurance agents, Governor Folsom distributed the agent commissions generated by the Alabama Insurance Fund. Because Alabama law prohibited the state from purchasing insurance, the fund insured every department and agency of the state government against unexpected financial losses. To protect itself from losses, the Alabama Insurance Fund purchased insurance protection directly from private companies. Since the Insurance Fund bought its coverage directly, the private insurer paid the commission that ordinarily went to its agent into the Alabama Insurance Fund. Because state law made no provision for the disposition of these agent commissions, the governor distributed the money to his political friends as if they were the agents who had sold the insurance to the Insurance Fund. The second Folsom administration delegated the job of dividing the commissions to John Overton of the Turner Insurance and Bonding Company. Between February 1955 and March 1956, Overton divided more than $210,000 in commissions among sixty insurance agents. More than $31,000 in commissions went to Hobart Key, a former Strawberry Picker. The Insurance Fund paid more than $22,000 to an insurance agency owned by Representative Joe Dawkins of Montgomery and more than $11,000 to Folsom and Folsom, an agency to which the governor himself belonged. Speaker Rankin Fite's brother received $4,000 worth of commissions, and Senators Broughton Lamberth and E. L. Roberts collected $1,000 each. Altogether there were fifteen pro-Folsom legislators among the sixty agents who received commission checks from the Alabama Insurance Fund.[11]

The most lucrative favors distributed by the Folsom administration were the state contracts. Because Alabama did not have a comprehensive state purchasing law before 1957, the finance director, Fuller Kimbrell, negotiated state contracts with a relatively free hand. Except for construction contracts for more than $15,000 and contracts that involved federal matching money, Folsom's finance director could purchase almost anything from anyone at any price. The Folsom administration used this prerogative to reward the loyalty of political friends.[12]

Kimbrell purchased everything from office supplies to road construction machinery from political friends. When the state built new offices for the Department of Industrial Relations, the state purchased paint from a Folsom friend who owned a Montgomery hardware store. Because the state paid the full retail price for the paint, the store owner was able to convert his small hardware business into a booming building material dealership in less than two years. The Department of Agriculture and Industries contracted with the *Elba Clipper* for the printing of its monthly magazine. At the rate of eleven dollars for each one thousand copies, the *Clipper* cleared a profit of about $42,000 during each year of the contract. In 1956, the Southern Contracting and Supply Company of Elba sold one hundred aluminum rowboats to the Department of Conservation for $145.39 each. The price was excessive, but Kimbrell did not object, since Fred Folsom was the major stockholder in the company. When the ABC Board contracted for the services of a hauling company, only Winfield Moon and Company of Cullman submitted a bid for the job. Winfield Moon had not supported Folsom in every campaign, but his company was a subsidiary of the Folsom Hauling Company.[13]

The purchase of automobiles frequently allowed the Folsom administration to share the "emoluments of office" with friends. During the 1955–56 fiscal year, Kimbrell supervised the purchase of 171 cars. The basic state vehicle was a four-door sedan with an eight-cylinder engine and no optional equipment except a heater. One of these basic cars cost approximately $2,500 and allowed the dealer to make a profit of about $250. Of the cars the state purchased during 1955–56, 38 came from Lineville Motor Company, a dealership with which the assistant finance director, Ed Pepper, was associated, and 25 came from either Drinkard Pontiac or Drinkard Chevrolet in Cullman. Another 21 came from Fayette Motor Company, a dealership in Kimbrell's hometown. On some cars, the dealers earned higher profits by selling higher-priced models with a full complement of optional equipment. At least 4 of the cars purchased from Fayette Motor Company in 1955 were expensive Mercury models. The legislature tried to regulate the purchase of state vehicles in 1957 by requiring competitive bids for future acquisitions. However, Kimbrell circumvented the regulations by insisting that dealers who submitted bids be able to provide immediate delivery. Thus, the state purchased vehicles only from those political friends who had advance knowledge of purchases.[14]

The Folsom administration demonstrated its loyalty to political friends in a series of contracts it awarded to H&H Construction Company in 1956. H&H belonged to Robert Finney, the brother of Folsom's executive secretary, and to Olin Hearn, a prominent Folsom supporter in Marshall County. In May 1956, the state paid H&H $21,000 for the installation of air conditioners in five offices of the state employment service. H&H also won contracts to paint a new state office building and to build a cottage at the state fishing lake in Tuscaloosa County for 15 percent above the cost of materials and labor. The Finance Department did not take competitive bids for any of these jobs. When the cottage in Tuscaloosa County was complete, H&H requested total payments of $17,719. The Finance Department withheld payment while protesting that the Conservation Department had authorized the project without a written contract. H&H appealed to the State Board of Adjustment, a three-member panel of state officials who served ex officio to settle the claims of private citizens against the state. The members of the board included Fuller Kimbrell and the secretary of state, Mary Texas Hurt, who had been elected with Folsom's endorsement. Predictably, the Board of Adjustment voted to pay the $17,719 that H&H requested. In spite of the irregularity of this procedure, neither the Folsom administration nor H&H altered its business practice. In June 1956, H&H began two more state jobs without submitting a competitive bid or signing a written contract.[15]

No one in Alabama could have been aware of every occasion on which the second Folsom administration gave short shrift to ethical considerations in order to reward political friends. Ordinarily, those Alabamians who knew how the governor dispensed political patronage accepted it as part of the political process and hoped that Folsom would be discreet. Normally, only blatant or chronic violations of the public trust attracted protests. The second Folsom administration, however, was embroiled in continuous controversy. The controversy stemmed partially from Folsom's uninhibited personality and from the close scrutiny of the hostile daily press. Even more important were the actions of Attorney General John Patterson and the chief examiner, Ralph Eagerton, because their investigations legitimized the rumors of corruption. Eagerton and Folsom had been political opponents since the first Folsom administration when anti-Folsom legislators had established Eagerton's position in order to expose every misstep Folsom made. Attorney General Patterson inherited his antipathy for Folsom from his late father and added his own ambition to succeed Folsom in office. With the powers of his office, Patterson could simultaneously damage Folsom's reputation and promote his own political image as an enemy of corruption in government.

The transactions between the state government and H&H provided a perfect opportunity for Patterson and Eagerton. In September 1956, the attorney general filed a petition in the Fifteenth Judicial Circuit of Alabama requesting that the court enjoin the state comptroller, John Graves, from paying H&H Construction Company for improvements to the cottage at the Tuscaloosa County fishing lake. Patterson also sought injunctions to block payment to two road contractors for allegedly illegal road construction projects. In all three petitions, Patterson argued that the transactions were illegal because there had been no competitive bids or written contracts. Judge Walter B. Jones of the circuit court agreed with Patterson and issued the injunctions. Encouraged by this success, Patterson asked Judge Jones to stop a payment of $13,000 to Glencoe Paving Company for highway maintenance work and materials. Judge Jones sided with the attorney general again and enjoined Graves from paying Glencoe. In October, Patterson went after H&H again. He challenged an agreement between the Highway Department and H&H for the construction of a maintenance building in Centre. Before Judge Jones could rule on the petition, however, the director of the Highway Department, Herman Nelson, announced that the agreement with H&H had been canceled.[16]

While Patterson prosecuted suspicious state contracts, the Department of Public Examiners audited the Department of Conservation. On the basis of Judge Jones's rulings, the auditors declared illegal all jobs that were performed by private companies without written plans or specifications, without competitive bids, and without written contracts. Using these criteria, the public auditors decided that the conservation director, Bill Drinkard, was personally responsible for the illegal expenditure of $709,487. The official audit detailed irregularities in transactions between the Conservation Department and H&H Construction Company; J. W. Gwin, Jr., Inc.; Floyd H. Woodley Dredging Company; and R. K. Summersell Dredging Company. The audit also cited Drinkard for allowing lumber companies owned by Bryce Davis of Cullman and Olon Belcher of Centreville to cut timber illegally in state parks. Although the conservation director denounced the audit as a political attack, Attorney General Patterson filed suit against Drinkard in the Fifteenth Judicial Circuit.[17]

In spite of the work of the chief examiner and the attorney general, neither Folsom nor any of his appointees were convicted for illegal contracting practices. In November 1956, the case involving Glencoe Paving Company became the test case for all the prosecutions. With the support of the Folsom administration, Glencoe began *mandamus* proceedings in order to compel the state comptroller, Graves, to pay the $13,000 bill for highway maintenance. The company appealed the decision of Judge Walter Jones of the circuit court all the way to the Alabama Supreme Court, arguing that state law did not require competitive bids on highway maintenance projects. In a unanimous decision, the Alabama Supreme Court cited a 1947 statute which omitted highway maintenance projects from the list of items that could be purchased only after

competitive bidding. The decision was a victory for the Folsom administration and ended Patterson's efforts to prosecute cases of
alleged illegal spending. Even so, Patterson and Eagerton had successfully informed the public that the Folsom administration was
using state funds to grant favors to political friends.[18]

Even after the Glencoe case was decided, suspicions of corruption
undermined public support for a governor who, in the name of
political loyalty, allowed his cronies to profit personally from their
proximity to him. One high-ranking member of the administration
remained politically loyal to Folsom while he used state purchases to
build his concrete pipe and asphalt business into a multimillion
dollar operation. Ward McFarland, Folsom's director of the Alabama
State Docks, knew where Interstate Highway 59 would enter his
hometown of Tuscaloosa and took advantage of that information to
buy farmland on the western side of town. Later, McFarland sold a
portion of his acquisitions to the state for the construction of the
superhighway and made the remainder available to builders of service stations, fast-food restaurants, and other businesses along
McFarland Boulevard. Senator Broughton Lamberth traded his influence in the Highway Department for personal enrichment in his
hometown of Alexander City. After Lamberth secured extensive road
construction for the town in 1955, the city council sold 16.9 acres of
land to Lamberth for one dollar and "other considerations."[19]

Governor Folsom's effort to reward the campaign contributions
of Dr. Louis Friedman inspired the most intense public resentment.
Dr. Friedman joined Folsom's ranks in 1954 when campaign leaders
in Jefferson County needed contributions to fund local television
advertising. Dr. Friedman made a large gift on that occasion and
decided to become active in the Folsom campaign. In the months
that followed, Friedman made frequent appearances at the governor's home and office and cultivated the friendship of Bill Drinkard.
Constantly solicitous of Folsom's favor, he regularly presented
Folsom with small gifts and even lent the governor $7,400 without
interest for a business investment.[20]

Alabamians saw the darker side of Dr. Friedman's character in
1955. To combat outbreaks of polio, the United States government
appropriated funds for the purchase and distribution of the newly
developed Salk polio vaccine. The appropriation offered $1.3 mil-
lion for Alabama with the stipulation that up to 20 percent
($260,000) of the money could be used for administrative costs. On
behalf of Dr. Friedman, Folsom sponsored legislation to create a

special state agency that would distribute the vaccine. Folsom intended to appoint Dr. Friedman as the head of the new agency and give the doctor control of the funds allotted for administrative costs. The legislation was unnecessary because the state Health Department was able to distribute the vaccine much more cheaply than a new state agency and would spend the administrative savings on the purchase of additional vaccine. The plan was impolitic as well. Long after the legislature defeated the bill, Alabamians remembered that Folsom had attempted to play politics with money that would protect their children from polio.[21]

The most ambitious scheme that Folsom's cronies devised for self-enrichment was the Alabama General Insurance Company. Pitt Tyson Maner, Folsom's civil defense director, and six pro-Folsom legislators—Richmond Flowers of Dothan, Broughton Lamberth of Alexander City, Garet Van Antwerp of Mobile, E. L. Roberts of Gadsden, and Harlen Allen and Bryce Davis of Cullman—organized the company in 1955. Although the politicians knew very little about the insurance business, the superintendent of insurance, a Folsom appointee, granted their company a charter. Alabama General specialized in the sale of surety bonds for public officials, state contractors, and the state government. Not only did members of the Folsom administration post their bonds through Alabama General, but so did construction companies who sought to win lucrative state contracts. Also, whenever a private citizen had a claim against the state that involved litigation, the state posted a surety bond for the amount of the claim pending settlement. During the second Folsom administration, Alabama General sold a large number of these bonds to the state government.[22]

With its strong connections to the Folsom administration, Alabama General prospered for more than two years. Private contractors, elected officials, and the state government provided a steady income, and Alabama General paid few claims. Folsom's cronies, however, were not particularly concerned about the long-term solvency of their business. They drew generous commissions for the sale of surety bonds and charged travel, food, lodging, and entertainment to their Alabama General expense accounts. Instead of making proper investments with the insurance premiums it collected, the company spent most of its income on agent commissions and expense accounts. By late 1957 these abuses were threatening the firm's survival, and the end of the second Folsom administration promised to cut off Alabama General's primary source of income. Without public notice, the State of Alabama transferred all of its bonds to other companies in October. Shortly thereafter, Alabama General went into receivership and left the state with no guarantee that twenty-eight contractors would complete the sixty-one road construction contracts they held. The politicians, who had milked the company for two years, escaped without financial liability.[23]

Folsom's self-indulgence and his unquestioning loyalty to political friends were the primary causes for the exposés and official investigations that plagued his second administration. He violated the public trust more seriously, though less frequently, when he abused the powers of his office in order to augment his political influence. In some cases, such abuses of power were comical. During the fall of 1956, for example, Folsom campaigned anonymously for the reapportionment amendment. Though state law prohibited the use of state equipment or personnel in political campaigns, Folsom directed Marion "Skinny" Boyette, the assistant director of the Industrial Relations Department, to print campaign circulars on the office machines. Boyette produced circulars claiming that reapportionment would prevent Black Belt Negroes from winning control of the legislature. Rumors of Boyette's activity attracted investigative journalists to the Industrial Relations printing room on the morning of 29 October. There the reporters found printing plates and sample circulars. They summoned an assistant attorney general to gather the material as evidence and reported the story in their newspapers. Although Boyette's enterprise was blatantly illegal, Attorney General Patterson did not prosecute. Instead, he and everyone else in Montgomery ridiculed the ineptitude of the Folsom administration. Embarrassed, Folsom lectured Boyette sternly: "Skinny Boyette, the next time you drink beer, don't leave printing plates lying around."[24]

The political reporters who uncovered Boyette's escapade never gathered enough evidence to expose a more chronic abuse of power. Throughout Folsom's tenure, his department heads maintained a cash fund known as the "campaign kitty." The fund financed the administration's activities in political campaigns like the Democratic primary and the reapportionment referendum of 1956. A donation to the kitty constituted an unwritten part of every negotiation between the administration and those individuals or companies who did business with the state. Liquor agents, construction contractors, insurance agents who received commissions from the Insurance Fund, and companies that sold merchandise to the state regularly returned between 5 and 10 percent of their profits in cash to the kitty. Cautious to leave no record for investigators to find later, the managers of the kitty never discussed the fund in writing or in the presence of untrustworthy associates.

The best-kept secret of the Folsom administration led to the embarrassment of a high-ranking cabinet member. On one afternoon, a road construction contractor brought a contribution of forty thousand dollars for the kitty. Since it was already late in the day, the cabinet member placed the cash in his office safe and planned to move it to a more secure location the following day. For several months prior to that afternoon, the same official had carried on a romantic relationship with a secretary who worked in his office. Since the relationship was as clandestine as the campaign kitty, news of it had not leaked to his wife and family in northern Alabama. On the evening after the road contractor delivered his contribution, the official and his secretary quarreled and declared an end to their relationship. In the office the following morning, Folsom's man discovered that the contractor's contribution was missing from his safe. Even though he knew that his former secretary had taken the money and was bound for Texas, he did nothing to stop her. It was better, he reasoned, to let the secretary and the money go than to risk losing his wife or going to prison.[25]

By the time Governor Folsom left office in 1959, public suspicion of his administration's corruption had ruined his credibility. In later years, Folsom's friends attributed his troubles to a few unscrupulous men who surrounded him. Such friends maintained that Folsom was not personally responsible for most incidents of corruption and that he was never convicted of any crime in a court of law. However, even if he was personally innocent, he assumed public responsibility for the actions of his appointees and he never dismissed an appointee except for political disloyalty. Moreover, there were weaknesses in Jim Folsom's character that made graft within his administration possible. His self-indulgence and his unconditional loyalty to political supporters made him vulnerable to the designs of unscrupulous men. In the interest of promoting his program, Folsom tolerated abuses of his power as governor. Perhaps Folsom's most glaring personal weakness, his excessive use of alcoholic beverages, best demonstrated how his personal failings undermined public confidence in his political leadership.

From the year he won his first gubernatorial nomination, Jim

Folsom displayed an alarming lack of discipline with regard to alcohol. There were rumors during 1946 that Folsom made several campaign appearances while intoxicated. He allegedly stayed drunk throughout the first special session of 1947 when the Alabama senate rejected his nominations for the API Board of Trustees. Folsom's appetite for liquor disillusioned political liberals who had believed that Big Jim would be a great southern leader. Malcolm Dobbs wrote to a fellow member of the Southern Conference for Human Welfare, "When Big Jim has a choice of doing one of two things—acting correctly politically or reaching for a drink—he does the latter." Dobbs recognized that Folsom did not have the strength of character to stop drinking and fulfill his promise to "clean house at the Capitol." Folsom's drinking received notoriety after *Life* reporters described him drinking during a fishing trip near Mobile and enjoying beer for breakfast in Texas. During the first administration, however, Alabamians focused their attention on his running battle with the legislature and his affair with Christine Putman Johnston. His drinking did not affect his performance enough to divert public notice from these more prominent concerns.[26]

After his second inauguration, Folsom's fondness for drink became a matter of public record. In October 1955, the governor played host to the Southern Governor's Conference at Point Clear, Alabama, and presided over a formal banquet while tipsy. After a Baptist minister delivered an eloquent invocation, Big Jim slapped the clergyman on the back and thanked him for "a damn good Baptist prayer." On another evening during the conference, Folsom agreed to answer the questions of news reporters in his suite. As a preliminary to the impromptu press conference, he announced, "Boys, I'm sorry I can't offer you a drink, but old Big Jim is going to have one, and you can quote me on that." Alabamians were still upset about the Governor's Conference when Adam Clayton Powell visited the governor's mansion and shared cocktails with Folsom. The governor was equally uninhibited when he and Congressman Frank Boykin invited Governor Averell Harriman of New York to Alabama for a weekend of deer hunting. Harriman, a candidate for the 1956 Democratic presidential nomination, was hunting political support as well as deer. Knowing this, Folsom took refuge in the bar at Boykin's hunting lodge and avoided Harriman for most of the weekend. On the last day of his visit, Harriman addressed a crowd of five hundred persons from the porch of the lodge. As Harriman began speaking, Folsom stood behind the New Yorker, leaning against the wall. As the speech continued, an inebriated Folsom sank slowly to the floor of the porch. He seemed to be unconscious in his horizontal position until Harriman made an adulatory reference to Franklin Roosevelt. Folsom lifted his head from the porch long enough to exclaim, "Truman too!" before returning to his inanimate state. After Harriman finished, no one could rouse Folsom to say a few words to the crowd.[27]

Governor Folsom's drinking did not interfere with his legislative success in 1955, but it increasingly upset his administration thereafter. In March 1956, he attended a morning cabinet meeting while intoxicated. In the minutes of the meeting, Ralph Hammond noted that it was the first time Folsom had presided over his cabinet while drunk. Unfortunately, it would not be his last. During April and May of 1956, Folsom appeared at his office irregularly. "Gone fishing" became a euphemism for drinking binges that could last for several days at a time. An embarrassed O. H. Finney regularly had to tell exasperated visitors that the governor had "gone fishing" and would not show up for an appointment. Finney's inability to cope with this kind of pressure contributed to his resignation as executive secretary. Other members of the administration reacted differently to the leadership vacuum that Folsom's alcoholism created. The press secretary, Ralph Hammond, assumed responsibility for supervising the governor's office and for speaking in Folsom's name in times of emergency. The finance director, Fuller Kimbrell; the Speaker of the house, Rankin Fite; and the director of the Highway Department, Herman Nelson, asserted themselves as the administration's decisionmakers on routine legislative and patronage matters. Men who resented the leadership of Hammond, Kimbrell, and the others gravitated toward the frequently incapacitated governor. Stories circulated throughout the state of late-night gatherings at the governor's mansion at which ambitious men plied Folsom with liquor in hope of winning political recognition or patronage favors.[28]

Folsom's alcoholism led to pathetic incidents of public drunkenness. Typical was the day he went to dedicate a new land drainage system in Geneva. Folsom invited a northern Alabama legislator; the public safety director, Bill Lyerly; Senator Neil Metcalf; and another cabinet member to join him for the trip. As soon as the party left Montgomery, Folsom began drinking. When they arrived in Geneva, Big Jim was too intoxicated to climb the steps of the speaker's platform alone. And instead of giving a speech, all he could do was mumble a few words. Although the other members of the party filled the time allotted for the governor's address with unrehearsed comments, they could not hide Folsom's condition from the disappointed audience.[29]

On another occasion, Governor Folsom accepted an invitation to review a new aircraft carrier at the U.S. Naval Air Station in Pensacola, Florida. As usual, Folsom began drinking as soon as his party left Montgomery, and he arrived in Pensacola so drunk that aides had to assist him to his seat on the carrier's deck. He sat with about fifty other dignitaries—including the governor of Florida, state and local officials, and U.S. Navy officers—while they watched the ship's crew move planes from below deck, place them into catapults, and launch them into the air in rapid succession. The exhibition proceeded without incident until one plane showered sparks on the carrier deck as it left the catapult. Approximately two hundred feet above the deck, the plane burst into flames. A series of booms shook the ship as the pilot ejected from his craft, the fuel tanks on the plane exploded, and wreckage fell into Pensacola Bay. The pilot parachuted safely into the water where he waited for a helicopter to fish him out. When the noise subsided, Governor Folsom rose from his seat to declare, "Ladies and gentlemen, I'll kiss your ass if that ain't a show!"[30]

Friends and associates of the governor all gave different reasons for his excessive alcohol consumption. His influence over the ABC Board assured him of an unlimited supply of free booze, a circumstance that facilitated his vice. Some said the pressures of his office were an overwhelming burden on him. By early 1956, it was obvious that the legislature would not approve a legitimate reapportionment plan or any of the other basic reforms Folsom favored. At the same time, because Folsom would not mouth segregationist rhetoric, he could do nothing to prevent the civil rights movement from destroying his political base. The pain of dealing with dishonorable friends also distressed him. The prospect of severing relationships with men who had stood behind him in the past may have been too unpleasant for a self-indulgent man like Folsom to confront while sober. Personal problems compounded the pressures of public life. During 1955, outside investors took control of the Emergency Aid Insurance Company, which Folsom had helped build. The struggle for power within the company contributed to the suicide of Folsom's brother-in-law Ross Clark, and it undoubtedly affected the governor as well. Folsom's two oldest daughters, the only children of his first wife, reached adolescence during the second administration. Domestic life promised no tranquility, since neither girl felt sure of the love of a father who spent every waking moment with political associates and a stepmother who had responsibility for six other children and a full social calendar. The girls' teenage years became even more difficult as they entered Sidney Lanier High School and experienced the social ostracism that Folsom's family had first encountered when they moved to Montgomery in 1947.

Other contemporaries of Folsom denied that mounting pressure led Folsom to seek solace in a whiskey bottle. His was an optimistic, ebullient personality. He thrived on the companionship of friends and the excitement of being the governor. Troubles did not penetrate the soul of anyone as easygoing as Big Jim. Instead, problems rolled off Folsom like water off a duck's back. Besides, by 1956 Governor Folsom had decided that the legislature had already enacted the most important portions of his campaign program, and no major unachieved political objectives remained to frustrate Folsom. He drank too much, contemporaries said, because he liked to drink. He liked the taste of liquor, he enjoyed the sensation of intoxication, and he treasured the fellowship of his drinking buddies.[31]

Although his friends never agreed on the cause of Folsom's alcoholism, its consequences were plain. From early 1956 until his second term in office ended, Folsom did not provide leadership for the men who supported him, and the solidarity of his administration disintegrated steadily as a result. The evidences of decline were legion. Aides who were crucial to Folsom's reelection in 1954 disassociated themselves from him. As Ralph Hammond took charge of the governor's office and Fuller Kimbrell dominated patronage decisions, the Folsomites squabbled among themselves for positions of power and wealth. In the legislature, respect for the administration declined as six or eight different men claimed to represent the governor. As the gubernatorial campaign of 1958 began, Folsomites divided their support among all the major candidates in the race. By the time he left office in 1959, Folsom's failure to provide leadership—because of his alcoholism, his racial views, his self-indulgence, and his loyalty to political cronies—had thoroughly demoralized the political organization that had supported him in 1954.

The decline of Folsom's ability to lead manifested itself as close associates and members of his cabinet committed acts of political disloyalty. The first signs of dissension came from the director of industrial relations, Eugene Wells, and the Labor Department director, Luke Barnett. Both men were influential members of the AFL-CIO in Alabama and had joined the Folsom administration in 1955 with the understanding that Big Jim would work for the repeal of Alabama's right-to-work law. After the 1955 legislative session, the labor leaders realized that Folsom would not back the repeal legislation vigorously and risk a fight with Speaker Rankin Fite. Angry that Folsom had forgotten his promise, Wells and Barnett publicly opposed the Goodwyn tax bill after the governor had announced his administration's support for it. Instead of seeking a rapprochement with the labor leaders, Folsom told the rest of his cabinet, "When the horses want to run away, just unhitch the traces and let them go. Then they won't wreck the buggy!"[32]

A major defection from Folsom's ranks occurred in March 1956, when George Wallace declared his political independence from Big Jim. The ambitious circuit judge had been Folsom's southern Alabama campaign director in 1954 and had provided invaluable assistance during the legislative sessions of 1955. Intent on occupying the governor's office himself, Wallace perceived that Folsom's problems might become a political liability for him in the future. He began complaining in 1955 that Folsom had lied when he promised to support the abolition of liquor agents in Alabama, the repeal of the right-to-work law, and the enactment of a comprehensive state purchasing law. Patronage disputes aggravated Wallace's dissatisfaction in early 1956 when Folsom appointed the nominee of the Barbour County legislative delegation to a local office instead of following Wallace's recommendation. Wallace decided to break with Folsom while attending the Young Democrats Convention in Oklahoma City during February 1956. At the convention, Folsom controlled the Alabama delegation and was sponsoring Senator Neil Metcalf as a candidate for president of the organization. In the interest of Metcalf's candidacy, Folsom wanted the Alabama delegation to take a noncontroversial position on the segregation issue. Wallace, however, wanted to speak against any resolution that criticized segregation. Fearing that he could not control Wallace, Folsom arranged to deny Wallace a delegate seat after the Alabama delegation arrived in Oklahoma City. Wallace returned home early determined to break with Folsom. When the Alabama Legislature met for its second special session of 1956, Wallace stationed himself in the lobby of a downtown Montgomery hotel and told every politician and journalist who walked through that he was finished with Folsom. He could no longer support a governor, Wallace explained, who had always been "soft on the nigger question."[33]

George Hawkins drifted from his allegiance to Folsom for essentially the same reason that Wallace did: he aspired to sit in the governor's chair. Although Hawkins accepted the post of administration floor leader, he was disappointed that Folsom had not chosen him to be Speaker of the house. By early 1956, Hawkins realized that Folsom's problems might jeopardize his own political future and sought to establish an independent political record. During the first special session of 1956, Hawkins ignored Folsom's wishes and sponsored a comprehensive state purchasing bill. The legislature did not enact Hawkins's bill in 1956, but he reintroduced it during the 1957 biennial session. Similar to a bill written by an anti-Folsom senator, Hawkins's proposal required competitive bids for any state purchase of more than five hundred dollars. With substitute bills, amendments, and filibusters, the Folsom administration fought the purchasing bill and attempted to preserve the finance director's ability to reward political friends with state contracts. The legislature passed a purchasing bill anyway. The whole process angered Folsom: "None of this mess on the purchasing bill would be up now except for George Hawkins' political aspirations." Hawkins retained the title of administration floor leader, but Representatives Joe Dawkins and Bryce Davis became the administration's spokesmen on the house floor.[34]

The rift between Folsom and Hawkins exposed a second symptom of the administration's political decline. Unable to rely on the administration floor leader, members of the house did not know which of their colleagues was actually Folsom's spokesman. When Hawkins first defected, Joe Dawkins of Montgomery, the vice-chairman of the Ways and Means Committee, assumed the task of directing legislative maneuvers for the administration. Because of his long friendship with Folsom, Bryce Davis also assumed some of the tasks of the administration floor leader. J. H. Kelly, chairman of the Public Welfare Committee, and W. E. Oden, chairman of the Business and Labor Committee, both believed that Folsom had confidence in them and attempted to speak for the governor. Throughout 1956 and 1957, legislative leadership changed regularly as various men rose or fell in Folsom's estimation. Eventually, very few of the legislators followed the leadership of anyone claiming to be Folsom's spokesman.

The same kind of confusion developed in the Alabama senate. President pro tem Broughton Lamberth never abandoned the Folsom administration, but he was not an aggressive floor leader. Other senators eagerly attempted to take advantage of the apparent leadership vacuum. Neil Metcalf occasionally attended cabinet meetings, heard Folsom and his aides discuss policy questions, and carried instructions back to the senate. Kyser Leonard of Talladega occupied the chair of the powerful Rules Committee, a position of such great influence that Folsom frequently bypassed Lamberth to communicate directly with Leonard. Richmond Flowers of Dothan, another young politician with aspirations of political advancement, asserted himself as the senator who best knew what the governor wanted to do. Since some of the senators colored Folsom's instructions with their own interpretations, no one knew for certain which administration senator, if any, actually spoke for the governor. Because of his alcoholism and his unwillingness to discipline anyone loyal to his leadership, Folsom was incapable of maintaining discipline among the pro-Folsom senators.[35]

The confusion in the legislature was part of a more general chaos that gripped the second Folsom administration. Many friends, political allies, and department heads vied with one another to become the governor's closest associates. The promise of monetary or political reward drew crowds of ambitious men because Folsom had repeatedly demonstrated his generosity with patronage. Some supporters wanted to be close to Folsom because the proximity to a celebrity and his power was exhilarating. Members of the administration took pride in the ability to assert that they exercised influence over the governor's decisions. Because he supervised the office during Folsom's absence, Ralph Hammond felt that he was often Alabama's acting governor. The finance director, Fuller Kimbrell, believed that he enjoyed the same status because he controlled state purchasing procedures. Kimbrell also developed the ability to anticipate events, a talent that allowed him to give the governor immediate solutions to most problems as soon as they became important. Senator Richmond Flowers also aspired to be known as Folsom's primary adviser. During 1955, the editor of the *Dothan Eagle,* Horace Hall, nicknamed the senator "Little Sir Echo" because of his unswerving loyalty to the administration. Flowers responded in a way that revealed his ambition for recognition: "Horace just doesn't know the score. If he did, he'd have called me 'Assistant Governor.' "[36]

The struggle for primacy among the Folsomites alarmed Alabamians who knew of the governor's problem with alcohol. Widely circulating rumors described frequent drinking bouts at the governor's mansion. According to the stories, Folsom's "friends" got him drunk and then persuaded him to give them state contracts, political appointments, or exceptional grants of authority. Allegedly, Folsom drank most frequently with the officers of the Alabama General Insurance Company, Bill Drinkard, and Dr. Louis Friedman. Occasionally, Folsom's executive decisions appeared to have been altered as a result of his drinking. On one occasion, the governor promised to appoint a Birmingham attorney to a local public office and asked the lawyer to pick up his commission in the governor's office. During a drinking bout on the night before the commission was ready, "friends" changed Folsom's mind about the appointment and informed the press that another man had been appointed. The Birmingham attorney was already en route to the capitol before he heard the name of the appointee on a radio newscast.[37]

Most reports of Folsom's associates' manipulating him with liquor attributed the drinking to the quest for money or political influence. In one instance, Folsom's drinking may have been responsible for the execution of a Negro prison inmate. In spite of inconclusive evidence, the black man had been convicted of assaulting and raping a white woman and had been sentenced to die in Alabama's electric chair. Whites suspected the same man in the rapes of six or seven other white women, including a relative of one of Folsom's cabinet members. Everyone knew that Folsom had a long record of commuting death sentences to terms of life imprisonment whenever an inmate's conviction seemed the least bit irregular. Folsom himself had stated, "My policy has always been to try and find an excuse to turn somebody loose. I always look for an excuse to reprieve a man." To prevent Folsom from commuting the death sentence of the alleged rapist, the cabinet member whose relative had been a victim conspired with other Folsom aides to take Folsom "fishing." For three or four days, the governor's men kept him drunk and prevented him from hearing any news. By the time Folsom returned to sobriety, the execution had been accomplished.[38]

In the growing confusion of his administration, Jim Folsom's weaknesses exaggerated his eccentricities and alienated Alabama voters. He strained his relations with the legislature by regularly missing scheduled appointments in his office. During the summer of 1955, Folsom played tennis on the People's Court one morning instead of showing up for an appointment with the Montgomery County legislative delegation. Later in the administration, Folsom asked a northern Alabama legislator to come to the capitol for a meeting. The legislator rushed to Montgomery and appeared at the capitol for the meeting only to learn that Folsom had forgotten what they were supposed to discuss. A senator from northeastern Alabama traveled to Montgomery twice for meetings that the governor had requested. In both instances, the governor's secretary apologized profusely and explained that Folsom had "gone fishing." Thereafter, the senator insisted that if Folsom wanted to have a meeting, he would have to drive to the senator's hometown. Folsom made the same mistakes in his relations with the press. Repeatedly his office summoned reporters with the announcement that the governor was preparing to make a statement. The reporters would hurry to the capitol in time to hear that Folsom's statement would be late. Sometimes the minutes turned into hours before a secretary announced that Folsom had left the office or before Folsom emerged to say that he had no statement to make. After witnessing Folsom's irresponsibility, the executive secretary, O. H. Finney, believed that Folsom's irresponsibility would cause him to dissipate all of his financial resources before his sons were ready to attend college. To protect the boys' future, Finney purchased insurance policies that guaranteed money for their educations.[39]

Such carelessness proved to be embarrassing for Folsom's closest friends and associates. The governor rarely carried cash with him to pay the incidental expenses of traveling. During one trip to Hot Springs, Arkansas, Folsom needed cash immediately and no one in his party had enough money to fulfill the need. So, Folsom secured a counter check from a hotel clerk, crossed out the name of the local bank, and wrote the check on the funds of the "State of Alabama." On a trip to New York, Folsom and his party stopped at a small bar in a railroad station. Everyone in the group assumed that the governor would pay for the drinks, but Folsom surprised them by handing the bill to Rowan Bone, a judge on the Alabama Court of Appeals. Totally unprepared, Bone did not have enough cash to cover the bill. Only the generosity of the bar's owner saved Bone and the governor from embarrassment. Folsom alienated the residents of one Montgomery neighborhood on mornings when he impulsively decided to go hunting. Before dawn, the governor's limousine would pull up in front of Folsom's hunting companion's home. While his chauffeur, Winston Craig, went to knock on the door, Folsom would sit in the car honking the horn and hollering, "Hey, Bubba! Get your ass out of bed! We're going hunting!"[40]

Jim Folsom led the Alabama Legislature to compile an outstanding record of accomplishment in 1955, but his attitudes toward racial relations, his self-indulgence, his excessive loyalty to supporters, his tolerance for abuses of power, and his alcoholism eroded his political base over the next three years. At the time, it was difficult to assess exactly how much damage Folsom had done to his political base. The newspapers criticized him incessantly, but they had done that even when he was the most popular gubernatorial candidate in Alabama. The Democratic primary elections of 1958 provided an accurate gauge of the extent to which Folsom's opinions concerning civil rights and his personal weakness had affected his appeal to Alabama voters.

The professional politicians in 1958 gave the first indication of how Folsom's behavior had affected his popularity. As the gubernatorial campaign began, his department heads scattered into the camps of almost every viable candidate. Folsom did not endorse a candidate, but he favored the election of Jimmy Faulkner. Bill Drinkard, O. H. Finney, and Pitt Tyson Maner made their support for Faulkner public. George Wallace, a Folsom campaign leader in 1954, had the backing of LaRue Horn, the revenue commissioner, and Frank Boswell, the former prison director. Representative George Hawkins was a candidate in 1958 and had the endorsement of Jimmy Jones, Folsom's director of the Selective Service in Alabama. Commissioner of Agriculture A. W. Todd was also running for governor and received the endorsement of Ralph Hammond. Among the major gubernatorial candidates only John Patterson did not have the support of at least one prominent Folsomite. Not only did this demonstrate the absence of solidarity within the second Folsom administration, but it also suggested that few of Folsom's men wanted to be identified with the governor during an election year.[41]

In spite of his political unpopularity, Big Jim Folsom influenced the way candidates conducted their campaigns in 1958. Like Folsom, the leading candidates took their musical groups and their campaign programs to the folks at the "brush arbors and the forks of the creeks." Each campaign program promised the same types of progressive state service that Folsom had promised. Jimmy Faulkner pledged to realize Folsom's goal of old-age pensions of fifty dollars per month. A. W. Todd promised pensions of sixty dollars, only to be outbid by John Patterson's pension pledge of seventy-five dollars. In a sardonic observation, Grover Hall wrote, "It's a safe bet nowadays that if you hear a hillbilly band or a gospel quartet, a candidate for governor is bound to pop up with a promise of $100 per month for the old folks." Although the candidates adopted Folsom's most appealing promises, they emphasized that they had no ties with the incumbent governor. It was for this reason that George Wallace broke with Folsom in 1956. George Hawkins repeatedly reminded voters that he had proposed a competitive bid law in 1956 and promised that there would be no political "hacks" in his administration. Candidate John Patterson enjoyed a great advantage. Not only did his father's death identify him as an enemy of corruption in government, but as attorney general he had diligently investigated graft in the Folsom administration.[42]

As they nominated Democratic candidates on 6 May and 3 June 1958, Alabama voters registered their opinion of Jim Folsom. In the first primary, John Patterson won a plurality and George Wallace placed second. Both men had campaigned on their opposition to the integration of public schools and their independence from Jim Folsom, and both continued to denounce Folsom vigorously during the run-off campaign. Because both Patterson and Wallace held essentially the same position with regard to racial issues, Patterson's opposition to Folsom since 1954 helped give him the decisive edge over Wallace when the voters returned to the polls on 3 June. The repudiation of Folsom was even more obvious in legislative races. The Speaker of the house, Rankin Fite, lost his seat to a political novice in Marion County. Representative Joe Dawkins of Montgomery not only lost his seat in 1958, but he also lost every other political race he ever entered. In spite of many public works that Folsom gave to Dothan on their behalf, Senator Richmond Flowers and Representative Bob Stembridge began compulsory, though temporary, political retirements. All over the state, incumbent legislators who had remained loyal to the Folsom administration suffered defeats.[43]

At the end of his first administration, the paternity suit and the Pardon and Parole Board scandal had made him unpopular with Alabama voters. Folsom had regained his popularity during the Persons administration, when legislative investigations failed to link him with specific incidents of corruption. When Jim Folsom ended his second gubernatorial administration, his racial views and his personal weaknesses dominated all accounts of his public service. These circumstances, over which Folsom had exercised no control, overwhelmed the significant record of legislative leadership he had compiled in 1955. As he had at Persons's inauguration, Governor Folsom gracefully surrendered his power to John Patterson on 19 January 1959. Leaving Montgomery after the inauguration, Folsom was already thinking about another gubernatorial campaign with confidence that his popularity would rebound as he retired to Cullman.[44]

12

"The Little Man's Big Friend"

When Jim Folsom finished his second term as governor, he talked like a man who was ready to retire. He told his cabinet not to expect him to seek reelection in 1962. He had already won the highest office in the state twice, Folsom explained, and had won legislative approval for most of his original campaign program. The frustrations of the last years had discouraged Folsom, especially the civil rights movement and the dissension and graft within his own administration. Even though he was only fifty years old and too young to consider full retirement, Folsom doubted that he would want to be governor enough in 1962 to conduct a successful reelection campaign.[1]

If Governor Folsom spoke sincerely of retirement in 1958, he changed his mind before 1962. He entered the gubernatorial race seeking an unprecedented third term as governor of Alabama. Competing with a younger generation of Alabama politicians, Folsom was the old politician whose administrations had produced legends of corruption and political favoritism. He was the professional politician against whom the younger candidates campaigned. Worst of all, Folsom was the former governor who urged compromise on the racial issues on which southern whites refused to compromise. By the end of the 1962 gubernatorial campaign, the new generation, with Folsom's inadvertent assistance, succeeded in discrediting Jim Folsom and forcing him into permanent political retirement.

Jim Folsom did not seek reelection in 1962 for financial reasons. Despite pro-Folsom myths that spread after his second term, Big

Jim was not a poor man when he left office in 1959. During his second administration, he had invested wisely in the stock of an airline, an electric utility, a textile mill, a heavy machinery manufacturer, a Montgomery bank, and at least three insurance companies. Folsom's business enterprises included a brand of poultry feed that bore his name, the Winfield Moon Hauling Company, and his own insurance agency in Cullman. Folsom's two largest investments, Emergency Aid Insurance Company and the Workall Battery Company, continued to earn profits for the former governor.

These investments and businesses could have provided a comfortable life for Folsom and his family. Properly managed, they might have afforded the Folsoms a luxurious standard of living. His interest in the Peoples Bank and Trust Company of Montgomery, one of his smaller investments, was worth $10,500 when he sold the stock in 1959. During 1959, Emergency Aid Insurance Company merged with National Selective Life Insurance Company, a firm headquartered in Montgomery. When Folsom's share of Emergency Aid was converted into the stocks of National Selective Life, his investment was valued at almost $185,000. Folsom's interest in the Workall Battery Company was his largest asset. At the time he sold his portion of the business in the early 1970s, his investment was worth approximately $400,000.[2]

Folsom's wealth in 1959 also included some scattered real estate. He owned a farm in Marshall County near Guntersville and had inherited a portion of his family's farm in Coffee County. The Folsom homestead in Cullman was a two-story white frame house located on a large town lot. When he left the governor's mansion, the former governor's friends paid to remodel and refurbish his Cullman home. Folsom's political appointees and businessmen who had profited from state contracts pledged to make "monthly contributions" for the work on the house. The contributions ranged in size from $25 to $100, and some contributors sent single gifts of up to $1,000. The chance that Big Jim might return to the governor's office motivated friends to be generous, but Ed Pepper presented his gift with a nobler rationalization: "Public service is not a very rewarding endeavor. You have spent eight years as Governor. I know that you have been deprived of eight of your most productive business years. Please let me make a small one hundred dollar contribution to you and your wonderful family to help you get re-established in private life."[3]

Despite Folsom's financial well-being, the conduct of the Patterson administration made him tire of retirement. Three new ship berths at the Alabama State Docks remained uncompleted because they had been planned by Folsom's administration. The Patterson administration diverted money raised for inland docks construction to other projects. Folsom believed that Alabama's criminal laws and its penal system needed thorough reform, but Patterson placed priority on the construction of a $10 million penitentiary. When Patterson's popularity sagged, one Folsomite explained, Governor "Jittery John" returned to the issue that launched his political career. He claimed that gangsters were trying to regain power in Phenix City and that his own life was in constant danger. Seemingly impressed by the threat, Patterson built fences and posted armed guards at the governor's mansion while making himself less accessible to members of the legislature. Patterson's behavior even moved Walter Givhan, a Black Belt legislator who had always opposed Governor Folsom, to remember the Folsom years favorably. "Your office was always kind enough to let me in to see you," Givhan wrote. Most disturbing to Folsom were reports that his programs had "come to a screeching halt" under the direction of Governor Patterson.[4]

At the same time the Patterson administration upset Folsom, friendly messages of support encouraged him to enter the 1962 gubernatorial campaign. An elderly woman in Munford wrote Folsom to thank him for her old-age pension and to wish "that some day Alabama will be able to meet the needs of everyone." A Negro post office employee wrote his first letter to a political leader to congratulate Folsom for being "one of the few Governors of Alabama who has demonstrated the ability to serve all the people in the true sense of democracy." An Alabama State Docks employee promised to support Folsom in 1962 because "you are the only governor that has ever done anything for little folks like me." The owner of a crossroads store near Abbeville explained his loyalty to the former governor when a visitor wanted to talk about politics. The merchant was emphatic: "Mister, let me tell you something. Jim Folsom is the only candidate that ever came by our store and sat in that old chair and reached in that sack and took a handful of peanuts and talked to us as if he belonged here and was one of us. I want you to know we will vote for him every time he runs." Friends in every section of the state relayed similar stories of loyalty to the former governor.[5]

During the summer of 1961, Folsom began identifying himself as a candidate for reelection. In a Labor Day speech at Talladega, Big Jim announced that the political campaign had already started. He knew the campaign had begun, Folsom said, because "the political smear artists already have started lying about what old Jim has said, and sometimes what he didn't say." Folsom cautioned the voters about the political rumors they would hear: "I want to ask you not to believe anything they say I said, and only half of what I tell you myself. After all, it is an election year and I've got to do a heap of promising."[6]

As his Labor Day speech suggested, Folsom's campaign style remained fundamentally similar to his earliest campaigns. Big Jim still attempted to project himself as an ordinary fellow with ordinary language and vivid imagery taken from daily experience. He continued to rely on the criticisms of the daily newspapers and his political opponents. With such opposition, it was easier for Folsom to campaign as the champion of the underdog and the common man who lacked influence among the powerful. Even as he called himself "old Jim" and admitted that he would overpromise during the upcoming campaign, Folsom still promoted himself as "the little man's big friend."

Folsom's campaign program and campaign organization also bore striking resemblances to those of his earlier campaigns. Where he had previously advocated appropriations for education, Folsom now supported state-furnished textbooks for all public school students and a raise of $15 per month for all teachers. Still promising to build paved roads, Folsom urged the construction of four-lane highways between county seats. Claiming that his second administration brought more than $700 million worth of new industry to Alabama, Folsom called for more industrial development, more inland docks, and the construction of the Tennessee-Tombigbee Waterway. Instead of Governor Patterson's new penitentiary, Folsom recommended that Alabama abolish the fee system for paying local law enforcers, modernize its criminal code, and expand its parole system. Legislative reapportionment and constitutional revision appeared in the fine print of the Folsom program even though the candidate rarely mentioned them in his speeches.

Familiar faces appeared in the leading positions of Folsom's 1962 campaign organization. Herman Nelson, the former Highway Department director, held the title of campaign chairman and supervised Folsom's campaign from Huntsville. Bill Drinkard served for the fourth time as the coordinator of Folsom's campaign tour. Ralph

Hammond and Myra Leak Porter worked in the Cullman campaign headquarters. Dr. Louis Friedman, Johnny Stiefelmeyer, Jerry Gwin, and the "Meat Grinders" accompanied Folsom on his speaking tour through the state.

In all previous campaigns, Jim Folsom had rarely commented on controversial racial issues. Big Jim spoke regularly and ambiguously to racial concerns during 1962. Throughout the campaign, Folsom declared his opposition to the racial desegregation of public schools and boasted that there had been no desegregation during his second administration. On the day Folsom campaigned in Talladega, two hundred Negro students from Talladega College marched to the county courthouse where Folsom was scheduled to speak. Folsom delayed his appearance long enough for local authorities to disperse the demonstration and send the placard-carrying students back to their campus. In a reference to the Freedom Riders, the civil rights workers who rode desegregated interstate buses through southern states, Folsom criticized Alabama officials in language that sounded segregationist to his Anniston audience. "Those responsible for law and order knew that the Freedom Riders were coming through and they didn't do nothing. . . . I would have put fifty of the biggest, blackest, country bucks I could find in the jail cells with them and the next morning those integrators would have come out saying 'Lord! Give us segregation!'" In Alexander City, Folsom reminded whites that they had learned valuable lessons from Negroes: the Black Bottom, the Charleston, and the Twist.[7]

These statements notwithstanding, Big Jim also promised to defend the civil rights of all Alabama citizens. Folsom courageously urged voters, "I tell you folks, the Civil War is over. We got to join together." When Folsom promised to promote "law and order," he was promising to abide by the decisions of the federal courts. To his 1954 campaign slogan "Y'all come!" Folsom added an appeal for "Peace in the valley." Taken together, the two expressions communicated Folsom's hopes for racial relations. He looked forward to the time when Alabamians would resolve all the differences that divided them and make "Peace in the valley" a reality. At that time, he believed, everyone would greet his neighbor with a friendly, sincere "Y'all come!" Folsom's appeal for "Peace in the valley" won him the respect of politically liberal Alabamians. Neil Davis wrote in the Lee County *Bulletin*, "Some will call this good politics, others will say it proves Big Jim is soft on integration and will lose him votes. Regardless of these considerations, what Folsom says makes sense. This paper is glad he is saying it." A frustrated Pike County voter shared Davis's admiration for Folsom's position and wrote to the *Alabama Journal,* "I don't like Jim Folsom and the people he has around him. But somehow, when I examine the statements of all the candidates on taxation, welfare measures, and civil rights, I always wind up in Folsom's corner."[8]

Folsom's ambiguity concerning racial relations suggested that he himself remained ambivalent. In his ambivalence, the campaigns of other gubernatorial candidates in 1962 may have influenced him to adopt rhetoric that was more racist than any he had ever used before. Folsom faced a strong field of opponents that included the circuit court judge George C. Wallace, the legislator Ryan de-Graffenried, Attorney General MacDonald Gallion, and Senator Albert Boutwell. Both Wallace and Gallion conducted aggressive campaigns on the issue of desegregation. Supported by the incumbent governor, Gallion's workers published racist attacks on Folsom. One Gallion advertisement reminded voters of the infamous meeting between Folsom and Adam Clayton Powell: "He said . . . Y'all come, but who came? . . . Adam Clayton Powell (Negro Congressman from New York)." Several unsigned anti-Folsom advertisements were also circulated by Gallion's campaign. One showed caricatures of Congressman Powell and Dr. Martin Luther King, Jr. Powell was asking King if he had ever had cocktails at the mansion with Big Jim. Dr. King was replying that he had never visited the mansion, but he could have had cocktails with "our good integratin' frien' Big Jim" any time he chose. In the face of such rabid racism, the ambivalence of Folsom may have led him to inject racism into his campaign talks with the idea of defending himself.[9]

Accompanied by the music of the Meat Grinders and supported by contributions to his "Hamsack," Jim Folsom campaigned for his third Democratic gubernatorial nomination. At times during the campaign, Folsom seemed cavalier about the outcome of the election. He told an audience in Decatur, "I'm not worried about what I'm going to do if elected. I'm worried about what I'm going to do if I'm not elected." Folsom's confidence seemed to be justified, however, because journalists in Alabama were calling him the frontrunner in the campaign. Big Jim was the candidate to beat during March and April, although Wallace's campaign steadily increased his chances of catching up with the former governor. On the eve of the Democratic primary, Bob Ingram, a reporter for the *Montgomery Advertiser,* predicted that Folsom would lead in the Democratic primary and would compete against Wallace in the run-off election. Ingram's forecast, however, could not have anticipated the disaster which befell the Folsom campaign.[10]

Big Jim planned to conclude his reelection campaign with a statewide television broadcast on the evening before the Democratic primary. He recorded the final campaign talk several days before the primary. For some reason, the videotape could not be broadcast at the scheduled time, and at the last minute Folsom and his family had to assemble at a television studio in order to broadcast the show live. Alabamians who tuned in Folsom's program witnessed a shocking sight. The former governor was obviously unable to control himself. When he began to introduce his family to the television audience, Folsom could not remember the names of his sons. During his campaign talk, most of which he mumbled, Folsom described his opponents as "Me, too!" candidates. The phrase appeared to catch his fancy and Folsom launched into a singsong chant of "Me, too, me, too, meee, toooo!" that continued for several moments. Viewers could not be certain whether Folsom was drunk or sedated, but it was obvious that he was one or the other.

Alabama voters reacted dramatically to Folsom's performance. In spite of predictions that he would lead the field, Jim Folsom finished third in the Democratic primary. George Wallace won a large plurality, and Ryan deGraffenried qualified to compete against Wallace in the run-off election. Folsom's strength all over the state had wilted instantaneously, and he trailed deGraffenried by approximately 1,100 votes. If Bob Ingram's forecast was accurate before the television broadcast, Folsom's mistake had knocked him out of contention and cleared the way for the election of George C. Wallace as Alabama's governor.

In the aftermath of Folsom's disaster, Alabamians wondered what caused the catastrophe. Supporters of George Wallace and the other candidates drew the obvious conclusions: on the night of the broadcast, Folsom was drunk, just as he had been drunk during most of his second administration. While Alabamians cast their ballots in the 1962 Democratic primary, campaign workers for Folsom's opponents asked voters all over the state, "Did you see Governor Folsom drunk on TV last night?"

Each of Folsom's supporters remembered the last day of the 1962 campaign differently. According to one version, Folsom had finished all of his campaign talks, assumed that the videotape was ready for broadcast, and began drinking. During the late afternoon, someone discovered that the videotape was missing from the television station from which the broadcast was to originate. Folsom was in no condition to do a live broadcast, but campaign aides decided that he had to do the show. In an effort to counteract the effects of the alcohol, Dr. Louis Friedman gave Folsom a sedative. The drug interacted with the alcohol to produce Folsom's disastrous appearance on television.

Another version of the affair explains that on the day of the broadcast, there was a wildcat strike of television technicians at the station from which the broadcast was to originate. Instead of crossing a picket line, Folsom decided to go to a station in another city and do a live broadcast. Upset by the confusion, however, the former governor demanded a drink. While driving Folsom to the new station Johnny Stiefelmeyer and Jerry Gwin could not resist Folsom's demands and allowed him to have a drink. After he began drinking, neither man could stop him. When they arrived at the television studio, Folsom's aides did not believe that Folsom's drinking had affected his appearance and allowed him to do the show. In making this decision, Folsom's aides did not realize that the television would distort Folsom's appearance and magnify the mistakes he made while speaking.

Members of Folsom's family and his closest friends insisted that Folsom had fallen victim to political sabotage. According to this version, Folsom aides who had sold out to George Wallace intentionally misplaced the videotape.[11] As Folsom prepared to do the live broadcast, the same aides stood guard while Dr. Friedman injected a large dose of a sedative. When Folsom's daughter Melissa arrived at the studio, the men would not let her see her father before he went on camera for the final campaign talk. While the broadcast was in progress, Dr. Friedman fled the studio and left town. Highway patrol officers had to apprehend him several hours later and force him to tell doctors attending Folsom what sedative he had used. After the Wallace administration took office, the men who had cooperated in the scheme received lucrative shares of the new governor's patronage.[12]

The truth of what happened on the day before the 1962 Democratic primary was never established, but the effect was unmistakable. After the television broadcast, James E. Folsom never came close to winning election to another office. He ran for a seat on the Public Service Commission in 1964 and won only one-fifth of the ballots cast. His name appeared on the ballot in 1966, 1970, 1974, and 1978 as a gubernatorial candidate, but he was not a serious contender in any of those races. The television show convinced Alabamians that Jim Folsom was not fit to serve as their governor again. At age fifty-three, Big Jim Folsom was forced into political retirement.

The succeeding years were not kind to Folsom. In a series of unsound business ventures, he exhausted most of his financial assets and alienated many of his old friends. By the 1970s, he had become a pathetic, lonely man who lobbied the Alabama legislature to enact a pension for him. He finally conquered his appetite for alcohol during the mid-1970s, but not before it contributed to his loss of vision and his failing health. Visitors to Folsom's home during the late 1970s listened to him ramble incoherently about the doctrine of the constitutional separation of powers and about the evils of the legal profession. After 1962, it seemed, the best part of Governor Folsom's life was the past.

A visitor to Alabama would search in vain for a monument celebrating the gubernatorial administrations of James E. Folsom. There is no James E. Folsom State Park, no James E. Folsom Community College and Technical School, no James E. Folsom Memorial Expressway, or even a James E. Folsom Prison. There is a Folsom bridge on a rural road in Coffee County, but it honors J. M. Folsom, the governor's father. In a state that proudly honors its heroes, warriors, and politicians, the absence of a James E. Folsom memorial suggests the embarrassment that many Alabamians feel toward a governor who was involved in a paternity suit, whose administrations were plagued with stories of rampant graft, who ended his political career in a drunken (or drugged) appearance on a statewide television broadcast, and who became a perennial candidate for office long after voters had lost confidence in him. To prevent the former governor from becoming a panhandler at the capitol, the Alabama Legislature voted him a pension and put one of his sons on the state payroll as his chauffeur.

The journalists and historians who have assessed the significance of Folsom's public life have depicted him as a disappointing hero.[13] He was an unpretentious champion of democracy with an instinctive understanding of the common man's interests; he directly challenged powerful political interests with appeals for substantive political reforms; he led the State of Alabama to implement an extensive array of public works. Most important, he was a post–World War II southern governor who was personally committed to defending the civil rights of Negroes even when this commitment alienated Alabama voters. However, Big Jim's loyalty to untrustworthy associates and his dependence on alcohol destroyed the integrity of his gubernatorial administrations and helped bring his public career to a premature end. And though he spoke of political reform and civil rights with conviction, the State of Alabama refused to reapportion the legislature, repeal the poll tax, or grant civil rights to Negroes for as long as the U.S. Constitution and the federal courts would allow. James E. Folsom had the potential to lead Alabamians to deal constructively with the pressing issues of the late 1940s and 1950s, but he never realized that potential.

Without ignoring any of Jim Folsom's political blunders, it is necessary to recognize that institutional factors were largely responsible for his failure to obtain basic political reform. Folsom promised legislative reapportionment and constitutional revision in every state election campaign of his career. Without considering the justice or prudence of Folsom's recommendations, Black Belt legislators knew that the proposed reforms would reduce their influence within the state government and increase state taxes on large landholdings. Legislators from small rural counties feared that reform would reduce the share of state funding they received for public works and services. Representatives of Alabama's industrial corporations saw Folsom's reforms as threats to their favored tax status and their management of employees. Between them, men who represented these interests held a majority of seats in the Alabama Legislature. Even the most skilled leader would have found it difficult to get the legislature to consider the sweeping reforms Folsom advocated.

The same was true on all issues relating to racial relations. Although he did not see any injustice in segregation, Governor Folsom's faith in democracy led him to believe that Negro citizens were entitled to suffrage, justice, and equal educational and economic opportunities. Most white Alabamians, however, believed that Negroes were inherently inferior to Caucasians and that racial segregation was fundamental to the survival of civilized society. Without segregation, they feared, there would be no way to prevent racial intermarriage or to curb the naturally uninhibited conduct of blacks. Even if he had been cold sober for eight years and the conduct of every member of his administration had been beyond reproach, Jim Folsom could not have altered the racial prejudices of Alabamians. He could not have stopped the Alabama Legislature from enacting segregationist legislation during his second administration, nor could he have escaped electoral defeat in the 1956 Democratic primary. In Alabama during the time of Folsom's public career, there was simply no tolerance for compromise on issues involving race.

Within these parameters—the interests of powerful groups and the racism of white Alabamians—Governor Folsom still left concrete evidence of his legislative leadership all over Alabama. In Marion County, all roads leading to the county seat are lighted, four-lane highways; all school buildings constructed during the late 1940s and 1950s were built solely with state, not local, funds; and the town of Hamilton is served by an airport with a runway long enough to accommodate commercial jets. Dothan was one of the first American cities to have a four-lane highway around its perimeter, the J. Ross Clark Circle. State Highway 69 originates at Guntersville, in the hills of Marshall County, and ends in Jackson, in the pine forests of Clarke County. But instead of following a direct line from northeast to southwest, the highway winds through Cullman, Jasper, Fayette, Tuscaloosa, and Grove Hill. Motorists on Interstate Highway 59 find that the primary exit ramp in Tuscaloosa intersects McFarland Boulevard less than one block from McFarland Mall. These and agricultural coliseums, National Guard armories, public school buildings, and secondary roads and state highways scattered across the state are the monuments Folsom left after two gubernatorial administrations.

The roads, schools, and other public works not only tell what Folsom accomplished, but they also reveal how he exercised leadership. When the legislators were alarmed by Governor Folsom's performance in early 1947, public education had broad support in all Alabama communities, and the legislature enthusiastically enacted salaries of $1,800 for public school teachers. While the Economy Bloc threatened to restrict his prerogatives with their "economy bills" in 1949, Folsom found friends among the leaders of the League of Municipalities and the Association of County Commissioners. Folsom's most successful year of legislative leadership began with a special session that enacted a $50 million road construction bond issue. Using local road construction projects as patronage, the Folsom administration won legislative approval for proposals concerning old-age pensions, the Alabama State Docks, industrial expansion, and education. During both of his terms in office, Governor Folsom led the legislature most effectively when his administration allied itself with the concerns and interests of community leaders throughout Alabama.

Ironically, even though Jim Folsom relied on the influence of Alabama's community leaders, he participated in the sweeping social and cultural changes that were breaking down the isolation of Alabama's island communities. Paved farm-to-market roads not only helped rural residents to move farm products to the towns, but they also offered access to the factories, schools, shopping centers, and entertainments of the towns and cities. Rural electrification brought laborsaving appliances to every farmhouse and gave rural people a chance to approximate the lifestyle of suburbanites in every section of the nation. Alabamians who learned the job skills that industry demanded were earning wages in paper mills, chemical plants, and other new industries that matched the pay of workers anywhere. Under the direction of President Ralph Draughon, Alabama Polytechnic Institute was growing from a school that sent farmers and veterinarians back to farms in rural Alabama to a university that prepared young Alabamians for careers in multinational corporations. The expanding welfare state was taking the responsibility of caring for the poor, the disabled, and the elderly away from local charities and giving it to distant bureaucrats. Most dramatically, the civil rights movement was seeking to apply national definitions of justice and equality to the personal relations between blacks and whites. In every area of change, Jim Folsom's actions, proposals, and attitudes belonged more to the emerging mass society than to the isolated, locally oriented world that was disappearing.

It was on the campaign trail that Big Jim contributed most directly to the forces of change. Before Folsom, candidates for state office planned their campaigns around the efforts of local campaign committees. Since political factionalism was strong in most Alabama counties, the candidate's hopes for winning majority support in a particular county hinged on whether or not members of the courthouse ring belonged to his local committee. When Jim Folsom entered state politics, he did not have a network of county committees. Instead, he had an engaging personality, a talent for communication, a hillbilly band, and an office staff that blanketed the state with campaign circulars. Big Jim went to the "branchheads," to "the brush arbors and the forks of the creeks," delivering campaign talks and convincing voters that he shared their likes, their dislikes, and their interests. As he went, Folsom bypassed county and community leaders in every section of the state. Claiming to be independent of the "professional politicians," he led Alabamians to sever their political ties with traditional leaders and to vote in state elections as individuals. His success in 1946 established a pattern for state election campaigns that Alabama candidates emulated until the late 1970s.

Notes

Chapter 1

1. Robert Wiebe, *The Search for Order, 1877–1920* (New York: Hill and Wang, 1967).

2. Alabama Department of Archives and History, *Alabama Official and Statistical Register, 1903, 1907, 1911, 1915, 1919, 1923, 1931, 1935, 1939, 1943, 1947, 1951, 1955,* and *1959* (hereinafter cited as ADAH, *Alabama Official and Statistical Register*).

3. V. O. Key, Jr., *Southern Politics in State and Nation* (New York: Knopf, 1949), pp. 555–643.

4. Cornelia Wallace, *C'nelia* (New York: Holman, 1976), pp. 160–61; ADAH, *Alabama Official and Statistical Register, 1947,* p. 29.

5. *Elba Clipper,* 22 December 1921; ADAH, *Alabama Official and Statistical Register, 1923;* James E. Folsom, interview with author, Cullman, 10 October 1979.

6. *Elba Clipper,* 1 December 1921, 19 January, 2 February, 13, 27 April 1922, 30 January 1936.

7. Wallace, *C'nelia,* p. 163; *Birmingham Post,* 17 January 1947.

8. *Birmingham Post,* 17 January 1947; James E. Folsom, 10 October 1979; "Vita," James E. Folsom Papers, Division of Maps and Manuscripts, Alabama Department of Archives and History, Montgomery (hereinafter cited as Folsom Papers).

9. James E. Folsom, 10 October 1979; "Vita," Folsom Papers.

10. James E. Folsom, 10 October 1979.

Chapter 2

1. V. O. Key, Jr., *Southern Politics in State and Nation* (New York: Knopf, 1949), pp. 37–41.

2. Ibid., pp. 41–46.

3. *Birmingham Post,* 16 January 1947; Carl Grafton, "James E. Folsom's First Four Election Campaigns: Learning to Win by Losing," *Alabama Review* 34 (July 1979):164–66.

4. Carl Grafton, "James E. Folsom and Civil Liberties in Alabama," *Alabama Review* 32 (January 1979):10; Grafton, "Election Campaigns," pp. 168–69.

5. James E. Folsom, interview with author, Cullman, 10 October 1979; S. Fleetwood Carnley, interview with author, Elba, 2 October 1979.

6. *Birmingham Post,* 17 January 1979; James E. Folsom, 10 October 1979; O. H. Finney, Jr., interview with author, Albertville, 5 September 1979.

7. *Elba Clipper,* 27 January 1936; James E. Folsom, 10 October 1979.

8. *Elba Clipper,* 5 March, 23 April 1936; Grafton, "Election Campaigns," pp. 166–67.

9. *Elba Clipper,* 19, 26 March 1936; Grafton, "Election Campaigns," p. 170.

10. James E. Folsom, 10 October 1979; *Elba Clipper,* 31 December 1936.

11. James E. Folsom, 10 October 1979; S. Fleetwood Carnley, 2 October 1979.

12. James E. Folsom, 10 October 1979; Wallace, *C'nelia,* pp. 123–24.

13. William D. Barnard, "The Old Order Changes: Graves, Sparks, Folsom, and the Gubernatorial Election of 1942," *Alabama Review* 28 (July 1975):163–84.

14. James E. Folsom, 10 October 1979.

15. ADAH, *Alabama Official and Statistical Register, 1943,* pp. 754–55.

16. James E. Folsom, 10 October 1979.

17. ADAH, *Alabama Official and Statistical Review, 1947,* pp. 436–38.

Chapter 3

1. James E. Folsom, interview with author, Cullman, 10 October 1979.

2. *Birmingham News,* 13 January, 3, 5, 8, 9 March 1946; *Huntsville Times,* 13 January, 5, 8, 10 March 1946.

3. *Birmingham News,* 3, 17, 23 March 1946; *Huntsville Times,* 3 May 1946; *Montgomery Advertiser,* 10, 25 March 1946; William D. Barnard, *Dixiecrats and Democrats: Alabama Politics, 1942–1950* (University: University of Alabama Press, 1974), pp. 23–24.

4. *Montgomery Advertiser,* 9 March 1946; Barnard, *Dixiecrats and Democrats,* pp. 25–26; ADAH, *Alabama Official and Statistical Register, 1943,* p. 39.

5. *Montgomery Advertiser,* 9 March 1946.

6. George B. Tindall, *The Emergence of the New South, 1913–1945* (Baton Rouge: Louisiana State University Press, 1967), pp. 224, 232–33.

7. Gordon Persons limited his 1946 campaign to addresses broadcast over statewide radio. He explained his limited activity as a consequence of a heart condition and of the need to give daily attention to the work of the Alabama Public Service Commission.

8. Carl Grafton, "James E. Folsom's 1946 Campaign," *Alabama Review* 35 (July 1981):176, 198.

9. *Birmingham News,* 14 April 1946; *Birmingham Post,* 20 August 1947; William V. Lyerly, interview with author, Montgomery, 23 November 1979.

10. James E. Folsom to Gilbert Stanford, 28 February 1946, Folsom Papers.

11. Neil O. Davis, "The Mystery of Big Jim," *Nation* 163 (31 August 1946):240–41; Barnard, *Dixiecrats and Democrats,* pp. 31–33; Hallie Farmer, *The Legislative Process in Alabama: Legislative Reapportionment,* Alabama Bureau of Public Administration Publications, no. 14 (University: Bureau of Public Administration, 1944), pp. 19, 33–36; *Huntsville Times,* 3 March 1946; *Montgomery Advertiser,* 3 March 1946.

12. Larry Brittain Childs, "Alabama Giant, Recollections of Jim Folsom" (honors thesis, University of Alabama, 1974), pp. 2–4; William Dewey Murray, "The Folsom Campaign of 1946" (master's thesis, University of Alabama, 1949), pp. 46–48; Davis, "Mystery of Big Jim," pp. 240–41; Barnard, *Dixiecrats and Democrats,* pp. 31–33; *Montgomery Advertiser,* 3 March 1946.

13. *Birmingham News,* 17 March 1946; *Huntsville Times,* 3 March 1946; *Montgomery Advertiser,* 3 March 1946.

14. Grafton, "Folsom's 1946 Campaign," pp. 184–88.

15. Charles Morgan, Jr., *A Time to Speak* (New York: Harper and Row, 1964), pp. 29–31; *Huntsville Times,* 17, 31 March 1946; Barnard, *Dixiecrats and Democrats,* pp. 33–35.

16. Murray, "Folsom Campaign," pp. 49–62; *Montgomery Advertiser,* 24 March 1946.

17. Grafton, "Folsom's 1946 Campaign," pp. 189, 192.

18. Ibid., p. 176.

19. Folsom's use of the corn-shuck mop resembled the political campaign of Andrew Jackson, who used a similar mop to illustrate his slogan, "sweep the rascals out." William D. Barnard, "The Old Order Changes: Graves, Sparks, Folsom, and the Gubernatorial Election of 1942," *Alabama Review* 28 (July 1975):176.

20. Barnard, *Dixiecrats and Democrats,* pp. 31–37; Murray, "Folsom Campaign," passim; Morgan, *A Time to Speak.* pp. 29–31; James E. Folsom, 10 October 1979.

21. *Montgomery Advertiser,* 3 March 1979; *Huntsville Times,* 3, 10 March 1946; Barnard, *Dixiecrats and Democrats,* pp. 27–29.

22. *Huntsville Times,* 10, 21, 28 March 1946; *Montgomery Advertiser,* 3, 9, 10, 29 March 1946.

23. Murray, "Folsom Campaign," pp. 64–74; *Birmingham News,* 17

March, 7 April 1946; *Huntsville Times,* 19, 31 March 1946; *Montgomery Advertiser,* 17, 24, 27 March 1946.

24. *Birmingham News,* 31 March, 10, 11 April, 5 May 1946; *Huntsville Times,* 1, 2 April, 5 May 1946; *Montgomery Advertiser,* 23 March, 16 April 1946.

25. *Birmingham News,* 31 March, 17, 26 April 1946; *Huntsville Times,* 5, 26 April 1946; *Montgomery Advertiser,* 31 March 1946.

26. *Montgomery Advertiser,* 10 April through 1 May 1946; Ralph Hammond to James E. Folsom, 24 May 1946, Folsom Papers.

27. *Montgomery Advertiser,* 31 March, 2, 12 April 1946; *Birmingham News,* 31 March 1946; *Huntsville Times,* 6 May 1946.

28. *Montgomery Advertiser,* 15, 28 April, 24 April through 2 May 1946; *Huntsville Times,* 25, 26 April 1946; *Birmingham News,* 21, 28 April 1946.

29. *Huntsville Times,* 7 May 1946; ADAH, *Alabama Official and Statistical Register, 1947,* pp. 481–83.

30. *Gadsden Times,* 9 May 1946; *Montgomery Advertiser,* 9 May 1946; *Birmingham News,* 8, 9, 12 May 1946; *Huntsville Times,* 9 May 1946; *Alabama,* 10 May 1946.

31. *Birmingham News,* 12, 13, 16, 17 May 1946; *Huntsville Times,* 17 May 1946.

32. Barnard, *Dixiecrats and Democrats,* pp. 38–40.

33. *Birmingham News,* 13 May 1946; *Mobile Register,* 2 June 1946; *Montgomery Advertiser,* 28 May 1946; *Birmingham Post,* 10 May 1946; miscellaneous newspaper clippings, Folsom Papers.

34. *Birmingham News,* 13, 16 May 1946; *Montgomery Advertiser,* 16, 17, 18, 21 May 1946; *Huntsville Times,* 20, 30 May 1946; *Anniston Star,* 19 May 1946.

35. *Birmingham News,* 18, 19, 26 May 1946; *Montgomery Advertiser,* 19, 26 May 1946; *Anniston Star,* 26 May 1946; *Huntsville Times,* 23, 29, 31 May 1946; *Birmingham Post,* 31 May 1946.

36. *Birmingham Post,* 28 May 1946.

37. *Anniston Star,* 30 May 1946; *Birmingham News,* 14, 17 May 1946; *Gadsden Times,* 31 May 1946; *Huntsville Times,* 26 May 1946; *Montgomery Advertiser,* 29 May 1946; *New York Times,* 2 June 1946.

38. ADAH, *Alabama Official and Statistical Register, 1947,* pp. 490–91.

39. *Birmingham News,* 5 June 1946; *Montgomery Advertiser,* 9 June 1946; *Huntsville Times,* 5, 7 June 1946; *Anniston Star,* 5 June 1946; *Mobile Register,* 5 June 1946.

Chapter 4

1. *Montgomery Advertiser,* 23 June 1946.
2. *Huntsville Times,* 3 May 1946.
3. The example of Charles Dobbins, editor of the *Montgomery Adver-*

tiser, is instructive in this context. Dobbins actually liked Folsom's program and believed it addressed the most important of Alabama's needs. He withheld his support from Folsom, however, because he felt that Folsom was too inexperienced to be effective. Charles G. Dobbins, "Alabama Governors and Editors, 1930–1955: A Memoir," *Alabama Review* 29 (April 1976):135–54. A show of competent leadership during the second half of 1946 would have challenged Dobbins to change his mind about the coming Folsom administration.

4. The account of the relationship between Folsom and Mrs. Johnston is based on documents filed in support of the 1948 paternity suit and on Mrs. Johnston's description of the events as written by William Bradford Huie. Since Folsom neither denied Mrs. Johnston's allegations nor contested them in court, I assume that her account was essentially accurate. Interrogatories submitted by attorneys for Christine Putman Johnston, Folsom Papers; William Bradford Huie, *A New Life to Live: Jimmy Putman's Story* (New York: Nelson, 1977), pp. 22–31; William Bradford Huie, "Pregnancy and Politics in Alabama," *American Mercury* 72 (June 1951):754–61.

5. *Montgomery Advertiser,* 26 June, 17 July 1946.

6. *Birmingham News,* 29 August 1946; *Montgomery Advertiser,* 18 August 1946. Some of Folsom's friends recalled that Truman discussed making Folsom his running mate in 1948. Others claimed that Folsom taught Truman his technique for taking a campaign to the "brush arbors and the forks of the creeks," thereby inspiring Truman's 1948 "whistle-stop" campaign. Confidential communications with two of Folsom's 1946 campaign aides.

7. *Montgomery Advertiser,* 25, 30, 31 August 1946.

8. *Montgomery Advertiser,* 15 December 1946; James E. Folsom, 10 October 1979; William V. Lyerly, 23 October 1979.

9. *Birmingham Post,* 9 May 1946; *Montgomery Advertiser,* 16, 17 November 1946; Curtis DeLamar to James E. Folsom, 18 November 1946, Folsom Papers.

10. "Alabama Election," *Life,* 3 June 1946, pp. 43–46.

11. *Montgomery Advertiser,* 26 June, 24 November 1946; confidential communications from four former legislators.

12. *Montgomery Advertiser,* 17 July, 16 November 1946.

13. ADAH, *Alabama Official and Statistical Register, 1947,* pp. 189, 209, 224; *Union Springs Herald,* 2 May 1946.

14. *Montgomery Advertiser,* 21 July, 16 November, 15 December 1946; *Alabama,* 5 July 1946; ADAH, *Alabama Official and Statistical Register, 1947,* p. 220; C. H. Peen to James E. Folsom, 6 June 1946, Folsom Papers.

15. *Montgomery Advertiser,* 31 October, 5, 16, 20, 24 November 1946.

16. *Birmingham News,* 4 March 1947; Joseph N. Poole to James E. Folsom, 27 November 1946, Folsom Papers.

17. *Montgomery Advertiser,* 4 January 1947; *Alabama,* 3 January 1947; Folsom legislative notebook, J. H. Kelley to James E. Folsom, 20 December

1946, John A. Altman to James E. Folsom, 24 November 1946, Frank Boswell to James E. Folsom, 6 September 1946, William M. Beck to James E. Folsom, 4 November 1946, Folsom Papers.

18. *Alabama*, 3 January 1947; *Montgomery Advertiser*, 14, 15 January 1947.

19. Gessner T. McCorvey to James E. Folsom, 20 November 1946, Folsom Papers; *Montgomery Advertiser*, 21 January 1947.

Chapter 5

1. *Albertville Herald*, 24 January 1947; *Birmingham Age-Herald*, 22 January 1947; *Birmingham News*, 21 January 1947; *Birmingham Post*, 21 January 1947; *Birmingham World*, 24 January 1947; *Montgomery Advertiser*, 24 November 1946, 21 January 1947; James E. Folsom, *Speeches of Gov. James E. Folsom, 1947−1950* (Montgomery: Wetumpka Printing Company, 1951), pp. 1−7.

2. "Branchhead" was one of the terms Folsom used to describe the rural regions from which he drew much of his support. Since rural Alabamians commonly used "branch" to describe a creek or other small stream of water, they understood that Folsom was referring to remote rural areas when he talked about visiting the "branchheads." Folsom referred to the same remote rural areas whenever he talked of going to "the brush arbors and the forks of the creeks."

3. *Birmingham Post*, 4 December 1946; *Montgomery Examiner*, 6 February 1947; Cornelia Wallace, *C'nelia* (New York: Holman, 1976), pp. 132−43.

4. *Montgomery Advertiser*, 3 February 1947; *Birmingham World*, 21 January 1947; ADAH, *Alabama Official and Statistical Register, 1947*, pp. 30−31, 36, 57, 62, 66−67, 72−73, 92, 105, 109.

5. "Department Heads—General Letters," drawer 230, Official Papers of Governor James E. Folsom, Division of Civil Archives, Alabama Department of Archives and History, Montgomery (hereinafter cited as Governor's Papers); W. LaRue Horn to James E. Folsom, 14 January 1947, Phillip Hamm to James E. Folsom, 19 January 1948, O. H. Finney, Jr., to James E. Folsom, 20 January 1948, William V. Lyerly to James E. Folsom, 20 January 1948, Kenneth J. Griffith to James E. Folsom, 20 January 1948, Folsom Papers.

6. *Montgomery Advertiser*, 29 January, 4 May 1947; *Alabama*, 14 March 1947; ADAH, *Alabama Official and Statistical Register, 1955*, pp. 55−56; W. LaRue Horn to all investigators, undated, Edward G. Lee and Henry Sweet to Governor's Office, 26 February 1947; W. LaRue Horn to O. H. Finney, Jr., 7 April 1947, O. H. Finney, Jr., to Cecil Folsom, 10 January 1947; William Herring to Governor's Office, 19 February 1947, Edward G. Lee to O. H. Finney, Jr., 21 April 1947, Folsom Papers.

7. *Montgomery Advertiser,* 31 January 1947; ADAH, *Alabama Official and Statistical Register, 1943,* p. 337.

8. L. N. Duncan to Members of the Board of Trustees, 21 February 1947, folder 77, and D. E. Ponder to L. N. Duncan, 13 January 1947, folder 155, Auburn University Board of Trustees Papers, Auburn University Archives, Auburn (hereinafter cited as API Trustees Papers); Charles A. Stakely and Ed E. Reid to L. N. Duncan, 3 June 1946, folder "Alabama, State of, Governor 1947," Office of the President Papers: L. N. Duncan Papers, Auburn University Archives, Auburn; Frank W. Boykin to P. O. Davis, 13 February 1948, box 10-A-56, Alabama Cooperative Extension Records, Auburn University Archives, Auburn; *Alabama,* 7 March 1947.

9. *Alabama,* 7, 14, 21 February 1947; Judge F. W. Hare to L. N. Duncan, 14 February 1947, folder 77, API Trustees Papers.

10. *Montgomery Advertiser,* 22 February 1947; Minutes of API Board of Trustees meeting, 21 February 1947, API Trustees Papers; Folsom, *Speeches,* pp. 11–12.

11. *Montgomery Advertiser,* 23, 26, 27 February, 2, 3 March 1947; *Birmingham News,* 25 February 1947; *Alabama,* 28 February 1947.

12. *Montgomery Advertiser,* 26 February 1947.

13. Unsigned and undated legal brief, affidavits documenting the presence of Agricultural Extension agents at the capitol on 3 March 1947 signed by Neil O. Davis, Joseph B. Sarver, Jr., and John Tucker, Folsom Papers; *Birmingham News,* 4 March 1947; *Montgomery Advertiser,* 4 March 1947; *Alabama Journal,* 3 March 1947.

14. *Montgomery Advertiser,* 5 March 1947; *Birmingham News,* 5 March 1947; transcript of speech by Carleton Myers to API students on 4 March 1947, folder 78, API Trustees Papers.

15. *Montgomery Advertiser,* 18, 21 March 1947; P. O. Davis to the Board of Trustees of Alabama Polytechnic Institute, 17 March 1947, Minutes of API Board of Trustees meeting, 17 March 1947, folder 79, API Trustees Papers.

16. *Montgomery Advertiser,* 16, 21, 22, 24 January 1947.

17. Folsom, *Speeches,* pp. 23–29, 30–33; *Birmingham News,* 5 February 1947; United States Office of Education, *Biennial Survey of Education in the United States, 1946–1948,* chapter 2, p. 5; *Montgomery Advertiser,* 12 February, 12 March 1947.

18. W. LaRue Horn to James E. Folsom, 1 April and 3 April 1947, Folsom Papers.

19. *Birmingham News,* 6, 13 February, 7 May 1947; *Alabama,* 24 January, 28 February 1947; *Montgomery Advertiser,* 8, 29 June, 3 July 1947.

20. The term "floating debt" was used to refer to the debts incurred by the State of Alabama during the Reconstruction period.

21. ADAH, *Alabama Official and Statistical Register, 1935,* p. 754.

22. *Montgomery Advertiser,* 5, 12 February, 3 March, 4, 14 April 1947.

23. *Montgomery Advertiser,* 23, 24 April 1947; Folsom, *Speeches,* pp. 27–

28; W. LaRue Horn to James E. Folsom, 1 April 1947, E. C. Boswell to W. LaRue Horn, 28 March 1947, Folsom Papers.

24. Folsom, *Speeches,* pp. 44–66; *Birmingham News,* 7 May 1946.

25. *Montgomery Advertiser,* 11 through 23 May 1947; Alabama Legislature, House, *Journal, 1947,* Second Special Session, pp. 6–7.

26. *Montgomery Advertiser,* 5, 27 June, 9, 16, 18 July 1947.

27. Ibid., 12 June, 2 August 1947.

28. Ibid., 18 July, 2, 7, 8 August 1947.

29. Ibid., 5, 27 June 1947; Alabama Legislature, House, *Journal, 1947,* Regular Session, pp. 980–83; Alabama Legislature, Senate, *Journal, 1947,* Regular Session, p. 1997.

30. *Birmingham News,* 28 January 1947; *Montgomery Advertiser,* 22, 24 January, 1, 2, 7 February 1947; *Alabama,* 7 February 1947.

31. *Montgomery Advertiser,* 28 January, 11 March 1947; *Birmingham News,* 9 March 1947; *Alabama,* 25 April 1947; Division of Purchases and Stores of the Department of Finance to Governor Folsom, 3 February 1948, drawer 230, Governor's Papers.

32. *Birmingham News,* 30 March, 9 April, 2 May 1947; *Dothan Eagle,* 16 February 1947; *Roanoke Leader,* 30 January 1947.

33. Folsom, *Speeches,* pp. 18–22.

34. ADAH, *Alabama Official and Statistical Register, 1947,* p. 226; *Montgomery Advertiser,* 3 July 1949; confidential communications from a member of Folsom's office staff and two members of the Alabama Legislature.

35. *Montgomery Advertiser,* 26 March, 16, 29 November 1949.

36. *Alabama,* 27 June 1947; *Montgomery Advertiser,* 22 May 1949; confidential communications from two members of the Alabama Legislature.

37. *Montgomery Advertiser,* 12 September 1947; ADAH, *Alabama Official and Statistical Register, 1947,* pp. 196–98; confidential communications from two members of the Alabama Legislature.

38. ADAH, *Alabama Official and Statistical Register, 1947,* pp. 185, 188–89, 193; *Montgomery Advertiser,* 14 September 1947; *The Martindale-Hubbell Law Directory,* 74th annual edition, vol. 1 (Summit, N.J.: Martindale-Hubbell, 1942), pt. 2, p. 11.

39. *Montgomery Advertiser,* 3 February, 22, 24 July, 19 September 1947; *Alabama Journal,* 3 March 1947.

40. *Montgomery Advertiser,* 6, 10, 17 August, 4, 11, 13 September 1947; Folsom, *Speeches,* pp. 89–91.

41. *Montgomery Advertiser,* 20 May, 1, 6, 18, 21 June, 19 July, 10, 13 August 1947; *Alabama,* 8 August 1947; "Executive Order Concerning the use of State Vehicles," drawer 230, Governor's Papers; Hallie Farmer, ed., *A Handbook of Alabama State Agencies,* Alabama Bureau of Public Administration Publications, no. 9 (University: Bureau of Public Administration, 1942), p. 20.

42. *Montgomery Advertiser,* 10, 17, 19 September 1947; ADAH, *Alabama Official and Statistical Register, 1947,* p. 549.

43. *Montgomery Advertiser,* 19 September, 1 October 1947.

44. *Montgomery Advertiser,* 1, 3 October 1947.

Chapter 6

1. *Montgomery Advertiser,* 1 September 1947; *Birmingham Post,* 21 August 1947.

2. *Montgomery Advertiser,* 16 October 1947; W. W. Ward, "Devil's Island, U.S.A.," *Reader's Digest,* October 1950, pp. 23–27. Folsom was wrong in declaring the investigative committees to be unprecedented encroachments on the governor's powers. Although investigations were rare, the Alabama Legislature had used them in the past to investigate "gross betrayal of public trust." Hallie Farmer, *The Legislative Process in Alabama: Recess and Interim Committees,* Alabama Bureau of Public Administration Publications, no. 23 (University: Bureau of Public Administration, 1946), pp. 11–13.

3. *Montgomery Advertiser,* 5, 6, 16 October 1947.

4. Ibid., 9, 16, 27 November 1947, 6 December 1947, 22 January, 12 March 1948.

5. *Montgomery Advertiser,* 26 November, 18 December 1947, 14 October, 21 December 1948; George Bliss Jones to Governor Chauncey Sparks, 13 November 1946, J. E. Searcy to James E. Folsom, 21 July 1950, Folsom Papers.

6. Robert Folsom, interview with author, Elba, 1 October 1979; Phillip J. Hamm, interview with author, Napier Field, 3 October 1979. It is difficult to estimate precisely how effective these enforcement procedures were because both the income tax and the sales tax should have produced more revenue as a result of inflation. However, stricter enforcement contributed to the growth of state revenue from $64,401,000 in 1946 to $94,091,000 in 1950. James E. Folsom, *A Four Year Report to the People* (Montgomery, 1951), p. 10.

7. Foreign corporations were corporations which held charters under the laws of other states but operated within Alabama.

8. O. H. Finney, Jr., interview with author, Albertville, 6 September 1979; *Montgomery Advertiser,* 30 October 1947.

9. *Montgomery Advertiser,* 28 June, 28 September 1947, 20 August, 17 September 1948.

10. *Montgomery Advertiser,* 30 July 1948; B. C. Goode, "The Effect of Highway Design and Operational Practices Related to Highway Safety on Secondary Roads," *Mr. County Commissioner,* December 1967, pp. 5, 9, 13, 18.

11. *Montgomery Advertiser,* 19, 29 May, 9 November, 17, 19 December 1947, 12 October 1948.

12. Ibid., 9, 30 October 1947; ADAH, *Alabama Official and Statistical Register, 1947,* p. 71; Charles G. Dobbins, "Alabama Governors and Editors, 1930–1955: A Memoir," *Alabama Review* 29 (April 1976):147–48.

13. *Montgomery Advertiser,* 30 October, 2, 8, 11 November, 6 December 1947; Dobbins, "Alabama Governors," pp. 147–48.

14. *Montgomery Advertiser,* 7 December 1947, 15, 21 January, 21 April 1948.

15. Ibid., 25 September, 12 October 1947; *Birmingham Post,* 5 January 1948; *Birmingham World,* 6 January 1948.

16. *Montgomery Advertiser,* 13 October, 21 November, 10, 13, 19, 20, 21, 24 December 1947.

17. Ibid., 28 October, 21 November, 2 December 1947, 1 January 1948; *Alabama,* 5 December 1947.

18. *Alabama,* 7 November 1947; *Montgomery Advertiser,* 28 October, 21 November, 13, 18, 20, 29 December 1947, 3 January 1948.

19. *Montgomery Advertiser,* 13, 29 December 1947, 3 January 1948; *Birmingham Post,* 27 October 1947.

20. *Alabama,* 21 November 1947; *Montgomery Advertiser,* 30 October 1947 through 4 January 1948.

21. *Alabama,* 21 November 1947; approximately 3,000 Hope Chest letters with attached replies, Folsom Papers.

22. *Montgomery Advertiser,* 30 October, 5 November 1947; *Folsom's Forum,* 29 October 1947 through April 1950, Division of Civil Archives, Alabama Department of Archives and History, Montgomery.

23. *Alabama,* 7, 21 November 1947; *Montgomery Advertiser,* 28, 29 October, 27 November, 5 December 1947.

24. ADAH, *Alabama Official and Statistical Register, 1947,* pp. 554–56; *Montgomery Advertiser,* 7 January 1948; *Birmingham News,* 7 January 1948.

25. Paul E. Deutschman, "Outsize Governor," *Life,* 15 September 1947; *Montgomery Advertiser,* 9, 24 October 1947.

26. "Kissin' Jim's Busy Weekend," *Life,* 10 November 1947, pp. 40–41.

27. *Montgomery Advertiser,* 5 October, 5 December 1947, 12 March 1948; *Birmingham Post,* 3 March 1948.

28. *Montgomery Advertiser,* 24 November, 16 December 1947, 22 January, 12 March, 22 May, 15 July, 5 October, 15 December 1948.

29. Ibid., 16, 18, 23, 29 November 1947, 1, 7, 20 May, 13 June 1948; O. H. Finney to All Department Heads, 17 April 1948, drawer 230, Governor's Papers.

30. *Alabama,* 7 November 1947; *Montgomery Advertiser,* 19 November 1947, 30 September 1948; Hugh Sparrow articles, Folsom Scrapbooks, Division of Maps and Manuscripts, Alabama Department of Archives and History, Montgomery.

31. *Montgomery Advertiser,* 24 January, 11 March, 20 April, 29 June, 1, 13 July, 10 August, 14 September, 2, 5, 24 October 1948.

32. Ibid., 14 March, 21, 23 May 1948.

33. Ibid., 23 May, 1, 17 July, 19 August 1948.

34. Ibid., 9, 22 June, 19, 22 August 1948.

35. Ibid., 27 January 1948; William D. Barnard's *Dixiecrats and Democrats: Alabama Politics, 1942–1950* (University: University of Alabama Press, 1974) provides an excellent account of the 1948 Democratic primary campaign in Alabama.

36. Barnard, *Dixiecrats and Democrats,* pp. 97–100.

37. Ibid., pp. 104–105.

38. *Montgomery Advertiser,* 28, 29 January, 20, 24 March 1948.

39. Ibid., 19 February, 2, 6, 11 March 1948.

40. Ibid., 3, 4, 7 March 1948; *Birmingham Age-Herald,* 9 March 1948; *Birmingham Post,* 3 March 1948; William Bradford Huie, *A New Life to Live: Jimmie Putman's Story* (New York: Nelson, 1977), pp. 31–32; confidential communications.

41. *New York Daily News,* 3 March 1948; confidential communications.

42. James E. Folsom, *Speeches of Gov. James E. Folsom, 1947–1950* (Montgomery: Wetumpka Printing Company, 1951), pp. 102–103; *Birmingham Post,* 4 March 1948; *Montgomery Advertiser,* 4, 11 March, 2 April, 1 May 1948; *Birmingham Age-Herald,* 4 March 1948; Barnard, *Dixiecrats and Democrats,* pp. 106–107.

43. *Montgomery Advertiser,* 2 March, 2, 6, 7 April 1948; Barnard, *Dixiecrats and Democrats,* p. 109.

44. *Montgomery Advertiser,* 13, 26, 27, 28 March, 2, 29 May 1948; James E. Folsom to All Department Heads, 27 April 1948, drawer 230, Governor's Papers.

45. *Montgomery Advertiser,* 6, 15 May, 2 June 1948; ADAH, *Alabama Official and Statistical Register, 1951,* pp. 449–75; Barnard, *Dixiecrats and Democrats,* pp. 109–10.

46. *Montgomery Advertiser,* 27 April, 6 May, 3 June 1948.

Chapter 7

1. *Montgomery Advertiser,* 5, 20 May, 13 August 1948.

2. Ibid., 6 May 1948; James E. Folsom, 10 October 1979; confidential communications from two members of Folsom's office staff and from one member of the Alabama Legislature.

3. *Montgomery Advertiser,* 20 May 1948, 21 January 1949.

4. *Alabama Journal,* 2 April 1948; *Montgomery Advertiser,* 7 April, 18 June, 9 July 1948; confidential communciations.

5. William D. Barnard, *Dixiecrats and Democrats: Alabama Politics, 1942–1950* (University: University of Alabama Press, 1974) is the best

available account of the role Alabamians played in the formation of the States' Rights party.

6. Ibid., p. 121.

7. Ibid., pp. 103–104; *Montgomery Advertiser,* 8, 15, 17 October, 2, 12 November 1948; James E. Folsom, *Speeches of Gov. James E. Folsom, 1947–1950* (Montgomery: Wetumpka Printing Company, 1951), pp. 113–18.

8. ADAH, *Alabama Official and Statistical Register, 1951,* pp. 478–79; Barnard, *Dixiecrats and Democrats; Montgomery Advertiser,* 4, 12 November 1948.

9. *Montgomery Advertiser,* 15 September, 19 December 1948.

10. Ibid., 30 August, 10, 18, 21 December 1948.

11. W. W. Ward, "Devil's Island, U.S.A.," *Reader's Digest,* October 1950, pp. 23–27; Hugh Sparrow articles, Folsom Scrapbooks, Division of Maps and Manuscripts, Alabama Department of Archives and History, Montgomery.

12. *Montgomery Advertiser,* 26 August, 25 November 1948.

13. Ibid., 18, 21, 22, 28 August, 13 October, 17 November 1948.

14. O. H. Finney, Jr., interview with author, Albertville, 6 September 1979.

15. Folsom, *Speeches,* pp. 119–25; *Montgomery Advertiser,* 2 January 1949.

16. *Montgomery Advertiser,* 22 September 1948, 19, 26 January, 8 February, 8 April 1949.

17. Ibid., 9, 23 January, 10 July 1949; Barnard, *Dixiecrats and Democrats,* p. 132.

18. *Montgomery Advertiser,* 22 April, 10 July 1949.

19. Ibid., 12 February, 10 July 1949; *Alabama,* 18 February 1949; Bruce Henderson to John Patterson, December 1957, J. Bruce Henderson Papers, 1892–1971, Division of Maps and Manuscripts, Alabama Department of Archives and History, Montgomery (hereinafter cited as Henderson Papers).

20. *Montgomery Advertiser,* 11, 25, 27 March, 16 April 1949; *Birmingham News,* 24 April 1949.

21. *Montgomery Advertiser,* 3 May 1949; Folsom. *Speeches,* pp. 139–54. The *Montgomery Advertiser* and the *Birmingham News* reported legislative action daily throughout the 1949 biennial session. The account here of that legislative session is based on newspaper reports from 3 May through 10 September 1949.

22. *Montgomery Advertiser,* 3, 4, 5, 7, 8, 11, 13, 18, 25, 28 May 1949.

23. Ibid., 6, 19, 22, 25, 29 June, 1, 7 July 1949.

24. Ibid., 29 May, 1, 4, 8, 10, 11 June, 2, 3 July 1949.

25. Ibid., 7, 9, 13, 16, 20, 23, 27, 30 July, 3, 6, 10, 12 August 1949.

26. Ibid., 7, 17, 21, 27, 29 July, 3, 4, 5, 6, 10, 14 August 1949.

27. Ibid., 9, 10, 16, 17, 24, 27 August, 3, 9, 10 September 1949.

28. Ibid., 26 September 1948, 4 March, 8 April, 28 July, 2 August 1949, 12 July 1950; *Alabama,* 11 March 1950.

29. *Birmingham News,* 5 June 1949; *Montgomery Advertiser,* 10 April, 12 June, 19 August, 8 September 1949.

30. *Montgomery Advertiser,* 4 August, 16 September 1949, 2 February, 29 September 1950; Folsom, *Speeches,* p. 181.

31. *Montgomery Advertiser,* 1, 8, 15, 29 November, 6, 13, 20 December 1949, 10, 17, 24, 31 January, 7, 25, 26 February 1950.

32. Ibid., 18 October 1949, 3, 4, 17 February 1950; confidential communications from two members of Folsom's cabinet.

33. *Montgomery Advertiser,* 12 March 1950.

34. "In Alabama: Anything to Draw Some Attention," *Life,* 27 March 1950, pp. 32–33.

35. *Montgomery Advertiser,* 16, 29 November 1949, 9, 28, 31 March, 11 April 1950; Folsom, *Speeches,* p. 172; Ira B. Thompson to William V. Lyerly, April 1950, and William V. Lyerly to Ira B. Thompson, 17 April 1950, Folsom Papers.

36. ADAH, *Alabama Official and Statistical Register, 1951,* pp. 527–29; *Montgomery Advertiser,* 10, 12 May 1950.

37. Barnard, *Dixiecrats and Democrats,* pp. 139–40; *Montgomery Advertiser,* 5 May, 1 June 1950.

38. Folsom, *Speeches,* p. 189; *Montgomery Advertiser,* 27 May, 5, 6 June 1950.

39. *Montgomery Advertiser,* 20, 21, 22, 23 June 1950.

40. Ibid., 28 June 1950. Attorney Files Crenshaw researched previous efforts to obtain court-ordered reapportionment and discovered that neither the state nor the federal courts had accepted questions of legislative apportionment as subjects for judicial decision. Files Crenshaw to James E. Folsom, 8 September 1950, Folsom Papers. Two legislative candidates from Blount County filed suit in Alabama's Fifteenth Judicial Circuit challenging the Alabama Legislature's apportionment in 1950. Judge Walter B. Jones dismissed the suit with the argument that his court had no jurisdiction over the matter. *Montgomery Advertiser,* 7 September 1950.

41. *Montgomery Advertiser,* 29 June 1950.

42. Ibid., 6, 8, 12, 14, 26, 28 July, 1, 2, 3, 4, 5 August 1950.

43. Ibid., 10, 11, 15 August, 11, 26 October 1950.

44. Ibid., 1, 30 July, 1 September, 10, 17 October, 15, 29 November 1950; James E. Folsom to William V. Lyerly, 29 June 1950, Folsom Papers.

45. *Birmingham News,* 20 November 1949; *Montgomery Advertiser,* 10, 24, 30 December 1949, 22 December 1950, 16 January 1951; Alabama Legislature, Special Investigative Committee to Investigate Pardons and Paroles, *Report of the Special Legislative Committee Investigating Pardons and Paroles,* Regular Session, 1954, Legislative Document no. 4: 13, 15 (hereinafter cited as Alabama Legislature, *Pardons and Paroles*).

46. Folsom, *Speeches,* pp. 176–77.

47. *Montgomery Advertiser,* 10, 24, 30 December 1949, 14 January 1951; Alabama Legislature, *Pardons and Paroles,* pp. 34–35; J. W. Brassell to Glen

Vinson, 18 May 1950, F. E. Throckmorton to James E. Folsom, 24 July 1950, Folsom Papers.

Chapter 8

1. *Montgomery Advertiser,* 10 October 1950, 16 January 1951.
2. Ibid., 19 March 1950.
3. Confidential communications from one member of Folsom's office staff and two members of the Alabama Legislature.
4. ADAH, *Alabama Official and Statistical Register, 1951,* pp. 605, 607; ADAH, *Alabama Official and Statistical Register, 1955,* pp. 534–35; E. C. Boswell to James E. Folsom, 26 February 1953, Folsom Papers.
5. E. C. Boswell to James E. Folsom, 26 February 1953, Folsom Papers; *Montgomery Advertiser,* 2, 16 January 1955.
6. *Alabama,* 2 March 1951; *Montgomery Advertiser,* 2, 16 January 1955; Charles M. Pinkston to James E. Folsom, 8 February 1956, Folsom Papers.
7. Alabama Legislature, *Pardons and Paroles,* pp. 38–39.
8. Ibid., pp. 19, 34–35, 54–57.
9. Ibid., p. 60; Ralph Hammond to James E. Folsom, 13 March 1951, Folsom Papers; *Montgomery Advertiser,* 22 August 1954.
10. W. LaRue Horn to James E. Folsom, undated, Folsom Papers.
11. William M. Beck to James E. Folsom, 27 July 1951, E. C. Boswell to James E. Folsom, 26 February 1953, W. LaRue Horn to James E. Folsom, 15 September, 15 March 1952, Folsom Papers.
12. *Montgomery Advertiser,* 15 May 1949; O. H. Finney, interview with author, Albertville, 6 September 1979; confidential communications.
13. Miscellaneous mats for printing product labels, sample feed bags bearing the Folsom label, W. LaRue Horn to James E. Folsom, 29 December 1951, Bert Thomas to James E. Folsom, 1 May 1954, Folsom Papers; confidential communication from freelance journalist.
14. George D. Patterson to James E. Folsom, 30 October 1953, Folsom Papers; *Montgomery Advertiser,* 31 December 1954; James E. Folsom, interview with author, Cullman, 10 October 1979; confidential communications.
15. S. H. Moore to James E. Folsom, 9 January 1951, Sam C. Jones to James E. Folsom, 6 November 1951, Folsom Papers.
16. ADAH, *Alabama Official and Statistical Register, 1955,* pp. 489–91, 500–501; Joseph N. Poole to James E. Folsom, 22 May 1952, Folsom Papers.
17. Ed E. Reid to James E. Folsom, 13 February 1953, S. G. Johnson to James E. Folsom, 20 August 1953, George C. Wallace to James E. Folsom, 13 June 1953, Folsom Papers; confidential communication from a weekly newspaper editor.
18. Grover C. Hall to James E. Folsom, 12 January 1953, Folsom Papers.
19. Fred E. Gill to James E. Folsom, 21 March 1954, William J. Watson to

James E. Folsom, 16 September 1953, George E. Trawick to James E. Folsom, 3 September 1953, Folsom Papers.

20. Undated list of county campaign leaders written on stationery of the Ed Pepper Motor Company, Frank Boswell to O. H. Finney, Jr., 17 July 1954, Coma Garrett, Jr., to Myra Leak Porter, 24 March 1954, Myra Leak Porter to George W. Ewing, 3 February 1954, Folsom Papers.

21. Thomas J. Gilliam, "The Second Folsom Administration: The Destruction of Alabama Liberalism, 1954–1958" (Ph.D. dissertation, Auburn University, 1975), pp. 57–58; George C. Wallace to Murray Battles, 11 March 1954, George C. Wallace to O. H. Finney, Jr., 13 April 1954, Folsom Papers; confidential communications from two members of Folsom's cabinet during the second administration.

22. Charles M. Pinkston to James E. Folsom, 22 April 1953, W. LaRue Horn to James E. Folsom, 27 September 1953, Escar Marley to Myra Leak Porter, 13 February 1954, Alva Register to James E. Folsom, 13 March 1954, Bart B. Chamberlain, Jr., to James E. Folsom, 27 April 1954, Jim Buford to James E. Folsom, 11 March 1954, Folsom Papers.

23. W. LaRue Horn to James E. Folsom, 25 February 1954, Neil Metcalf to O. H. Finney, Jr., 12 May 1954, Folsom Papers.

24. ADAH, *Alabama Official and Statistical Register, 1955,* p. 548; *Montgomery Advertiser,* 18 April 1954; Ira B. Thompson to James E. Folsom, 30 January 1954, Folsom Papers.

25. *Montgomery Advertiser,* 27 February, 4, 12 March, 1, 25 April 1954.

26. *Montgomery Advertiser,* 25 February, 28 March, 3 April 1954.

27. Transcript of speech delivered by Bruce Henderson at Dothan, 9 February 1954, Henderson Papers.

28. *Montgomery Advertiser,* 25 February, 5, 10 March, 6, 10, 23, 29 April 1954; *Alabama Journal,* 10 March 1954; *Birmingham News,* 3, 16 March 1954; *Huntsville Times,* 22 March, 6 April 1954.

29. *Montgomery Advertiser,* 4, 27 March 1954; Gilliam, "The Second Folsom Administration," pp. 62–65; undated draft of speech delivered by James E. Folsom at Hamilton, on stationery of Murray Battles, Folsom Papers.

30. *Montgomery Advertiser,* 26 January 1954; James E. Folsom, 10 October 1979.

31. Gilliam, "The Second Folsom Administration," p. 63; James E. Folsom, 10 October 1979. The theme song "Y'all Come!" was adapted from a contemporary song of the same name recorded by Bing Crosby.

32. James E. Folsom, 10 October 1979.

33. Ibid.; *Montgomery Advertiser,* 1 May 1954. Grover Hall turned Folsom's confession into a nickname for the first administration, the "Shore I Stole" administration. *Montgomery Advertiser,* 30 April 1954.

34. *Montgomery Advertiser,* 1 May 1954; draft of speech delivered by James E. Folsom in Montgomery, 1 May 1954, Folsom Papers.

35. ADAH, *Alabama Official and Statistical Register, 1955,* pp. 548–49.

36. Ibid., pp. 558–60, 575–76; *Montgomery Advertiser,* 12, 30 May 1954.

37. Newspaper clipping kept under the glass on Governor Folsom's desk during his second administration, n.d., Folsom Papers.

38. Mimeographed list of advisory committees, undated, Folsom Papers; *Montgomery Advertiser,* 1 August, 21, 26 November 1954; confidential communications from one member of the Alabama Legislature and one member of Folsom's cabinet.

39. *Montgomery Advertiser,* 8, 14 May 1954.

40. Ibid., 14 May 1954; Ed E. Reid to James E. Folsom, 12 May 1954, 12 May 1954 (two letters on the same day), Folsom Papers.

41. *Montgomery Advertiser,* 11, 12, 13, 16 May, 8, 9, 10, 16, 17, 18, 19 June, 26 September 1954; legislative notebook for 1954–1958, O. H. Finney, Jr., to George Hawkins, 1 December 1954, Folsom Papers; confidential communications from two members of the Alabama Legislature.

42. *Montgomery Advertiser,* 13 May, 24 June, 16 August, 2 October, 8 December 1954, 2 January 1955; O. H. Finney, Jr., to Leslie L. Gwaltney, Jr., 2 September 1954, O. H. Finney, Jr., to James E. Folsom, 19 November 1954, W. D. Partlow to James E. Folsom, 29 November 1954, Folsom Papers.

43. *Montgomery Advertiser,* 26 August 1954; "Herman Nelson—vita," Folsom Papers; confidential communications.

44. *Montgomery Advertiser,* 26 September 1954; Ralph Hammond to Claude N. Know, 2 July 1954, and lists of nominees for local offices with the agreement of legislators and local supporters certified by Frank Boswell, Folsom Papers.

45. *Montgomery Advertiser,* 4 June 1954; Dave Birmingham to James E. Folsom, 4 June 1954, Folsom Papers. The Folsom Papers contain evidence of similar squabbles among Folsom supporters in Mobile, Houston, Geneva, and Walker counties.

46. *Montgomery Advertiser,* 14, 29 July 1954.

47. Ibid., 18 May, 11 June, 9 January 1954; *Huntsville Times,* 26 September 1954. J. Tyra Harris's "Alabama Reaction to the Brown Decision, 1954–1956: A Case Study of Early Massive Resistance" (Ph.D. dissertation, Middle Tennessee State University, 1973) discusses this topic in much greater detail. Numan Bartley surveys reactions in all the southern states in his *The Rise of Massive Resistance: Race and Politics in the South during the 1950s* (Baton Rouge: Louisiana State University Press, 1969).

48. *Montgomery Advertiser,* 14 November 1954; *Huntsville Times,* 26 September 1954.

49. "A Sawdust Trail Brings New Days," *Life,* 4 October 1954, p. 47; "The Odds Were Right," *Time,* 28 June 1954, p. 22; "Up in Arms," *Newsweek,* 27 December 1954, p. 18; John Patterson, "I'll Get the Gangs That Killed My Father," *Saturday Evening Post,* 27 November 1954, pp. 20–21; confidential communications. The most complete account of the Phenix City investigation appeared in the *Columbus* (Georgia) *Ledger* beginning 19 June

1954. The *Ledger* won a Pulitzer Prize for its investigative journalism, and its reporters often led law enforcement officials to relevant evidence.

Chapter 9

1. *Montgomery Advertiser,* 16 January 1955.
2. Ibid., 30 December 1954, 18 January 1955.
3. ADAH, *Alabama Official and Statistical Register, 1955,* pp. 262, 264–67, 282, 287–88; James E. Folsom to Cabinet Members, 5 November 1954, Ralph Hammond Papers in the personal possession of Ralph Hammond, Arab (hereinafter cited as Hammond Papers); minutes of cabinet meeting, 6 February 1955, Ralph Hammond Notebook, in the personal possession of Ralph Hammond, Arab (hereinafter cited as Hammond Notebook, Cabinet Minutes).
4. ADAH, *Alabama Official and Statistical Register, 1955,* pp. 77, 251; *Montgomery Advertiser,* 10 April 1955.
5. *Montgomery Advertiser,* 21 January 1955; "Message to the Alabama Legislature," 25 January 1955, Folsom Papers; confidential communications from one member of the Alabama Legislature and one member of Folsom's cabinet.
6. "Message to the Alabama Legislature," 25 January 1955, Folsom Papers; Hallie Farmer, ed., *A Handbook of Alabama State Agencies,* Alabama Bureau of Public Administration Publications, no. 9 (University: Bureau of Public Administration), p. 85.
7. Thomas J. Gilliam, "The Second Folsom Administration: The Destruction of Alabama Liberalism, 1954–1958" (Ph.D. dissertation, Auburn University, 1975), pp. 140–42; *Montgomery Advertiser,* 30 January 1955.
8. Confidential communications from three members of the Alabama Legislature and two members of Folsom's cabinet.
9. O. H. Finney, Jr., to All Department Heads, undated, Hammond Papers; confidential communications from two members of the Alabama Legislature and one member of Folsom's cabinet.
10. File box containing punched computer cards on which Ed Pepper recorded legislative votes, Folsom Papers; Hammond Notebook, Cabinet Minutes, 6 February 1955; confidential communications from two members of the Alabama Legislature.
11. Hammond Notebook, Cabinet Minutes, 31 January, 6 February 1955; *Montgomery Advertiser,* 2, 3, 5, 6, 13, 15 February 1955; Gilliam, "The Second Folsom Administration," pp. 144–46.
12. Alabama Legislature, House, *Journal, 1955,* First Special Session, pp. 6–7, 29, 47, 52–59, 69, 72.
13. *Montgomery Advertiser,* 20 February 1955; Gilliam, "The Second Folsom Administration," pp. 146–48; confidential communications from two members of the Alabama Legislature.
14. Confidential communications from two members of the Alabama Legislature.

15. Alabama Legislature, Senate, *Journal, 1955,* First Special Session, pp. 119–36; House, *Journal, 1955,* First Special Session, pp. 148–55, 157–64.

16. *Montgomery Advertiser,* 25 February 1955; Gilliam, "The Second Folsom Administration," p. 147.

17. Hammond Notebook, Cabinet Minutes, 23 February 1955; *Montgomery Advertiser,* 25 February 1955.

18. House, *Journal, 1955,* Second Special Session, pp. 201–202; Senate, *Journal, 1955,* Second Special Session, pp. 7, 54–55; *Montgomery Advertiser,* 5, 12 March 1955; Press Release by Welfare Commissioner J. S. Snoddy, 2 March 1955, Hammond Papers.

19. "Message to the Alabama Legislature," 8 March 1955, Hammond Papers; Hammond Notebook, Cabinet Minutes, 7, 21 March 1955; Gilliam, "The Second Folsom Administration," pp. 148–51; *Montgomery Advertiser,* 17, 18, 24 March 1955.

20. House, *Journal, 1955,* Second Special Session, pp. 171–78, 185–98, 255–56; *Montgomery Advertiser,* 17, 18, 24, 27, 30 March 1955; confidential communications from two members of the Alabama Legislature.

21. *Montgomery Advertiser,* 21 March, 6, 8 April 1955; Hammond Notebook, Cabinet Minutes, 7, 11 March 1955.

22. Senate, *Journal, 1955,* Second Special Session, pp. 179–86, 188; Gilliam, "The Second Folsom Administration," pp. 151–56; *Montgomery Advertiser,* 9 April 1955.

23. Hammond Notebook, Cabinet Minutes, 11 April 1955; *Montgomery Advertiser,* 13, 16, 17, 18, 20, 21, 23 April, 22 July 1955.

24. *Montgomery Advertiser,* 4 May 1955.

25. Ibid., 29 June, 1 December 1955; W. Cooper Green to James E. Folsom, series of letters during July and August 1955, Clarence B. Hanson, Jr., to James E. Folsom, series of letters during July and August 1955, Hammond Papers.

26. *Montgomery Advertiser,* 16, 22 January 1956; Otto E. Simon, interview with author, Mobile, 18 July 1979; A. K. Wakman to James E. Folsom, 2 September 1955, "Planning and Industrial Development" file, Folsom Papers.

27. *Mobile Register,* 4, 12, 18, 22 May, 1, 2, 3, 17 June 1955; Otto E. Simon, 18 July 1979; House, *Journal, 1955,* Regular Session, p. 176.

28. House, *Journal, 1955,* Regular Session, pp. 419, 648; Senate, *Journal, 1955,* Regular Session, pp. 356–69; *Mobile Register,* 11 June 1955; *Montgomery Advertiser,* 25 June, 14 July 1955; Otto E. Simon, 18 July 1979.

29. Alabama, State Docks Board, *Annual Report to the Governor, for the Fiscal Year Ended 30 September 1954,* pp. 13–14; Alabama, State Docks Department, *Annual Report to the Governor, for the Fiscal Year Ended 30 September 1957,* pp. 1, 7, 9, 12.

30. Alabama, State Docks Department, *Annual Report, 1957,* pp. 10–11; Alabama, State Docks Department, *Annual Report to the Governor, for the

Fiscal Year Ended 30 September 1962, pp. 27–28; ADAH, *Alabama Official and Statistical Register, 1959,* pp. 546, 562–63.

31. William H. Stewart, Jr., *The Tennessee Tombigbee Waterway: A Case Study in the Politics of Water Transportation,* Alabama Bureau of Public Administration Publications, no. 73 (University: Bureau of Public Administration, 1971), pp. 1–2, 48–54, 65.

32. *Montgomery Advertiser,* 18 May 1955, 17 August 1955; *Mobile Register,* 24, 26 May 1955; Alabama Legislature, *Acts of Alabama, 1953,* pp. 637–44.

33. *Montgomery Advertiser,* 30 June, 1, 6, 8, 14, 16 July 1955.

34. Ibid., 9, 14, 16, 27 July, 5, 10, 12, 17 August 1955.

35. "Message to the Alabama Legislature," 1 March 1956, Governor's Papers.

36. Gilliam, "The Second Folsom Administration," pp. 164–67; James E. Folsom to Lew White, 3 May 1955, "Speeches and Press Releases" folder, Hammond Papers.

37. Gilliam, "The Second Folsom Administration," p. 163; *Montgomery Advertiser,* 5 April, 15 May, 28, 30 July 1955.

38. James E. Folsom to the Alabama Legislature, undated, Folsom Papers; Hammond Notebook, Cabinet Minutes, 15, 18 April 1955.

39. *Montgomery Advertiser,* 1, 24 December 1955; confidential communication from a member of the Alabama Legislature.

40. "Message to the Alabama Legislature," 3 January 1956, Folsom Papers; *Montgomery Advertiser,* 4 January 1956; Gilliam, "The Second Folsom Administration," p. 311.

41. *Montgomery Advertiser,* 11, 12, 13, 18, 19, 20 January 1956.

42. Ibid., 20, 21, 22, 23, 24 January 1956; confidential communications from two members of the Alabama Legislature.

43. *Montgomery Advertiser,* 27 January 1956; ADAH, *Alabama Official and Statistical Register, 1959,* p. 538; Gilliam, "The Second Folsom Administration," pp. 313–14.

44. *Montgomery Advertiser,* 3, 4, 5, 29 February 1956.

45. Ibid., 30 October 1956; Gilliam, "The Second Folsom Administration," p. 375; reapportionment amendment campaign posters, Folsom Papers; Hammond Notebook, Cabinet Minutes, 29 October 1956; ADAH, *Alabama Official and Statistical Register, 1959,* pp. 543–45.

46. *Montgomery Advertiser,* 4 September 1955; U.S. Department of Health, Education, and Welfare, Office of Education, *Biennial Survey of Education in the United States: 1956–58,* chapter 2, *Statistics of State School Systems,* p. 70; "Governor Folsom's 1956 Report to the People," James E. Folsom to T. Herman Vann, 25 January 1956, Hammond Papers; "Message to the Alabama Legislature," 7 May 1956, Folsom Papers.

47. "Message to the Alabama Legislature," 1 March 1956, drawer 334, Governor's Papers.

Chapter 10

1. Fuller Kimbrell, interview with author, Fayette, 30 October 1979.

2. The charge that Folsom was "soft" on the "nigger issue" was the most publicized explanation of why George C. Wallace disassociated himself from Folsom in 1956.

3. *Montgomery Advertiser,* 13 October 1947; James E. Folsom, interview with author, Cullman, 11 October 1979. Carl Grafton retells the same family stories in his article "James E. Folsom and Civil Liberties," *Alabama Review* 32 (January 1979):3–27.

4. James E. Folsom, 11 October 1979; confidential communications with two of Folsom's boyhood friends.

5. *Montgomery Advertiser,* 25, 31 August 1946; J. A. Carnley to James E. Folsom, 18 September 1946, Folsom Papers.

6. *Birmingham World,* 21, 24, 31 January 1947.

7. C. G. Gomillion to James E. Folsom, 9 May 1954, Folsom Papers.

8. *Birmingham News,* 24 January 1947; *Birmingham World,* 17 October 1947; Austin R. Meadows, interview with author, Montgomery, 8 June 1979; William D. Barnard, *Dixiecrats and Democrats: Alabama Politics, 1942–1950* (University: University of Alabama Press, 1974), p. 128.

9. James E. Folsom, *Speeches of Gov. James E. Folsom, 1947–1950* (Montgomery: Wetumpka Printing Company, 1951), pp. 175–77.

10. Ibid., pp. 182–86.

11. *Montgomery Advertiser,* 16 January 1955; confidential communication from a member of the Alabama Legislature.

12. Confidential communications from three members of Folsom's cabinet.

13. "Segregation" file, James E. Folsom to Winston Craig, 16 March 1954, James E. Folsom to Rev. M. C. Griffin, 22 March 1954, Folsom Papers; Thomas J. Gilliam, "The Second Folsom Administration: The Destruction of Alabama Liberalism, 1954–1958" (Ph.D. dissertation, Auburn University, 1975), pp. 51–52; confidential communications.

14. A. G. Gaston to James E. Folsom, 15 March 1954, O. Z. Vickers to James E. Folsom, 11 May 1954, C. G. Gomillion to James E. Folsom, 6 May 1954, Folsom Papers.

15. Confidential communications from two members of Folsom's cabinet.

16. Gilliam, "The Second Folsom Administration," pp. 111–13; *Montgomery Advertiser,* 18 May 1954; E. C. Boswell to James E. Folsom, 30 September 1954, Folsom Papers; Vincent F. Kilborn to James E. Folsom, 27 May 1954, Hammond Papers.

17. "Segregation" file, Folsom Papers; *Montgomery Advertiser,* 4 October 1955; "Address to the Alabama Education Association," 24 March 1955, "Statement on the United States Supreme Court Decision on Segregation," 31 May 1955, Hammond Papers.

18. *Montgomery Advertiser,* 18 January 1955; *Birmingham World,* 21 January 1955.

19. *Birmingham World,* 4, 7, 11 January 1955; O. H. Finney, Jr., interview with author, Albertville, 6 September 1979.

20. *Montgomery Advertiser,* 20 October 1955; Gilliam, "The Second Folsom Administration," pp. 192–96.

21. Gilliam, "The Second Folsom Administration," pp. 192–96; *Birmingham World,* 12, 15 April 1955; *Montgomery Advertiser,* 12 August, 1 October, 18 November 1955; Mr. and Mrs. L. L. Penn to James E. Folsom, 22 September 1955, W. C. Patton to Ralph Hammond, 27 January 1955, Folsom Papers.

22. Gilliam, "The Second Folsom Administration," p. 109; J. Tyra Harris, "Alabama Reaction to the *Brown* Decision, 1954–1956; A Case Study of Early Massive Resistance" (Ph.D. dissertation, Middle Tennessee State University, 1978), pp. 202–17; *Montgomery Advertiser,* 1, 15 June, 2 July 1955.

23. Alabama Legislature, House, *Journal, 1955,* Regular Session, pp. 270, 816–22; Alabama Legislature, Senate, *Journal, 1955,* Regular Session, pp. 358–61, 643–44; Gilliam, "The Second Folsom Administration," pp. 175–81; *Montgomery Advertiser,* 28 June, 13, 23 July 1955; *Birmingham World,* 15 July 1955.

24. Gilliam, "The Second Folsom Administration," pp. 175–83; *Montgomery Advertiser,* 29 June 1955; Harris, "Alabama Reaction," pp. 202–17.

25. Senate, *Journal, 1955,* Regular Session, pp. 708, 714, 852–53, 1120, 1414; House, *Journal, 1955,* Regular Session, pp. 490–92, 598–600, 1403, 1708–709, 1784; Gilliam, "The Second Folsom Administration," pp. 219–21; Harris, "Alabama Reaction," pp. 202–17; *Birmingham World,* 12 August 1955.

26. Senate, *Journal, 1955,* Regular Session, pp. 883–84, 1569; Gilliam, "The Second Folsom Administration," pp. 219–21; *Birmingham World,* 12, 16 August 1955; *Montgomery Advertiser,* 14 August 1955; Hammond Notebook, Cabinet Minutes, 15 August 1955.

27. Gilliam, "The Second Folsom Administration," p. 285; *Birmingham World,* 24 June 1955; "Statement on Wadley Raid," 21 June 1955, "Speeches and Press Releases" folder, Hammond Papers.

28. *Montgomery Advertiser,* 16 July 1956; Hammond Notebook, Cabinet Minutes, 20 March 1956. Neil R. McMillen, *The Citizens' Council: Organized Resistance to the Second Reconstruction, 1954–64* (Urbana: University of Illinois Press, 1971) provides a detailed account of the origins and spread of the citizens' councils in Alabama.

29. *Montgomery Advertiser,* 4 November 1955; *Nashville Tennessean,* 4 November 1955.

30. Larry Brittain Childs, "Alabama Giant: Recollections of Jim Folsom" (honors thesis, University of Alabama, 1974), p. 13.

31. Hammond Notebook, Cabinet Minutes, 17 October 1956; Virginia

Durr to Aleine Austin, 19 June 1956, letter in the possession of Mrs. Aleine Austin Cohen, Baltimore, Maryland; confidential communications from two members of Folsom's cabinet.

32. *Montgomery Advertiser*, 5 November 1955; memorandum on Governor Folsom's personal stationery describing Congressman Powell's visit, Folsom Papers; James E. Folsom to J. D. Crow, 29 November 1955, "National Political" file, Hammond Papers; Hammond Notebook, Cabinet Minutes, 20 March 1956; Gilliam, "The Second Folsom Administration," p. 287.

33. Gilliam, "The Second Folsom Administration," pp. 222–28; J. Mills Thornton III, "Challenge and Response in the Montgomery Bus Boycott of 1955–1956," *Alabama Review* 33 (July 1980):163–235. The *Montgomery Advertiser* provided daily coverage of the Montgomery bus boycott from 2 December 1955 through 21 December 1956.

34. *Montgomery Advertiser*, 31 December 1955.

35. Gilliam, "The Second Folsom Administration," pp. 252–53, 258–60; *Pittsburgh Courier*, 24 March 1956; Thornton, "Challenge and Response," p. 215, n. 52; Childs, "Alabama Giant," p. 21. Childs attributes his account of the secret meetings between Governor Folsom and the Negro leaders to Jeff Norrell, a student of Paul Gaston at the University of Virginia. Norrell heard the story from Gaston, to whom Dr. Martin Luther King, Jr., told it during 1963. In a conversation with me in 1980, Gaston confirmed the gist of the account but could not confirm that Folsom actually said, "Why go after a few crumbs when you can have the whole loaf?" Since the meetings were confidential, no documentary evidence exists to substantiate the content of the conversations between Folsom and the boycott leaders.

36. Gilliam, "The Second Folsom Administration," pp. 282–83; O. H. Finney, Jr., 6 September 1979; Otto E. Simon, interview with author, Mobile, 18 July 1979.

37. *Montgomery Advertiser*, 3 through 9 February 1956; Austin R. Meadows, 8 June 1979.

38. "Statement by President Oliver C. Carmichael to University Convocation," 16 February 1956, Andrew J. Thomas to H. H. Grooms, 1 March 1956, Andrew J. Thomas to Robert Steiner, Jr., 3 March, 29 August 1956, Gessner T. McCorvey to Andrew J. Thomas, 1 September 1956, "U of A—Autherine Lucy" file, drawer 341, Governor's Papers. Ultimately, the University of Alabama trustees were able to expel Autherine Lucy because Judge H. H. Grooms subscribed to a narrow interpretation of his authority. Grooms confided to University of Alabama trustee Gessner T. McCorvey that his only responsibility was to judge the legality of the university's admissions policies. He had no authority, Grooms believed, to decide who should be admitted or denied admission to the University of Alabama. Gessner T. McCorvey to Andrew J. Thomas, 1 September 1956, "U of A—Autherine Lucy" file, drawer 341, Governor's Papers.

39. Gilliam, "The Second Folsom Administration," p. 273.

40. Ibid., pp. 284, 296–97; Otto E. Simon, 18 July 1979; Benjamin Muse,

"Confidential Memorandum: Visit to North Alabama, Birmingham, and Tuscaloosa," 13 July 1961, box 41, Southern Regional Council Papers, Department of Archives, Birmingham Public Library, Birmingham.

41. *Montgomery Advertiser,* 7, 27 February, 5 September 1956; Hammond Notebook, Cabinet Minutes, 10 February, 11 March 1956.

42. McMillen, *The Citizens' Council,* pp. 43–44.

43. *Montgomery Advertiser,* 25 February 1956.

44. Senate, *Journal, 1956,* First Special Session, pp. 52, 173; House, *Journal, 1956,* First Special Session, pp. 537, 582–85; Gilliam, "The Second Folsom Administration," pp. 316–19; Harris, "Alabama Reaction," pp. 220–28; ADAH, *Alabama Official and Statistical Register, 1959,* pp. 527–29; *Montgomery Advertiser,* 18, 20 January, 8 February 1956.

45. *Montgomery Advertiser,* 18, 21, 22, 24, 26 January, 2 February 1956; House, *Journal, 1956,* First Special Session, pp. 182, 255; Harris, "Alabama Reaction," pp. 220–28; Gilliam, "The Second Folsom Administration," pp. 324–26.

46. *Montgomery Advertiser,* 2, 11, 18 March 1956; House, *Journal, 1956,* Second Special Session, p. 34; Gilliam, "The Second Folsom Administration," pp. 333–34; Harris, "Alabama Reaction," pp. 231–37.

47. Gilliam, "The Second Folsom Administration," pp. 327–33; "Message to the Legislature on the Opening Day of the Second Special Session," 1 March 1956, Folsom Papers; House, *Journal, 1956,* Second Special Session, p. 34; "Bi-Racial Commission" file, drawer 341, Governor's Papers; *Montgomery Advertiser,* 25 February 1956; *St. Louis Post-Dispatch,* 24 February 1956.

48. Hammond Notebook, Cabinet Minutes, 11, 20 March, 2, 16 April 1956.

49. *New York Herald Tribune,* 21 September 1956; Gilliam, "The Second Folsom Administration," pp. 333–34; *Montgomery Advertiser,* 18, 19, 22 March, 25, 26, 27 April.

50. *Montgomery Advertiser,* 10, 28 March 1956; Hammond Notebook, Cabinet Minutes, 20 March 1956; posters advertising Charles McKay's candidacy, Folsom Papers; Montgomery County Citizens' Council to James E. Folsom, 13 March 1956; "Miss Lucy—University of Alabama" file, drawer 341, Governor's Papers.

51. ADAH, *Alabama Official and Statistical Register, 1959,* pp. 524–25.

52. *Montgomery Advertiser,* 15 May 1957.

53. James E. Folsom to Estes Kefauver, 26 May 1956, "VIP Letters" file, Hammond Papers; James E. Folsom to Jim Battles, 9 May 1956, Folsom Papers; *Birmingham News,* 12 January 1957; *Montgomery Advertiser,* 7 November 1957.

54. *Montgomery Advertiser,* 11 January, 25 September 1957, 27 August 1958; Dwight D. Eisenhower to James E. Folsom, 23 January 1957, "VIP Letters" file, Hammond Papers; Gilliam, "The Second Folsom Administration," pp. 534, 545.

55. Confidential communication from a member of Folsom's cabinet.

Chapter 11

1. William Bradford Huie to James E. Folsom, 18 June 1954, Folsom Papers; clipping from the *Birmingham News*, "Folsom Articles and Materials" file, n.d., Hammond Papers.

2. *Montgomery Advertiser*, 2 October 1956; "A True Southerner" to James E. Folsom, "Bad Letters" file, Hammond Papers.

3. "1955–56 State Docks Boat" file, drawer 334, Governor's Papers; *Montgomery Advertiser*, 19 June, 26 August, 15 September 1955, 11 September 1956, 27 February, 12 June, 12 October 1958.

4. *Montgomery Advertiser*, 25 September, 27 November, 1, 2 December 1955; confidential communications from one member of the Alabama Legislature and one Folsom appointee.

5. *Montgomery Advertiser*, 26 August, 1, 25 September 1955, 2 January, 6 May 1956, 1 June 1958.

6. Ibid., 12, 16, 19, 23, 25, 31 October, 17, 27, 28 November 1956, 17, 20 January 1957.

7. Ibid., 31 January, 15 June, 18, 20 November 1956, 31 March, 6 July, 6 August 1958; Thomas J. Gilliam, "The Second Folsom Administration: The Destruction of Alabama Liberalism, 1954–1958" (Ph.D. dissertation, Auburn University, 1975), pp. 338–48.

8. Confidential communications.

9. *Montgomery Advertiser*, 30 September 1955, 27 October 1957.

10. Ibid., 21 September 1955, 10 January, 14 December 1956, 27 November 1957; Arthur D. Kelley to James E. Folsom, 7 April 1959, Folsom Papers; confidential communications.

11. John W. Overton to O. H. Finney, Jr., 2 March 1956, Folsom Papers; "1955–56 Insurance Allotments" file, drawer 333, Governor's Papers.

12. *Montgomery Advertiser*, 5 January 1957.

13. Ibid., 13 March 1956, 12 September 1955; Bert S. Cross to Fuller Kimbrell, 7 October 1954, Folsom Papers; confidential communication from long-term Montgomery resident.

14. *Montgomery Advertiser*, 2 October 1955, 13 March, 18 October 1956, 14 June 1957, 19 January 1958; confidential communication from Folsom supporter who owned an automobile dealership.

15. *Montgomery Advertiser*, 9 May, 19 June, 6 September, 3 October 1956.

16. Ibid., 6, 19, 26 September, 4, 5, 7 October 1956; Robert R. Finney to Herman Nelson, 25 September 1956, press release by Herman Nelson, 3 October 1956, "Herman Nelson vs. Patterson Case" file, Hammond Papers.

17. *Montgomery Advertiser*, 5, 12 October, 18 December 1956, 5 January

1957; press release by William H. Drinkard, 4 October 1956, "Herman Nelson vs. Patterson Case" file, Hammond Papers.

18. *Montgomery Advertiser,* 19 September, 15 November 1956, 22 February, 26, 27, 30 April, 1 May 1957.

19. Ibid., 17 July 1955; confidential communications.

20. Copy of promissory note for $7,400 witnessed by Frank Long, 13 July 1955, Folsom Papers; confidential communications from one member of Folsom's cabinet.

21. *Montgomery Advertiser,* 13, 17, 18 August 1955, 25 March 1956.

22. *Montgomery Advertiser,* 27 November 1957, 12 January 1958; bond abstracts for Alabama General Insurance Company bonds no. CJ-138 and no. CJ-139, Folsom Papers.

23. *Montgomery Advertiser,* 29 December 1957, 12 January 1958; confidential communications.

24. *Montgomery Advertiser,* 30, 31 October 1956; Hammond Notebook, Cabinet Minutes, 30 October 1956.

25. The account of this incident is based on four confidential communications from members of the Folsom cabinet and the Alabama Legislature. In each of the four versions of the story that I heard, the amount of the highway contractor's contribution differed. All four informants estimated that the contribution was between $10,000 and $50,000.

26. Confidential communications from two members of the Alabama Legislature and two members of Folsom's cabinet.

27. Malcolm Dobbs to Clark Foreman, 24 March 1947, box 51, Southern Conference of Human Welfare Papers, Tuskegee Institute, Tuskegee.

28. *Montgomery Advertiser,* 19, 20, 21, 23, 25 October, 2, 3 December 1955; Gilliam, "The Second Folsom Administration," p. 349.

29. Hammond Notebook, Cabinet Minutes, 11 March 1956; *Montgomery Advertiser,* 22 July 1956; confidential communications.

30. Confidential communications with a member of the Alabama Legislature.

31. Confidential communications from a member of the Alabama Legislature, a member of Folsom's cabinet, and a political journalist.

32. Confidential communications from a member of Folsom's cabinet, a political journalist, and a member of the Alabama Legislature.

33. Hammond Notebook, Cabinet Minutes, 19 November 1955.

34. *Montgomery Advertiser,* 12 December 1954, 1 February, 4 March 1956; Gilliam, "The Second Folsom Administration," pp. 351–53; confidential communications.

35. *Montgomery Advertiser,* 12 January 1956, 5, 23 May, 7, 23 June, 27 July, 17 August 1957; Gilliam, "The Second Folsom Administration," pp. 335–36; Hammond Notebook, Cabinet Minutes, 10 February 1956.

36. Hammond Notebook, Cabinet Minutes, 15 August 1955; confidential communications.

37. *Montgomery Advertiser,* 6 January 1957; *Alabama,* 25 February 1955; confidential communication from a member of Folsom's cabinet.

38. Confidential communications.

39. *Montgomery Advertiser,* 27 August 1958; confidential communications.

40. *Montgomery Advertiser,* 25 March, 1 September 1955; O. H. Finney, Jr., to James E. Folsom, 30 January 1957, O. H. Finney, Jr., to J. L. Kerr, 28 September 1955, Folsom Papers; confidential communications from two members of the Alabama Legislature.

41. Confidential communications from a member of the Alabama Legislature, a Folsom appointee, and a long-term Montgomery resident.

42. *Montgomery Advertiser,* 18 March, 24 April 1958.

43. Ibid., 21 February, 2 March, 10 April 1958.

44. Ibid., 25 May, 1 June 1958; ADAH, *Alabama Official and Statistical Register, 1959,* pp. 568–69, 592–93.

Chapter 12

1. Hammond Notebook, Cabinet Minutes, 30 December 1957.

2. Miscellaneous brochures, company reports, and investment information, Folsom Papers; confidential communication from a freelance journalist.

3. Arthur D. Kelley to Carolyn Burnham, undated, Melvin Dawkins to James E. Folsom, 21 July 1959, James E. Folsom to R. E. Ellzey, 17 December 1959, Ed Pepper to James E. Folsom, 17 February 1959, Folsom Papers.

4. Luke Barnett to James E. Folsom, 13 July 1959, Theodore J. Richter to James E. Folsom, 12 May 1959, Walter C. Givhan to James E. Folsom, 20 August 1960; speech delivered by James E. Folsom at Talladega, Labor Day, 1961, Folsom Papers.

5. Hugh H. Jacobs to James E. Folsom, 9 August 1959, W. DeWitt Ellis to Louis Friedman, 15 September 1958, W. H. Drinkard to James E. Folsom, 8 July 1958, Glynn Jones to James E. Folsom, 1 March 1960, Folsom Papers; Mary Parnell to James E. Folsom, 5 November 1958, William L. Riles to James E. Folsom, 6 November 1958, Hammond Papers.

6. Speech delivered by James E. Folsom at Talladega, Labor Day, 1961, Folsom Papers.

7. *Alabama Journal,* 7 April 1962; *Anniston Star,* 7 April 1962; *Alexander City Outlook,* 5 April 1962; 1962 campaign posters, Folsom Papers.

8. W. Bradley Twitty, *Y'all Come!* (Nashville: Hermitage Press, 1962); *Alabama Journal,* 5 April 1962; *Lee County Bulletin,* 5 April 1962; Benjamin Muse, "Confidential Memorandum: Additional Notes, April Travels, 1962,"

2 May 1962, Field Reports 1962, Southern Regional Council Papers, Birmingham Public Library, Birmingham.

9. *Montgomery Advertiser,* 27 April 1962; miscellaneous campaign materials for 1962, Folsom Papers.

10. *Decatur Daily,* 29 April 1962; *Montgomery Advertiser,* 27 April 1962.

11. Governor Folsom himself insisted that the men who were responsible for his appearance on television were agents of President John Kennedy. According to Folsom, Kennedy was angry because Folsom had opposed his nomination at the Democratic National Convention in 1960. James E. Folsom, interview with author, Cullman, 10 October 1979.

12. Confidential communications from four members of the Alabama Legislature and three members of Folsom's cabinet.

13. Neil O. Davis, interview with author, Auburn, 24 October 1979; William D. Barnard, "James E. Folsom," in *The Encyclopedia of Southern History,* ed. David C. Roller and Robert W. Twyman (Baton Rouge: Louisiana State University Press, 1979), p. 463; Thomas J. Gilliam, "The Second Folsom Administration: The Destruction of Alabama Liberalism, 1954–1958" (Ph.D. dissertation, Auburn University, 1975).

Essay on Sources

In my study of the political career of Governor James E. Folsom of Alabama, I have relied heavily on the information found in a small number of major sources. The following essay seeks to describe those sources. This bibliographic essay is neither an exclusive nor an exhaustive list of works cited in the text, since complete bibliographic information appears in the notes.

Newspapers

The basic chronology of James E. Folsom's gubernatorial administrations is recorded in the *Montgomery Advertiser*. I examined every issue of the *Advertiser* from January 1946 through January 1951 and from January 1954 through January 1959. The *Advertiser*'s own reporters and correspondents of the Associated Press in Montgomery wrote eyewitness accounts of the major events in Alabama state politics during this period. Similarly thorough coverage of Alabama state political affairs can be found in the *Birmingham News*.

For the reactions of journalists outside the state capital, I consulted the *Huntsville Times*, the *Anniston Star*, the *Dothan Eagle*, and the *Mobile Register*. For an estimate of the perspectives of Alabama business leaders, *Alabama: The News Magazine of the Deep South* proved to be a valuable source. The *Birmingham World* provided a clear picture of how black Alabamians felt about Governor Folsom. The *Albertville Herald* and the *Union Springs Herald*, weekly newspapers whose editors were members of the Alabama Legislature, revealed the reactions of two legislators to Folsom's leadership. All of these publications may be found on file in the Division of Civil Archives of the Alabama Department of Archives and History.

I also inspected copies of *Folsom's Forum,* the campaign newspaper that the first Folsom administration began printing in late 1947. *Folsom's Forum* was published at irregular intervals and under several different titles between 1947 and 1950, but all issues have been bound together in a single volume by the Division of Civil Archives of the Alabama Department of Archives and History.

Manuscript Collections

The personal papers of James E. Folsom make up one of the largest collections of manuscripts available for the study of Folsom's career. The Folsom Papers have been donated by the former governor to the Alabama Department of Archives and History and are housed in the Division of Maps and Manuscripts. The papers fill more than forty file drawers and are arranged in roughly chronological order. The collection had not been inventoried or catalogued when I used it during 1978 and 1979. Anyone willing to wade through the collection will find a wealth of information in personal and official correspondence, state documents, records of appointments, campaign literature, and miscellaneous personal effects.

A collection of scrapbooks containing newspaper clippings accompanies the Folsom Papers in the Division of Maps and Manuscripts of the Alabama Department of Archives and History. The clippings were taken from various Alabama newspapers and include most of the articles concerning Folsom that appeared in the *Birmingham News* and the *Montgomery Advertiser.* Two scrapbooks—one devoted to the columns of John Temple Graves and the other filled with Hugh Sparrow's writings—make the views of these journalists easily accessible to the researcher.

To a certain extent, the materials in the Folsom Papers duplicate the contents of the Official Papers of Governor James E. Folsom, housed in the Division of Civil Archives of the Alabama Department of Archives and History. The Governor's Papers are arranged in folders by executive department or state agency for each fiscal year of the two Folsom administrations. The Governor's Papers contain official correspondence, interoffice memoranda, records of appointments, official proclamations of the governor, and some personal correspondence.

Several other collections in the Division of Maps and Manuscripts complement the information contained in the Folsom Papers and the Governor's Papers. The personal papers of former governor Frank Dixon offer insights into Alabama political life at the time of Folsom's first election. A small collection of the personal papers of Senator J. Bruce Henderson provides evidence of how a leading opponent of Governor Folsom viewed political affairs during the 1940s and the 1950s.

The archives of Auburn University, located in the Ralph B. Draughon Library, house collections that reveal the involvement of the Agricultural

Extension Service in Alabama politics. The Auburn University Board of Trustees Papers, the Office of the President Papers, and the Alabama Cooperative Extension Records include documents that detail Governor Folsom's controversial leadership of the Alabama Polytechnic Institute's trustees in 1947.

The papers and notes in the personal possession of Ralph Hammond of Arab, Alabama, make up a valuable source of information concerning the second Folsom administration. The documents in Hammond's possession include correspondence, newspaper clippings, and the minutes of cabinet meetings that Hammond recorded as Governor Folsom's press secretary and executive secretary. I gained access to these materials through the courtesy of William D. Barnard of the University of Alabama.

Interviews

The richest sources of information concerning James E. Folsom's political career are the recollections of Folsom, his friends and family, and contemporary politicians. The notes to the text of this study do not adequately reflect the contributions of personal interviews to my understanding of the subject. The interviews not only provided information about Folsom that was not available in manuscript collections or printed sources, but they also gave me an appreciation of the significance of personal interaction between Alabama political leaders.

In many cases, individuals who agreed to be interviewed did not grant me permission to cite them as sources. Information from these sources has been cited as a "confidential communication." Information that might reflect personally on Folsom or another individual has not been incorporated into this study unless two or more individuals provided the same information. Because many of my informants have not permitted me to cite them as sources under any circumstances, I am not at liberty to disclose the origins of confidential communications now or in the future.

The following is a list of all persons who were interviewed by the author with the location and date of the interview. All of the interviews were conducted in Alabama.

Woodrow Albea, Anniston, 1 August 1979
L. G. Bassett, Troy, 28 November 1979
William M. Beck, Fort Payne, 5 November 1979
J. J. Benford, Albertville, 5 September 1979
Chester Black, Jasper, 26 September 1979
Rowan Bone, Gadsden, 6 September 1979
Jake Bonneau, Elba, 26 November 1979
A. L. "Pat" Boyd, Troy, 28 November 1979
L. W. Brannan, Jr., Mobile, 6 August 1979

James Branyon, Fayette, 30 October 1979
S. Fleetwood Carnley, Elba, 2 October 1979 and 26 November 1979
Thelma Folsom Clark, Elba, 26 November 1979
Thomas Cooley, Talladega, 27 August 1979
Dan Davis, Florence, 14 November 1979
Dr. Joe Davis, Albertville, 5 September 1979
Neil O. Davis, Auburn, 24 October 1979
Mrs. Ralph Draughon, Auburn, 24 October 1979
Bow Dunaway, Elba, 1 October 1979
Smith Dyar, Boaz, 5 September 1979
E. O. Eddins, Demopolis, 21 August 1979
O. H. Finney, Jr., Albertville, 5 September 1979, 6 September 1979, and 9
    October 1979
Robert Finney, Albertville, 5 September 1979
Rankin Fite, Hamilton, 11 December 1979
James E. Folsom, Cullman, 10 October 1979 and 11 October 1979
Robert Folsom, Elba, 1 October 1979
Mrs. Lowell Gregory, Boaz, 13 December 1979
E. B. Haltom, Florence, 18 November 1979
Phillip J. Hamm, Napier Field, 3 October 1979
Guy Hardwick, Dothan, 4 October 1979
Dr. J. L. Hardwick, Talladega, 28 August 1979
Norman Harris, Decatur, 6 November 1979
Olin Hearn, Albertville, 9 October 1979
Jack Huddleston, Muscle Shoals, 13 November 1979
William Bradford Huie, Hartselle, 12 December 1979
Bob Ingram, Montgomery, 12 June 1979
Fuller Kimbrell, Fayette, 30 October 1979
Jack Kirkham, Linden, 22 August 1979
Joseph Langan, Mobile, 8 July 1979
G. Kyser Leonard, Talladega, 27 August 1979
Pleas Looney, Montgomery, 12 September 1979
William V. Lyerly, Montgomery, 12 September 1979 and 23 October 1979
Juanita McDaniels, Montgomery, 12 September 1979
Roy Mayhall, Jasper, 26 September 1979
Austin R. Meadows, Montgomery, 8 June 1979.
J. Paul Meeks, Birmingham, 29 August 1979
James T. Merwin, Jr., Mobile, 27 December 1979
J. C. Monroe, Talladega, 27 August 1979
Wilbur Nolen, Montgomery, 11 September 1979
David U. Patton, Athens, 6 November 1979
Ben Reeves, Troy, 28 November 1979
Escar L. Roberts, Gadsden, 5 September 1979
Noble Russell, Decatur, 6 November 1979
Mrs. Florida Segrest, Tuskegee, 20 August 1979

T. K. Selman, Jasper, 27 September 1979
A. C. Shelton, White Plains, 1 August 1979
Alonzo Shumate, Jasper, 27 September 1979
Otto E. Simon, Mobile, 18 July 1979
Robert Stembridge, Dothan, 4 October 1979
Rex Thomas, Montgomery, 8 June 1979
John M. Tyson, Sr., Mobile, 9 August 1979
Carl Upchurch, Cuba, 22 August 1979
Graham Wright, Talladega, 28 August 1979

State Documents

Publications of the State of Alabama provide valuable sources of detailed, official information concerning public officials, the operations of
state departments and agencies, and the activities of the Alabama Legislature. For this study, the *Alabama Official and Statistical Register,* published
quadrennially by the Alabama Department of Archives and History, served
as an indispensable reference tool. The *Register* includes the names of all
state and local officials, biographical sketches of major state officials and
Alabama legislators, and the official returns for all primaries, general elections, and referenda.

Among the documents published by the Alabama Legislature, the *Acts of
Alabama* series provides the official text of all legislation enacted. The
house *Journal* and the senate *Journal* record the daily activities of the
legislative houses, including the texts of all substitute bills and local bills
and the record of action on every motion. The reports of interim study and
investigative committees supply occasional insight into the way in which
the legislators formulated legislation. *The Report of the Special Investigative Committee Investigating Pardons and Paroles,* prepared in 1951, is an
example of the work of an interim legislative committee. The audits issued
by the Department of Examiners of Public Accounts are classified as legislative documents because the department worked under the supervision of
the Alabama Legislature. Audits completed under the direction of the chief
examiner, Ralph Eagerton, detail charges of corruption leveled against the
Folsom administrations.

Regular reports published by individual state departments offer detailed
descriptions of the work of the Folsom administrations. Departmental reports that were helpful in this study of James E. Folsom included the
quadrennial reports of the Department of Finance and the Department of
Revenue and the annual reports of the Highway Department, the Alabama
State Docks and Terminals, the Alabama Alcoholic Beverage Control
Board, and the Alabama Department of Public Safety.

While governor of Alabama, James E. Folsom directed his office to pub-
lish several documents that advertised the work of his administration. In

the last year of his first administration, Folsom's office issued *Your State Finances, 1949–50; A Four Year Report to the People by Governor James E. Folsom;* and *Speeches of Gov. James E. Folsom, 1947–1950.*

Publications of the Bureau of Public Administration

Students of Alabama political history during the 1940s and 1950s are fortunate to have access to a wealth of contemporary political analysis compiled and published by the Bureau of Public Administration at the University of Alabama. The political scientists who contributed to the Bureau of Public Administration publications studied a great many of the institutions and problems within the state government and the local governments of Alabama. Studies published as a part of this valuable series include Hallie Farmer's *The Legislative Process in Alabama* (1949); Coleman B. Ransone's *The Office of Governor in the South* (1951); James E. Larson's *Reapportionment in Alabama* (1955); and Karl A. Bosworth's *Black Belt County* (1941) and *Tennessee Valley County* (1941).

Secondary Sources

The life of James E. Folsom has not been given complete, scholarly attention in any previously published work. The one work that claims to be a biography, Bradley Twitty's *Y'all Come* (Nashville: Hermitage Press, 1962), was written as campaign literature for Folsom's 1962 reelection campaign. Several students at Alabama universities have examined portions of Folsom's public life in theses and dissertations. They include William Dewey Murray, "The Folsom Gubernatorial Campaign of 1946" (master's thesis, University of Alabama, 1949); Osmos Lanier, Jr., "The First Administration of James E. Folsom, 1947–1950" (master's thesis, Auburn University, 1959); Thomas J. Gilliam, "The Second Folsom Administration: The Destruction of Alabama Liberalism, 1954–1958" (Ph.D. dissertation, Auburn University, 1975); and Larry Brittain Childs, "Alabama Giant: Recollections of Jim Folsom" (honors thesis, University of Alabama, 1974). William D. Barnard, who originally set out to write a Folsom biography, includes an insightful account of the initial years of Folsom's public career in his book *Dixiecrats and Democrats: Alabama Politics, 1942–1950* (University: University of Alabama Press, 1974).

Inasmuch as Jim Folsom's public career belongs to the history of Alabama, several excellent studies of topics in Alabama history help place the career of Governor Folsom in proper perspective. In addition to the already-mentioned work of William D. Barnard, *Dixiecrats and Democrats,* the works that have provided insights for this study include J. Mills Thornton III, *Politics and Power in a Slave Society: Alabama, 1800–1860* (Baton

Rouge: Louisiana State University Press, 1978); Jonathan M. Wiener, *Social Origins of the New South: Alabama, 1860–1896* (Baton Rouge: Louisiana State University Press, 1978); William Warren Rogers, *The One-Gallused Rebellion: Agrarianism in Alabama, 1865–1896* (Baton Rouge: Louisiana State University Press, 1970); and Sheldon Hackney, *Populism to Progressivism in Alabama* (Princeton: Princeton University Press, 1969).

Examinations of the southern states during the civil rights movement of the 1950s and 1960s have also illuminated the context into which the story of Jim Folsom's political career must be placed. Although these examinations, both journalistic and scholarly, focus on racial relations in the South, they often include brief references to the performance of Governor Folsom. The outstanding scholarly work of this type is Numan V. Bartley, *The Rise of Massive Resistance: Race and Politics in the South during the 1950s* (Baton Rouge: Louisiana State University Press, 1969). Journalistic accounts of the same period of southern history include Robert Sherill, *Gothic Politics in the Deep South: Stars of the New Confederacy* (New York: Grossman, 1968); Charles Morgan, Jr., *A Time to Speak* (New York: Harper and Row, 1964); and Marshall Frady, *Wallace* (New York: World, 1968).

Index

About the Author

George E. Sims teaches history at Wayland Baptist University, Plainview, Texas. He received his bachelor of arts degree from Samford University and his master of arts degree and doctorate from Emory University. This is his first book.